T0287471

Also available at all good book stores

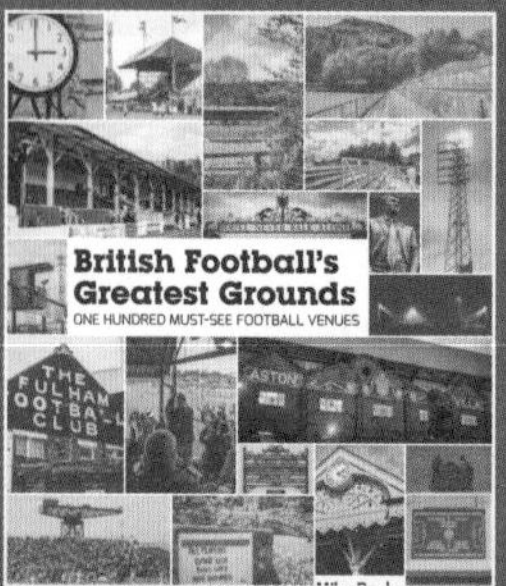

9781785316470

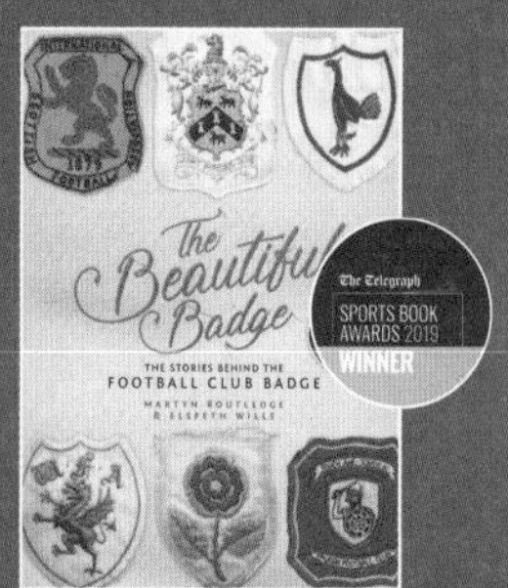

9781785313929

9781785315466

9781785315459

9781785310782

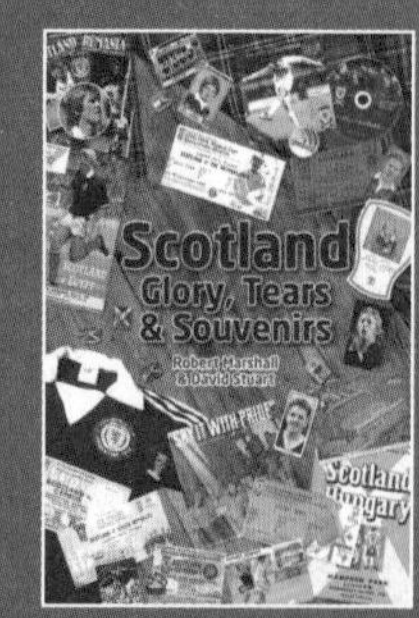

9781785313318

9781785314391

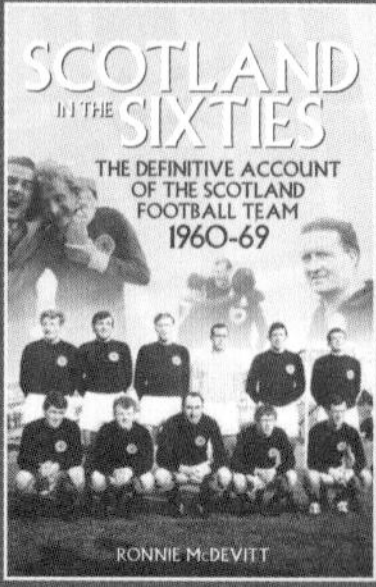

9781785311802

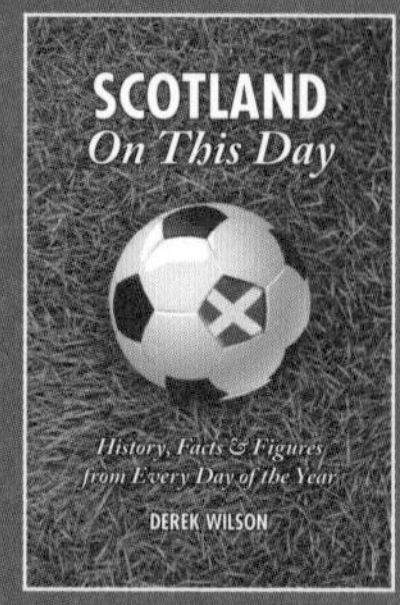

9781905411832

THE HIBS ARE HERE!

HIBERNIAN FC

92-99

THE HIBS ARE HERE!

MILLER TO MILLENNIUM

IAN COLQUHOUN

First published by Pitch Publishing, 2021

Pitch Publishing
A2 Yeoman Gate
Yeoman Way
Worthing
Sussex
BN13 3QZ
www.pitchpublishing.co.uk
info@pitchpublishing.co.uk

A CIP catalogue record is available for this book from the British Library.

ISBN 978 1 78531 829 0

Typesetting and origination by Pitch Publishing

Printed and bound in India by Replika Press Pvt. Ltd.

CONTENTS

Acknowledgments 8
Author's Note 9
Foreword 10
Forever and Ever 14
1. Prologue: Sit Down 16
2. Sound 19
3. Waltzing Along 33
4. Say Something 49
5. Born of Frustration 52
6. Ring the Bells – Season 92/93 – Part One. 57
7. Runaground – Season 92/93 – Part Two 69
8. She's a Star – Anderlecht Away 78
9. Hymn from a Village – Season 92/93 – Part Three. . 95
10. Just Like Fred Astaire – Off-Field Stuff 115
11. Laid – Season 93/94. 117
12. Come Home – Season 94/95 160
13. I Know What I'm Here For – Straiton 197
14. Destiny Calling – Bosman 203
15. Getting Away With It (All Messed Up) – Season 95/96 211
16. We're Going to Miss You – Season 96/97 244
17. Tomorrow – The Jocky Scott Years 259
18. Sometimes – Season 96/97 Continued 272
19. Bitter Virtue – Season 97/98. 300
20. La Petite Mort (Gone Baby Gone). 320
21. Moving On – The Great Adventure. 328
22. Nothing But Love – Hibernian Forever 339
23. Interviews 345

‘From little towns and Scotland’s capital we came
To save the Hibs from a world aflame
In little towns and in Scotland’s capital we sleep,
and trust that club we saved, for you to keep’

DEDICATION

In memory of former Garda Chief Superintendent John Courtney, Co. Kerry, 1928–2017. RIP

Fīat jūstitia ruat cælum

ACKNOWLEDGMENTS

FOR THEIR help, advice, encouragement, kindness and general inspiration over the last five years and in writing this book and others, I should like to thank the following people.

My family, my friends, Tony the Fish, Maggie, Ralph, Stephanie and Jessica, Bobby Sinnet, Jillian, Mark Strachan, The Coonster, Gerard Gough, Pitch Publishing, Sir Tom Farmer, Martin Ferguson, Jim Duffy, Keith Wright, Graham Mitchell, Kevin McAllister, Steven Tweed, Chris Jackson, David Farrell, Darren Jackson, Mark McGraw, David Hardie, Frank Dougan, John Campbell, Leeann Dempster, Maurice Dougan, Kieran Power, Ted Brack, Dougie Macleod, Andy MacVannan, St Patrick's Branch HSC, Paul Larkin, Elspeth, Gary Kerr, Spire Healthcare, David Hardie, the staff at my local gym, George Henry, Francesca, The Hiblogs, Alison the Hibby, Lawrence Fitzpatrick, Thomas Jamieson, Heather, Donnie Hill, Gemma, Garry O'Hagan, Tom McManus, Tommy McIntyre, Amanda, Jess, Eugene Gilligan, Ian Murray, Sarah, Mariyln Harkins, Coonster's dog, the late Bradley Welsh and all of the other Hibernian 'spirits in the sky'.

AUTHOR'S NOTE

THIS BOOK is written in a fan narrative, for fans. The interviews with ex-Hibees contained herein are completely separate from the main book – the legends were all kind enough to give me their time without actually reading my work first. So, if I've made a pig's ear of anything or have written something that any readers disagree with, it's my fault not theirs. Same goes for current Hibs employees and staff. They were kind enough to support me in this book's production but didn't have any say on my wee book's content. Two other wee things: if you want to read my account of the first half of Alex Miller's Hibs reign, from 1986–91, that book is called *From Oblivion to Hampden*. Lastly, I have the utmost respect and admiration for Alex Miller, Jocky Scott, Jim Duffy, Alex McLeish and every other Hibs person mentioned in this wee book. To me, all are legends. Thank you.

FOREWORD

BY BOBBY SINNET

A WISE woman once told me that you can never have too many books about Hibs. Up until now, there wasn't a book about one of the most fascinating periods in Hibernian Football Club's history – the 1990s. I'm pleased to be able to report that respected fan and author Ian Colquhoun has turned his attention to this period with his latest book. Unlike the Hibs books I grew up on in the 1980s, this book covers an era that I remember and in which I attended games.

Commercialism, which had eked its way into football in the 1980s, was now in full-blown takeover mode and the people's game was to change – rightly or wrongly, and we all have opinions on this – forever. One thing I'm sure we can all agree on is that there was nowhere quite like the East Terrace, and, despite the wonderful stadium we now have at Easter Road, a part of me still hankers after a more old-fashioned setting. The 1990s was a period of great change for stadiums of course, and not just Easter Road. The terrible Hillsborough disaster of 1989 set in motion a chain of events that saw the refurbishment of football grounds all over the United Kingdom – grounds that often were little changed over the previous 50 years. Hibs started the decade with terraces and ended it with a much reduced all-seated stadium and two completely new stands built in 1995 as the club sought to comply with the demands of Justice Taylor and his report. Of course, around this time Sir Tom Farmer investigated the possibility of moving Hibs away from their home of nearly 100 years and to Straiton in Midlothian. It never happened, but such were the financial considerations of the stadium development that every avenue was explored by Sir Tom Farmer and Douglas Cromb, in the interests of Hibernian FC. The Sir Tom Farmer era has of course now ended, and the reins have been passed to Ron Gordon to take the club forwards. The 90s were the period that Tom Farmer picked up the carnage that had been left by David Duff, and Wallace Mercer, and put the club back on a stable footing and nurtured the business back to a position of health and sustainability. There were some ups, and there were some downs, but this period was critical in providing the base for the club to re-establish itself as one of the top teams in Scotland. Largely there was progress, and Hibs were in a far better position on all fronts by the end of the 90s than they had been coming into the 90s. The 1990s was of course also the beginning of the 'Sky era', although in Scotland it had been slightly less heralded with a live football deal with BSB. This was an age when traditional football was under attack and Saturday 3pm kick-offs went from the norm to being much less usual as fans became accustomed to having their scheduled fixtures lists obliterated by the demands of television. Some chose to watch games on television, and rarely returned, even to this day. And then there was the little matter of the Belgian Jean-Marc Bosman affair, which led to the abolition of transfer fees for players out of contract. Bosman had made an unremarkable appearance at Easter Road for Royal Liege, in a game remarkable for Keith Houchen's missed penalty. Bosman's impact on the game has been likened to the shockwaves that were caused in the 1890s when the game moved from amateur to professional. By the late 90s, the predominantly Scottish squad that Hibs had utilised for a number of years gave way to a much more cosmopolitan blend, which eventually saw players from nearly all the different continents of the world wear the green. But there were still guys like Barry Lavety, too.

The 70s might have been scintillating for Hibbies and gave way to the post-modern bleakness of the 80s, and the false dawns. The 90s, though, were a time of renaissance for Hibs and the team gave the fans something that was close to being back in the upper echelons of the Scottish game. The 90s were a time of great change and turbulence – one such example being the job of Hibs manager. Hibs went from a team that rarely sacked managers, and managers having lengthy periods in the hot seat, to turning over managers frequently in search of that elusive blend, the opening six years of the decade under Alex Miller giving way to Jocky Scott, Jim Duffy and Alex McLeish in quick succession. But, if we thought that was chop and change, it was nothing compared to what we would see in the future. I've known Ian for a number of years and collaborated with him in the past. His work is insightful, thorough and captures a raw energy about what really happened that you often don't really capture from reading news reports or watching YouTube video clips. Ian is able to draw out elements of the storyline that would otherwise be lost. You might want to search out the YouTube clips after reading this, as it takes you for a pleasant meander down memory lane, if, of course, you were fortunate to be there. Jim Leighton, Darren Jackson,

Keith Wright, Kevin McAllister to Thorsten Schmugge and Juha Riippa. It's all here. There were some great games of football, some great cup ties, some fantastic European games and some great goals. There were some great victories and some painful defeats. Some laughs and some tears. Some oh so nears. It was never ordinary. One thing you learn as a Hibs fan, life is never ordinary.

Bobby Sinnet | @ihibs

FOREVER AND EVER

MY FIRST Hibs game was our 4-1 win over Chelsea at Easter Road in 1986. My first ever 'Hibs interview' came on Tuesday, 6 October 1992, aged 14, in the Weir Toyota Lounge at Easter Road.

As part of a SCOTVEC course on work studies at high school, two school friends and I had to arrange a day observing a workplace of our choosing. We wrote to Hibs and asked if we could do it there and they said yes, so we hung out at Easter Road all day. I took a tape recorder with me and interviewed the groundsman Pat Frost – a great guy – and asked him about working at Hibs, the new Bukta deal and other Hibby things. Darren Jackson and some other players came in and spoke to us, too. I was the only Hibby out of my party – my two pals were Rangers fans – but we all loved the day out. Did I use that course just to blag a day hanging out at Easter Road? Of course I did. We all passed the course.

The tape still exists; I might upload it to the internet just for a laugh. So, here I am, 29 years later, still interviewing Hibs folk and still writing about Hibs. I've come to the conclusion that I'll never stop. Oh, in case you're wondering, most of the chapter names are songs and albums by my favourite band, James.

There's only one
Human race
Many faces,
Everybody belongs here.

PROLOGUE: SIT DOWN

'Hibees here, Hibees there …'

WRITING A book about the football team that you love and support is enjoyable but comes with a certain amount of pressure. Writing *From Oblivion to Hampden* was a wonderful experience. This new work was a bit trickier to structure as it doesn't have a cup win or other significant triumph for the story to be built around. Indeed, some people have asked why I wanted to write a book about this period at all. There are three main reasons that I wrote it. One reason is artistic. My last Hibs book stopped in May 1992, bang in the middle of a manager's reign. It seems the right thing to do as a writer to tell the story of what happened next. However, I couldn't very well just write about the remainder of Alex Miller's reign, as that leaves the reader on a cliffhanger and without a happy ending. Ditto regarding ending the work when we were relegated. So, I put in a shorter, more summarised account of our beloved Hibs' story after the 1998 relegation right up until the end of the 20th century, when things were good again.

This leads us to the second reason for writing the book. Despite suffering catastrophic injuries and a multitude of illnesses and personal trauma since 2002, my memory of following Hibs from boyhood right up to 2002, when I was healthy and able-bodied, is still so vivid, photographic and detailed. I clearly remember songs, shouts and even smells, as well as events – *I was there.* I felt it a kind of duty to write it all down while I retain the faculties and finger strength with which to do so. The third reason is more pragmatic – lockdown because of COVID-19. It not only gave me a great opportunity for some uninterrupted writing, it also gave me a great opportunity to get interviews with some kind Hibs legends, while we were all stuck at home.

When you read this story, you may find the narrative sounds cynical at times. That's very deliberate. It doesn't mean that your author doesn't love, admire and respect every single person connected with Hibs and football who is mentioned herein – I do, just like you do. What I've done when writing this work is to regress myself partially, to regain the mindset of my teenage and young adult self who rarely missed a Hibs game. So, if descriptions of certain players, people or events sound coarse or harsh, they're supposed to, as that's how I and many of my peers felt at the time those players, people and events were current. No disrespect to anyone is intended, be they Hibs players/staff or otherwise. So, if I sound pissed off at anything or anyone in the book, that's because I was, and many Hibbies also were pissed off at the time, not now. Please remember, all of this happened over 20 years ago.

I'm not a posh boy; I watched Hibs from the terracing for most of my life and am proud to be working class. So, if at any time my account of things or my narrative sounds yobbish or makes me sound like a bit of an uncouth terrace Ned, I make no apologies for that, because in my younger days, that's what I was.

I was at a great many of the over 300 matches mentioned in this wee book. For the ones I wasn't at, or the handful that I was too drunk to remember properly, I've spoken to at least two people who were actually there. It would have been nigh on impossible to compile this work without my friend Bobby Sinnet's wonderful Hibs statistics resource, and his encouragement. I also dipped into various newspaper archives and utilised my own collection of books and programmes. Most of all, though, I used my memory, and I hope that you will, too.

It's my hope that you'll enjoy the read and will yourself regress through your own time following Hibs in the 90s while reading it. I sincerely hope that you will. If you're a younger Hibby, then I hope you enjoy the 'Hibstory'. It's a privilege to write a book about our Hibernian FC, but without you, dear reader, it would be a lonely, pointless exercise. In short, I *had* to write all of this down.

You may find this humble work to be a bit of a slog to read, particularly the extended season 92/93 part, but remember, season 92/93 was itself a slog of over 50 matches, and it was important to be expansive when it came to the season immediately after our SKOL League Cup-winning one, to create a written bridge to what happened next. I know you'll love the extra contributions by my friends Bobby Sinnet and Matthew Kane. They're much better writers than I am and without them this book probably wouldn't exist.

Drawn by the undertow
My life is out of control
I believe this wave will bear my weight
So let it flow
Oh sit down
Oh sit down
Oh sit down
Sit down next to me
Sit down, down, down, down, down
In sympathy.

SOUND

'Alex Miller's green and white army!
Alex Miller's green and white army!'

HIBS WERE formed in 1875 by and for Irish Catholic immigrants. Part of the reason was because clubs in Protestant Edinburgh wanted 'papists' and Irish immigrants to stay away from their own clubs. Newspapers from the time often cited how it was a good thing that Scotland at last had a 'sectarian' football team. 'Sectarian' actually had a positive meaning back in the 19th century, whereas today the word is used to mask racism in Scotland by people who don't want Scotland or some Scots to be thought of as racist. Hibernian provided the blueprint for and was copied by other Irish immigrant teams formed in Scotland thereafter, the most famous of which being Celtic and Dundee United (Hibernian), though there were scores of others. For example, Broxburn at one point had three 'Hibs-esque' teams: Broxburn Shamrock, Broxburn Harp and Niddry Celtic. Other similarly constituted clubs included St Roch's of Glasgow, Lochee Harp of Dundee, Larkhall Hibernian and Govan Hibernian.

A multitude of other similar clubs also sprang up around the country, though most remained small and either don't exist any more or have long since been merged with other teams in their locale.

The problematic thing for Hibs in the earliest days was that being an exclusively Irish/Catholic club in Edinburgh really wasn't sustainable. There wasn't enough of the Irish diaspora in Scotland's capital to *really* make it work. There was in Glasgow, though; that's how Celtic flourished. In the last decade of the 19th century Hibs went bust and had to go on a kind of hiatus, only playing friendlies for a while. When Hibernian resumed proper operations in 1892, resurrected thanks to two ancestors of Sir Tom Farmer, they did so as a non-sectarian club open to all and have remained so ever since.

People from Edinburgh and the surrounding area over the years who are from an Irish or Catholic background would still tend to choose Hibs as their team but Hibs fans nowadays tend to choose to support Hibernian because of family tradition or because of geography, i.e. because they are their local team. A good number of Hibs fans today belong to the socio-economic and religio-ethnic group for which the club was originally formed, or are at least descended from people who were, but many more have no links to these groups at all. In short, Hibernian is a football club for everybody, regardless of race, faith or class. It's all about the football. Some Hibs fans love and revel in the club's heritage, most find it pleasing but don't go on about it, some aren't that fussed about it, you even get the odd few who would rather the club's cultural history wasn't mentioned or celebrated at all. Regardless of that, Hibs fans aren't a homogenous group, but we are all united in one thing – our love of the team. That love transcends all of our differences and has stood us in good stead over the years as we have faced and overcome challenges together. When

Hibernian FC opened itself up to all of Edinburgh, that beautiful city's people welcomed her with open arms and she became a wonderful, integral part of Scotland's capital story and has remained so. Over the years the football club and its fans have formed their own unique identity, based on Edinburgh, Leith, the east coast and, well, coolness.

The attempted Mercer takeover of Hibs by Hearts in 1990 sealed a bond within two generations of the Hibs support, which has endured. It defined us as a club in the 1990s. We were, as Sky dubbed us, 'The team that wouldn't die.' That episode not only showed what Hibs fans could achieve together when our beloved team was under existential threat, it also strengthened our collective mentality. To be blunt, nothing negative that we have had to endure as Hibs fans in the last 30 years has come close to the trauma of 1990, and everything positive that we have experienced since 1990 has tasted all the sweeter because we know that we are lucky to be alive to experience those positives, 1990/91 proved an old adage true – what doesn't kill you makes you stronger.

Supporting Hibs in the 1990s was a wee bit different to following 'the Cabbage' today. Most games were at 3pm on a Saturday, and most matches weren't on television, though the number of televised matches increased substantially as the decade wore on. For most Hibs fans, particularly those outwith Edinburgh, the main source of Hibs news came from small columns in the 'weegie'-dominated daily newspapers and from the much better sources that were *The Scotsman* and the *Evening News* – particularly from the excellent David Hardie. Fans keen on extra titbits of midweek Hibs info could resort to Teletext/Ceefax or even the club's premium-rate information line, the number of which was 0898 70 70 70. Your humble correspondent, then a teenager, once listened to most of a midweek away match on that clubcall number, costing 50p per minute, and experienced a very long week when his mum got the telephone bill. I doubt he was the only one.

By far the biggest change which affected Hibs fans during the 1990s was the Taylor Report. From the summer of 1994 we had to sit down at matches, which was a bit of a culture shock to fans that were used to standing on terraces. Like all fans, we adapted and got used to it, but all-seater did make watching football slightly more sanitised and our game did lose some atmosphere irretrievably. One plus point of going all-seater was that the numbers of women, children and whole families attending games did increase, though there were always plenty of bairns and women at football before 1994 anyway.

The casual group, the CCS, obviously weren't anything to do with the actual football club, but they were part of the support. To ordinary Hibs fans and indeed ordinary fans of other clubs, casual movements were very much a double-edged sword. Their very existence forced police and football clubs to 'wise up' when it came to crowd safety, which actually improved the match-day experience and safety for all as the years went by. The casuals made fans of other clubs wary of Hibs fans; this could work either in favour of or against ordinary Hibbies. For instance, cops might see a group of Hibs fans who weren't wearing many colours but who weren't actual casuals, but would treat them with suspicion regardless. Same with opposing fans. Many would see Hibs fans and think 'casuals', 'trouble' and would either give us a wide berth, be nice to us, or, less often, try to give us a hard time. One negative about having casuals, other than inexcusable violence, *obviously*, was that their existence was sometimes used by the authorities as a stick with which to beat ordinary Hibs supporters and the club. When we almost died as a club in 1990, many people in Lothian and beyond wanted us to die, for two main reasons: because of the casuals and because of our club's heritage. We were seen, absurdly, as being 'fenian' because we wore green, or as all being a gang of hard men looking for a pagger, because of a small group of casuals. Most casuals at all clubs back then were just angry young men in the Thatcher/Tory years, looking for something deeper to belong to, and they were no more or no less Hibs fans than other supporters. In any case, whenever there was any sort of 'bother' at a match anywhere in the country, there was as much a chance that it was started by steaming drunk 'scarfer' fans as by organised hooligans. Every big club in Britain had a 'firm' back then. Fans today are lucky that they can attend football matches in such comparative safety. Society moves on.

By the mid 90s Scottish football clubs had finally cottoned on to just how much money could be made from merchandise and other club-related curiosities. The newer Hibs shop under The Famous Five Stand is testament to how football merchandising was finally embraced by the club and dragged into the 21st century. Hibs actually released three VHS videos in the 90s as well. One such video was called *Going for Glory* and it was a film about Hibs, released in late 1997 to commemorate the 25th anniversary of our 1972 League Cup win. It featured footage from that match and interviews with Eddie Turnbull and some players of that era. Tony Higgins presented part of it and, as Jim Duffy's Hibs side were flying high when it was filmed, it also featured interviews with the boss and some current players, as well as showing the goals from our good start to that campaign, up to the 3-4 loss against Rangers. It sold reasonably well but by that season's end was a bit of a cringe to watch as it showed our goals but not the opposition's and half of the players and the manager were gone by the end of the season *and* we ended up going down. Watched nowadays, it's nice; a good snapshot of Hibs history from what was a time of heady optimism at the club. Another VHS, released in 1995, was called *Hibee Hibernian*.

The first of the trio of VHSs came out just in time for Christmas in 1992. It was, of course, *The Team That Wouldn't Die*, which told a compressed story of our near-death in 1990 and our subsequent SKOL League Cup triumph of 1991. Though it largely ignored the three early rounds of that cup run, it was nevertheless a superb video, a must-have for any Hibs fan and remains a classic to this day. Narrated by Jim Hossack, this video is an important part of Hibernian's history, not only as a fine audio-visual catalogue of that historic cup win, its aftermath and of club personalities at the time, but for one other reason. That video brought new meaning to the song 'Sunshine on Leith'.

'Sunshine on Leith' by The Proclaimers was known to Hibs fans ever since its release in 1988 but prior to the release of that cup-winning video in 1992 you'd be stretching it to say that it was a Hibs song. At the Hands Off Hibs rally at Easter Road in 1990 The Proclaimers sang 'You'll Never Walk Alone' on the pitch with the fans. That was our 'dewy-eyed' club anthem at the time, sung at times of great emotion; however, 'Sunshine on Leith' was sung at the Hands Off Hibs rally in the Usher Hall in 1990. For the 1992 SKOL Cup VHS, 'Sunshine on Leith' was dubbed over crowd footage of that Easter Road Hands Off Hibs rally and it worked magnificently. As the beautiful, moving song played over the emotive footage of the rally, everything just clicked. 'Ma heart was broken' echoing over footage of what was a heartbreaking emotive time at Easter Road was artistic genius. The fact that the song is about Leith and sung by two good Hibbies, both of whom are actually in the clip, was the icing on the cake. It just clicked. In fact, it clicked so well in the Hibernian psyche that some fans to this day mistakenly associate the song with the Hands Off Hibs episode, even though it only really had a minor role in that drama. The song would continue to be a slow burner. 'You'll Never Walk Alone' remained our main celebration anthem right up until we sang it near the end of the 6-2 win over Hearts in 2000. We sang 'Sunshine on Leith' against AEK Athens in 2001 and then en masse after thrashing Kilmarnock in the 2007 League Cup Final, and, thereafter, 'Sunshine on Leith' has been our club anthem, and rightly so. It's awesome that we have a unique song that is ours and only ours. For that song we have The Proclaimers to thank, and that 1992 video about the SKOL Cup win which embedded it into many of our hearts. 'Sunshine on Leith' was, however, played regularly on the PA at Easter Road from the mid 90s, as well as on Hibs pub jukeboxes and on buses, at Hibby weddings, funerals, parties and social gatherings – and probably will be forever. A CD of Hibs songs appeared in the club shop in the late 90s, too. As well as 'Sunshine on Leith' and the 'Turnbull's Tornadoes' song, it featured tracks like 'Hibs Heroes' (the zoom zoom song), 'Glory Glory to the Hibees' and even a weird electro-dub track by The Jimmy Boco Experience, based on the terrace song 'We are Hibernian FC'.

At actual games in the 90s, our song repertoire was quite extensive.

Asides 'You'll Never Walk Alone', which was reserved for moments of triumph or adversity, or for when playing Hearts or Rangers, we had quite the eclectic mix of songs and chants in the 90s, some of which are still with us today.

'Hail Hail' was and is one of our main anthems, usually sung just after we have celebrated a goal and also usually to inspire the team just before or after kick-off. The chant comes from two tunes. The 'Hail Hail, the Hibs are here, all for goals and glory, all for goals and glory' part comes from Gilbert and Sullivan's famous 1879 comic opera *Pirates of Penzance* which has also been made into a movie. The actual song in question is called 'With Cat-like Tread' and the real lyrics are:

'Come friends, who plough the sea!
Truce to navigation
Take another station
Let's vary piracy
With a little burglary!'

The second part of 'Hail Hail' which goes 'For it's a grand old team to play for' comes from a totally different song. It's from a song called '76 Trombones', which first featured in a 1957 musical called *The Music Man* which has also been made into a movie. Several UK clubs sing versions of 'Hail Hail', most famously Hibs, Celtic, Fulham and Everton. There's some debate about who sang it first, not that that really matters. One story goes that Glasgow Celtic inherited the song when Belfast Celtic folded in 1949. That's only possible for the 'Hail Hail' part, as '76 Trombones', the 'grand old team' part, wasn't even written when Belfast Celtic folded. In any case, each club sings their own words to the tune.

Our other excellent club anthem, 'Glory Glory to the Hibees', is far easier to trace. Our version was recorded by Hector Nicol back in the day. Rather a lot of football teams sing songs to this tune, as it is taken from one of the most popular Christian hymns of all time, but Hibs were the first football team to make a record with the tune. The original tune was written in the early 1800s in America and was called 'Say Brothers Will You Meet Us?' It later became the abolitionist anthem 'John Brown's Body' then also became the US Civil War anthem 'Battle Hymn of the Republic' when new lyrics were written by American woman Julia Ward Howe in 1861. It's one of the most well-known songs in the Christian world, covered even by Elvis Presley, so it's no real surprise that the song made its way from churches onto football terraces, like so many others. The song had quite a journey – from the hills of Gettysburg in 1863 to the slope at Easter Road a century later and beyond.

Another big 90s Hibs terrace song that we got from Christianity is 'We are Hibernian FC'. It uses the tune to the chorus of the Easter hymn 'Lord of the Dance', written in 1963 by English composer Sydney Carter. For a time in the 80s, after 1986, we sang 'We love Dundee' instead of 'We hate Dundee' in the lyrics, because of Albert Kidd. An advantage of using old hymns and war songs at the time was that most people knew the tunes. The original hymn was about Christ's resurrection, so there's a nice irony that Hibs fans sang a song to the tune, as we ourselves were raised from the dead after the 1990 takeover episode.

I'm unsure of where the tune to 'Ooh to be a Hibbie' originally comes from. All I've been able to deduce is that fans the world over in the 60s started using that particular chant or pattern of clapping. It may have come from a 1966 UK chart hit by Dave Dee, Dozy, Beaky, Mick & Tich, 'Hold Tight'; then again that band might have borrowed the tune from football. We also sang 'Hibees' and clapped to that tune as well, and still do. Every team's fans use the tune.

Our song 'We hate Glasgow Rangers, we hate Celtic too …' is still sung today. Other teams' fans use that tune as well. The original tune 'Land of Hope and Glory' was written by the composer Edward Elgar in 1901. Elgar used to feature on British banknotes, but is probably most revered for writing the tune to a Hibs song. Probably.

'Triumphal March' from the Italian composer Verdi's opera *Aida* was sung a lot in the early to mid 90s by Hibs fans but also by most fans at that time. It doesn't have lyrics, you just sang 'do do …' to the tune. It's the song of the big entrance and when it filled a football stadium it sounded amazing. It went out of fashion, eventually.

After Euro 96, fans all over Britain started to use the 'It's coming home' line from Baddiel, Skinner and The Lightning Seeds' England song 'Three Lions'. It was usually used to tell other teams they were going down or that their manager would soon be on the dole. Another song which crept from the charts onto the terraces at Easter Road and elsewhere in the 90s was 'Go West'. This happened because the Pet Shop Boys had released a fairly successful cover of the song in 1993, which was originally recorded by The Village People in 1979. You know the tune. You may know it better as 'You're pish, and you know you are' or words to that effect. We also sang a version of it about Russell Latapy, and we also did it to 'Stand up if you hate jam tarts'.

Then there were more obscure songs, less frequently sung. The one about a fictitious 6-2 victory over Rangers at Ibrox and the one about Bill Shankly and the mental Hibees are examples. The latter still gets the odd outing, usually on big away days, and uses the tune from the 50s rockabilly hit 'Tennessee Wig Walk' by American singer Bonnie Lou.

'Forever and Ever' still gets sung by our fans now and then, not often. Back in the 90s we sang it on the terracing all the time, particularly against Hearts, Airdrie and Rangers. It's probably not PC any more, with its lyrics about being 'mastered by no ...' Almost every team in the country sang a version of that song as it's very catchy. The chorus of the song, the 'Bring on the Hearts ...' part, uses an old, old tune. It was originally an American Civil War song from the 1860s about Confederate POWs having to walk all the way to camps in Chicago, called 'Tramp Tramp Tramp', which later became 'God Save Ireland', the emerald isle's unofficial national anthem when it was part of the UK. 'God Save Ireland' was actually played by the band on the pitch after Hibs beat Celtic 1-0 in the 1902 Scottish Cup Final for that reason. The tune was later used for Scotland's 1978 World Cup song as well. As for the first part of that Hibs song, the 'Forever and ever' part, well, that's an old, old song. 'Forever and Ever' was written in the 1940s by Malia Rosa, using an old Austrian tune. In 1949 American crooner Perry Como had a smash hit with the song and it became so massive and well known that football fans later adopted it.

We also had songs for players. The manager only had one chant, 'Alex Miller's green and white army.' Keith Wright had 'Keef Keef Keef'. Mickey Weir had 'He's here, he's there'. Darren Jackson had 'Ooh ah Jacksona'. Jim Leighton's 'Scotland's number one' chant used the tune of the 1968 hit 'Helule Helule' by The Tremeloes. Joe Tortolano's song was 'Joe, Joe, Super Joe, Super Tortolano' sung to 'Skip to my Lou'. Steven Tweed's chant was 'Tweedy, Tweedy'; Chic Charnley's chant was the same as Tweed's but 'Chico' instead. Most of the rest of the squad, when they'd earned a chant, were serenaded with 'One [insert name], there's only one [insert name]', sung to the tune of 'Guantanamera'.

We did have some chants specific to certain teams. Celtic, Rangers and Partick all got treated to our 'In your

Glasgow slums' ditty, though we sang that to Hearts as well, changing Glasgow to Gorgie. Aberdeen got hit with 'sheepshagger' patter. For a brief time in the 90s some of our lot taunted fans of both Dundee clubs about the closure of the Timex factory up there, and we also once made fun of Motherwell fans because of Ravenscraig. Those last two were embarrassing chants but that's how football was. We got it back from all of those fans, AIDS 'banter' from the non-Edinburgh teams, songs about saunas, heroin and homosexuality. The odd dig at our club's roots as well. Aberdeen fans travelled the country taunting fans of every other club with 'sign on, sign on' during what was a time of high unemployment. Society was very different in the 90s; football is a microcosm of society, so that's how things were. Some songs are gone, some aren't.

Michael O'Neill's song was 'Oh Mikey Mikey, Mikey Mikey Mikey Mikey O'Neill', sung to the tune of Chicory Tips's 'Son of my father'. Hearts and Celtic both used the same tune about Mike Galloway.

The hymn 'Cwm Rhondda', also known as 'Bread of Heaven', was used for a lot of our other songs; most teams' fans used it. It provides the tune for chants like The referee baiting chant:

'Who's the bastard in the black?
We'll support you ever more
We can see you sneaking out
What the fucking hell is that?'

And other such ditties. There were others, of course. Nowadays most football chants come from chart songs rather than from hymns or army marching tunes. The pop group who have had the largest number of their songs adapted into football terrace chants is … Boney M. At least six of their songs have become widespread football chants in Europe – those songs being 'Mary's Boy Child', 'Daddy Cool', 'Brown Girl in the Ring', 'Rivers of Babylon', 'Sunny' and 'Rasputin'. That's right, 70s disco giants Boney M!

We didn't just have songs, we had fanzines. Fan-made independent magazines about the club were a superb source of both information and humour. Sold by mail subscription or in pubs and outside the ground, publications like *Mass Hibsteria/Hibs Monthly* and *TANEHSH* provided fans of the club with what one might compare to an early version of internet football forums and social media, neither of which were around for most of the 90s. *MHHM* gave us Grumpy Gibby the North Stand Hibby and had some wonderful contributors, even Irvine Welsh, who used the name Octopus, I think. All clubs had their own fanzines. Hearts' main ones were called *Always the Bridesmaid*, a reference to their long barren trophyless spell, and *No Idle Talk*. One featured a comic Gorgie-agro hardman called Chi who would spout threats of unrealistic violence.

As the 90s wore on and Hibs got gradually worse on the pitch, somewhat ironically the team was becoming a bit more famous culturally. The movie version of *Trainspotting* in 1996 started it; who can forget most of the characters wearing Hibs gear in the opening scenes, or the décor in Renton's bedroom? In 1997 you had that guy in the audience on a TV show singing the 'Leith San Siro' song. Then 1998 brought another movie version of an Irvine Welsh book, this time *The Acid House*. That, too, had numerous Hibs references in all three of the stories featured; Hibs legend Pat Stanton was even in it, playing a barman. The year 1998 also saw *Looking after JoJo* hit British screens. The gritty but intelligent drama set amid the drug-plagued atmosphere of 1980s Sighthill also had Hibs references.

In 1999 an Edinburgh-based pop group called The Lanterns released a pop song and video called 'High Rise Town'. The song, sung in Edinburgh accents, made it onto cable TV music channels and featured a promotional video showing the now demolished high-rise flats at Broomhouse and nearby street scenes full of adults, youths and children, many of whom were wearing Hibs gear.

We flew many flags. Green and white striped ones. Green saltire ones. Harp ones. The CCS flag. A weird, beautiful one like the CCS flag but done in purple and green. Even Irish tricolours – mostly when playing Rangers, Hearts or Airdrie. Most supporters' branches had a flag. There was, for a time, an enormous green and white flag that covered around half of the area between the TV gantry and the away end when unfurled. You tended to only see flags at half-time in the terracing days as they obstruct the fans' view of the pitch. Big flags could be a godsend at away trips when we were on open terracing in bad weather, as the lucky few could shelter under them. We even had one which said 'Oblivion to Hampden'.

So, by the end of the 90s, no matter how the team was actually doing, Hibernian FC was pretty cool and trendy and supporting the Hibs was a cool experience. Always has been. Always will be.

Do everything you fear
In this there's power
Fear is not to be afraid of…

WALTZING ALONG

'Joe, Joe, Super Joe, Joe, Joe Super Joe, Joe, Joe, Super Joe, Super Tortolano!'

THIS ISN'T a book about Alex Miller, Jim Duffy or any other manager or player, though they are all integral parts of the Hibs story. In *Oblivion to Hampden* we looked at Hibs from 1986–1992, so in this work we're looking at 1992–1999, the last few years of Hibernian's 20th-century story. Here's a brief recap.

Alex Miller was a hot managerial prospect when he came to Hibs late in 1986. He had taken St Mirren to Hampden and had led the Buddies into Europe, as well as consistently finishing above Hibs in the league table. In contrast, Hibernian FC had been somewhat uninspiring since being promoted back to the Premier Division in 1981 and had been largely mediocre under successive managers Bertie Auld, Pat Stanton and John Blackley. However, all three of those managers had played for Hibernian at one point in their careers, while Alex Miller was best known for his long spell as a Rangers player. He was the first Hibs manager who wasn't also an ex-Hibs player since Dave Ewing in the early 70s.

Season 85/86, John Blackley's last full campaign in charge, had seen Hibs reach the SKOL Cup Final and the

Scottish Cup semi-finals. Steve Cowan had scored 28 goals while Gordon Durie had bagged 14 – Hibs didn't have such a potent strike force again until Anthony Stokes and Derek Riordan in 09/10, with 23 and 17 goals respectively. The average home attendance in 85/86 at Easter Road was 9,135, the highest that it had been since the season Hibs ended up being relegated in 79/80, though in actual fact, Hibs hadn't had an average attendance of more than 10,000 since 76/77 anyway.

So, the cup runs and the two brilliant strikers, and the highest crowds since the 70s, were good points for Hibernian from season 85/86. Bad points were the league table position and the defensive record. Hibs might have scored 49 goals but they had conceded 63 – the third-worst defensive record of that league campaign – and Hibs had also finished third from bottom in the table, just eight points above bottom club Clydebank. Since promotion in 1981, no Hibs side had managed to finish in the top half of the table. Indeed, it's accepted by many Hibs fans and commentators that,4 were it not for having Alan Rough in goal, the Hibs sides of the early to mid 80s could easily have been relegated.

So, when Alex Miller arrived late in 1986, it seems that he had three things to improve: the defence, the league position and, hopefully, the attendances. There's a myth among some fans to this day that Alex Miller's teams drove some fans away – hard facts and statistics say otherwise. Of the nine full seasons that Alex managed Hibs for, average crowds were consistently higher than they had been since the late 70s, except in season 92/93 when they dipped to just under 9,000 and in season 94/95 when Easter Road had reduced capacity and was partly a building site. So, Alex Miller's time at Hibs saw increased crowds, he succeeded there.

After Miller took over in season 86/87, Hibs finished fourth from bottom in the table, one place better than the previous year but in a league extended that season from ten to 12 teams. The defence was just as bad that season as it had been in the previous, and Gordon Durie was gone; Steve Cowan only scored four without him and no Hibs player scored double figures that season. The manager did act decisively to tighten the defence and in his first 12 months in charge recruited Tommy McIntyre, Graham Mitchell, Neil Orr and Andy Goram, all of whom would greatly improve the side and would become legends at the club.

In Alex Miller's first full campaign as Hibs boss in 1987/88 the team improved and finished sixth in the table – narrowly missing out on Europe. They scored 41 goals in the league, so the goals-scored tally was still a problem but the number of goals conceded was greatly reduced, from 63 conceded in 85/86, 70 conceded in 86/87, to just 42 conceded in 87/88. That's a remarkable reduction in goals against and shows that the manager started to build his team from the back. Paul Kane was top scorer with 12 in 87/88; no other Hibs player managed more than six.

In season 88/89, with Gareth Evans having been added midway through the previous season, Steve Archibald donning the green and Keith Houchen joining late in the campaign, Hibs improved again, finishing fifth and qualifying for the UEFA Cup, as well as reaching the Scottish Cup semis. Just 36 league goals were conceded that season, another improvement, though the goals-for tally remained much the same as in the previous two seasons. Nevertheless, there was yet more improvement. Steve Archibald was top scorer in that campaign, with 16. The league that season had been reduced from 12 teams to ten again.

With 12 goals, Keith Houchen was the club's top scorer in season 89/90, a campaign which saw the green jerseys compete in Europe and finish seventh in the league, also winning the popular Tennents' Sixes indoor tournament. While the league position of the club regressed slightly that season, the defence stayed relatively tight again, remaining on roughly the same average number of goals conceded as in the previous two campaigns, 41 conceded to 34 scored.

So, by the time of that horrible summer of 1990, when Hearts supremo Wallace Mercer tried to do away with Hibernian, Alex Miller had built a better side than those of any Hibs manager since the great Eddie Turnbull. He'd fixed the leaky defence, crowds were up and the team wasn't finishing anywhere near a relegation spot. He had steadied the ship. We didn't score enough goals but we were by no means a bad side.

Season 90/91 was an anomaly statistically and a nightmare emotionally for Hibernian. We almost ceased to exist, we were in turmoil, we'd just lost the irreplaceable John Collins and we had no money for new players. Our threadbare squad won just six matches. We finished second bottom, though we only conceded ten more goals than in the previous campaign. Our main on-field problem in 90/91 was a lack of goals scored. We only scored 24 in the league; Paul Wright was our top scorer with just six, while no other player got more than three. We were fortunate that season that league reconstruction saved us the ignominy of a proper relegation battle, though it should be noted that, with the ten-team top flight, there was only one relegation spot and the team that would have gone down would have been St Mirren, not us. The league was reconstructed once more, to a 12-team top flight.

The summer of 1991 saw Hibernian reborn, simplified, minus the old PLC and all of the headache related to it. Andy Goram was gone but Keith Wright arrived. Keith's 17 goals in all competitions, along with a dozen apiece for Mickey Weir and Pat McGinlay, helped the team to finish fifth in the league, win the SKOL League Cup, and to qualify for the UEFA Cup once more. That season 91/92 saw our goal difference go into the black again for the first time since our season in Division One under Bertie Auld, with 53 scored to 45 conceded. The statistics for subsequent seasons up until Alex Miller left are contained within the season chapters in this book.

Alex Miller improved Hibernian's defence during his first three full seasons at the helm. Then, after the 90/91 'write-off' campaign, he did something else. Between 1991 and 1995, for four years, Alex Miller's Hibs were a good team. Here's why.

From season 91/92, our SKOL League Cup-winning campaign, to the end of season 94/95, when we split the old firm and finished third, we played 168 league matches and won 56, drew 62 and lost 50. A total of 209 league goals were scored, 194 conceded. In those four seasons, we averaged 1.25 goals per match, to 1.15 conceded. In other words, in that four-year period we did what all good football teams do, we scored a few more than we conceded. Given how things had gone for Hibs since the late 70s, that was a vast improvement. It's true that the average Hibs result under Alex Miller for his full decade in charge actually works out at 0-0, but that's largely down to the rebuilding job that he had to undertake in his first three years, the poor season 90/91 and the restricted player budget from 1995 onwards due to stadium redevelopment (hence why season 95/96 isn't included in the good period I've highlighted).

From the summer of 91 to the summer of 95, Hibs were a good side. We finished seventh in 92/93, but after that no Alex Miller Hibs side finished the campaign outside of the top five for the duration of his reign. In that four-year period we also scored 27 goals in the Scottish Cup, 29 goals in the League Cup and three in the UEFA Cup, which bumped the goals scored up to 268 in 198 matches in all competitions. That is an average of 1.35 goals per game from 91/92 to 94/95. That doesn't sound great, but for a non-old firm Premier League club, it actually is. Statistics don't tell the whole story, though.

During those four years we had some wonderful, unforgettable times as Hibs fans. We won the League Cup in 1991/92, the first time that many of us had seen Hibs win anything and a win that heralded a fine seven years of hilarious 'No cups in Gorgie' banter with our city rivals. We ran a crack European side close in the UEFA Cup in 92/93, not actually losing a game to them and doing ourselves and Scotland proud, as well as reaching the Scottish Cup semis that same season. In season 93/94 we topped the league for months and came within a whisker of winning the League Cup for the second time in just two years. In season 94/95 we again reached the Scottish Cup semis and we finished third in the table, becoming the first Hibs side to do so since 1976. Given that we operate in a domestic set-up where the two main Glasgow sides have a virtual duopoly on success, that period of Alex Miller's time at Hibs is almost a golden era. Were it not for the poor run against Hearts in that time, more would see it that way, though many already do. The 90/91 Hands Off Hibs battle and the HOH movement itself – Kenny McLean, Dougie Cromb, Tom Farmer and the Hibs fans – didn't just save the club; their interventions also contributed to giving us a no bad Hibs team for the next five years as well, better than anything from the 80s or even the late 70s. That's often overlooked. We Hibs fans who were but children or even unborn in 90/91 owe a lot to our older Hibs comrades for making sure that we got that.

So, not only did Alex Miller steady the ship when he came in, he gradually improved the team and its fortunes, with the exception of season 90/91. He made the defence better, he brought actual success and a trophy to the club, and helped give Edinburgh its first open-topped bus parade in a generation.

When we look at Alex Miller's signings at Hibs, we more often than not find that the manager struck gold. His first three signings, Dougie Bell, Tommy McIntyre and Graham Mitchell, gave us one decent bit-part player and two cup-winning club legends. Neil Orr, too, was a fine player whose contribution to the Hibernian cause perhaps deserves more recognition. Andy Goram went on to become a legend, Steve Archibald was a fine striker whom we were all lucky to get to see in the green, whilst the excellent Gareth Evans proved not only to be a bargain at £55k but also a great striker and fantastic club servant. Keith Houchen would have ended up a Hibs legend were it not for his temper, while Paul Wright was also a fine striker; his career at Hibs was ruined by injury but he proved at other clubs just what a good player he was and why Alex Miller was right to pay £300,000 to QPR for him. Mark McGraw was another fine talent. Like Paul Wright, his stint at Hibs was disrupted by injury. Brian Hamilton won a cup at Hibs and was an unsung hero in green, while Neil Cooper, signed at the same time, was a decent player. David Farrell was a very useful footballer player and Pat McGinlay, signed from Blackpool as a teenage full-back by Alex Miller, went on to become perhaps Hibernian's finest midfield player of the 1990s.

Murdo MacLeod came in and was an inspired choice as our cup-winning captain in 1991.

However, the later Alex Miller signings that contributed to our success in the 90s really show that the boss had an eye for a fantastic player. John Burridge came in to replace Andy Goram and was an inspired choice to do so, as not only was he a great goalie, he lifted spirits in the dressing room with his wonderful personality. Dave Beaumont is seen by some as a bit-part player, yet he scored for us in Europe and helped set up the goal which ended Hearts' unbeaten run in 1994, as well as proving himself a fine, versatile centre-back. Keith Wright was Hibernian's biggest impact signing of the late 20th century; perhaps our greatest 'old-school' number nine. Darren Jackson was an absolute revelation for Hibernian, whether starring up front or in midfield – but perhaps not as goalkeeper. He was our best player for five years. The three signings in 1993 were great choices: Jim Leighton was perhaps the last truly great Hibs goalie, while Kevin McAllister and Michael O'Neill were two of the most gifted players to wear the green in the modern era. Some of the later signings, guys like Lavety, Millen, Ian Cameron, Ray Wilkins, Brian Welsh, big Joe McLaughlin and a few others, may not have set the heather on fire at Easter Road, but all had a part to play and all were good football players. Alex Miller has his detractors among the Hibs support, that's only natural, especially for a boss who managed the club for such a long time, some of those times being difficult, but one truth is undeniable – he never signed a single bad football player.

While the manager was fairly quick to move along players who were at the club when he arrived but who he didn't think were suitable for the new Hibs – good talented guys like George McCluskey and Steve Cowan, for example, even club legends like Gordon Rae – he clearly saw that John Blackley, and before him Pat Stanton, had ensured that there was a backbone of excellent young but experienced players already at Hibs when he arrived late in 1986. Brilliant, talented Hibs legends like Mickey Weir, Eddie May, Joe Tortolano, Paul Kane, Gordon Hunter and the amazing John Collins all became better players under Miller and were a huge part of the post-1986 Hibs story, some for a couple of years, some for much longer. The boss also gave youth a chance. Guys like Willie Miller, Kevin Harper and Steven Tweed were first blooded by Alex Miller and became Hibs legends in their own right. Other great guys like Billy Findlay, Chris Jackson, Chris Reid, Davy Fellenger, Danny Lennon and Graeme Donald all played their parts, too.

Alex Miller was also fortunate to have some great coaches around him. Martin Ferguson, Peter Cormack, Murdo MacLeod, Jocky Scott, even Jim McLaughlin with the youth teams and the physio Stewart Collie, all played their part at various stages of that era.

Some Hibs fans claimed that Alex Miller's teams were defensive. His signings, most of whom were attacking players, prove otherwise. Part of the problem some Hibs fans had with the manager was this notion that there is a 'Hibs way' of playing football, a way of playing attacking, cavalier, entertaining football and scoring a barrowload of goals. The good Hibs teams of the 50s, 60s and 70s were certainly capable of that at times, but that wasn't really down to a specific 'Hibs way', it was down to having good players led by good managers; if you have that then it's easy to score goals and to entertain. Have you ever heard of a shite team with shite players and a shite manager who score a lot of goals and who entertain? Good players and a good manager lead to good results and lots of goals, ergo, good entertainment. Alex Miller didn't have his ideal squad at first, but when he did have his own team, particularly between 91 and 95, Hibs were as good and as entertaining as any other side in the UK.

So, all things considered, was Alex Miller a good Hibs manager? Believe it or not, that's not what this book is all about. It's just a story of Hibs from 1992–99, of which he happens to be a huge part. Of course he was a good manager: he had success managing St Mirren and Hibs, as well as at Scotland and Liverpool as a coach. Certain things are true of Alex's time at Easter Road.

Alex Miller's teams increased the crowds at Easter Road. He fixed a defence that had been leaking goals for six years under three different managers. He was the first 'modern' Hibs manager, as he was at the helm when cataclysmic events like Bosman and the Taylor Report struck football and was at the forefront of the introduction of modern coaching techniques and sports science in Scottish football. He was at Hibs when our stadium was first modernised, when Sky TV first showed an interest in our game and when our old rigid league set-up was finally modernised in 1994. He was the first 'modern' Hibs manager, yet he was also the last 'old-school'-style Hibs manager. Why? Well, he was the last man to manage Hibs when the old transfer system was still in use, a system where the manager's say on almost everything was final. The days when managers could have a real go at underperforming players and when more often than not those players would react positively to a ticking-off rather than, say, going blubbing to the press or to their agents or even to the chairman, as some vacuous crybaby footballers do nowadays when at odds with their gaffer. There was no posh training centre, no media training, no Sky Sports News lurking, waiting to find out which player had been fined for going out during the week or turning up late for training, and though the boss could and did delegate his duties when necessary, ultimately, the buck stopped with him on all matters. Alex Miller was both a truly modern coach and an authentic 'old-school'-style manager, the like of which we will never see in football again. He was the last Hibs manager who truly managed every aspect of football at the club. Football managers today have coaches, recruitment officers, a multitude of assistants and 'suits' at their beck and call and are really more akin to motivational speakers and PR guys, with a little bit of tactics thrown in. Alex Miller wasn't like that; he was a proper football manager.

His interview style, his attitude towards and his record in the derby fixture and the fact that he came from 'the west' and played for Rangers doubtless pissed off some Hibs fans at times, even your humble correspondent was exasperated by some of the team's performances in 1986–1996 and may have joined in with some anti-Miller chants, but that's all by the by, now. For my generation of Hibs fans, who were but boys and girls when Alex arrived at Hibs and were adults when he left, he is a Hibernian legend. We literally grew up watching him manage our team. He signed all of those wonderful players who wowed us on the terracing, players who made us cheer, roar, laugh, sing and cry. He stuck by us during the 1990 takeover attempt, he brought joy to Easter Road by winning us a major cup – at the time a feat managed only by Eddie Turnbull and Dan McMichael and since achieved only by John Collins and Alan Stubbs. He led us into Europe twice, and, for the most part, he helped make us proud to be Hibbies. Older Hibbies, too, now that time has passed, must surely look back and see how important his ten years at the helm were. He led our green jerseys for a decade and vastly improved on the poor

Hibs sides of the late 70s and early 80s. When thinking of Alex Miller, ask yourself, which memory of his time at Hibs will you take to the grave with you, what will truly stay with you? Is it a frustrating narrow defeat to Hearts? Is it an unexplainable 1-3 humping by Airdrie at Broomfield with all the players out of position for no apparent reason? Or, is it following your beloved Hibs to Hungary or to Belgium for your first European away trip? Is it big Tommy McIntyre and Keith Wright sending a green and white sea of scarves at Hampden into rapturous delirium, lifting the SKOL League Cup then heading back to Edinburgh for an unforgettable joyous party in the shadow of Arthur's Seat? You already know the answer to that question, don't you? Alex Miller is a Hibernian legend.

After Miller was sacked in 1996, Jocky Scott didn't do enough in his time as caretaker boss to justify being given the manager's job on a permanent basis. He lost six and won just three of his 13 matches in charge – that's relegation form. The players and some of the board wanted him to get the job as he was well liked, was a good coach and was highly respected. Appointing him wouldn't have been a revolution; it'd have been more of an evolution. As it turned out, revolution, under Jim Duffy, was to prove catastrophic for Hibs, in the short term at least, so perhaps we'd have been as well appointing Jocky. Truth is, we'll never know how that might've worked out. The highlight of his brief reign was that fine home win over a very good Rangers side.

Jim Duffy's spell in charge is a time that still today can provoke a luke-warm response from many Hibs fans when asked about it. Some still blame him for us being relegated in 1998. However, many Hibs fans also look fondly upon those few months in the late summer of 1997, when our boys in green jerseys played in that fearless, flowing, cavalier entertaining style that for a time had us all spellbound. We just wish that had lasted a bit longer. Jim was a young manager and the Hibs job is a massive one. The temporary intricacies of the transfer market around the time of Duffy's reign didn't help, nor did the spate of injuries the team suffered as the season moved into winter. With winter, we stopped scoring, kept conceding and the heads went down. Jim himself accepts the blame for that – I think that in doing so he's being a little harsh on himself, but we all have our own view as fans.

Jim Duffy, like Miller and Scott, did his best for Hibernian. He tried something new and it did work briefly, but ultimately it didn't work out. Despite the calumny poured on Jim by some since the 1998 relegation, Jim was no fool. Now, almost 25 years later, look back and remember the good times. After all, relegation wasn't solely Jim's fault and, in any case, relegation really isn't that big a disaster in Scotland. All it *really* meant was that we played some different teams for a season in a different league, then returned to our old league after a year, far stronger and with a much better side.

Alex McLeish was a great Hibs manager, but in the context of this book he's almost a footnote, simply by virtue of the fact that he came to the club at the very end of the century, when this book ends. He is most fondly remembered by Hibs fans for two things: signing Franck Sauzee and Russell Latapy, and his impressive (by Hibs standards) record of losing just one of the ten derbies in which he managed Hibs. Motherwell refused to let Eck (McLeish) speak to Hibs when Alex Miller left Easter Road in 1996, so we didn't get him until 1998.

Now, it's correct to say that Hibs didn't last 18 months in the top flight without Alex Miller, because we didn't.

It's easy to say that Miller should've stayed or that someone else should have replaced him: there are merits in both arguments. Ask yourself, did these changes really affect or ruin your life as a Hibs fan in the late 90s? Did they stop you from having pints, singsongs and a good time on a Saturday while watching the Hibs? Of course they didn't. It's all part of that Hibernian rollercoaster. In many ways, it doesn't matter one bit who the manager is, or what division we're in, we go along to watch our team regardless. Hibs weren't relegated because Alex Miller left and Jim Duffy came in. We were relegated because we had been largely pish for almost two years after our excellent early-to-mid 90s team ran out of steam and was broken up. That's football, that happens, relegation was just the coup de grace. Relegation didn't really do us any real harm, anyway; here's how.

Alex Miller left in 1996 and was replaced by Jim Duffy. Jim Duffy left in February 1998 and was replaced by Alex McLeish. Hibs were relegated. Hibs rebuilt in Division One, crowds soared, the team easily won the title and promotion and, en route, acquired Russell Latapy and Franck Sauzee. McLeish's reign in the top flight brought a much-needed dominant spell over Hearts, a third-place finish, two Scottish Cup semi-finals and a Scottish Cup Final, as well as a noble outing in the UEFA Cup against AEK Athens.

Eck's good work at Hibs saw him lured to Rangers. The board fecked up and appointed Franck Sauzee as manager, giving us what we, the fans, wanted, instead of what the club actually needed. It didn't work out for Franck as a boss so instead we employed the league's best manager outwith the old firm at the time, Bobby Williamson. Bobby came in just before the Sky deal collapsed and our league ended up with a pitiful TV deal and most clubs had to cut costs drastically. These cuts compelled Bobby to fully utilise youngsters Scott

Brown, Kevin Thomson, Derek Riordan, Garry O'Connor and Steven Whittaker, as well as relying more heavily on young Tam McManus. The youngsters were thrown in at the deep end and they all swam. Tony Mowbray came in later and let the five younger players express themselves. They managed a third-place finish and got into Europe again, as well as reaching two Scottish Cup semi-finals. By 2007 all of those five players had done exceptionally well and had been sold, though two remained long enough at the club to win the 2007 League Cup, when John Collins turned a very talented but 'boybandish' Mowbray team into true winners. The cash raised from the sale of those great young players helped fund our new out-of-town training centre.

The global economy began to crash in 2007 and was in full meltdown by 2008 when Mixu Paatelainen took over. We did alright under Mixu and then under John Hughes but then Colin Calderwood came in and didn't do as well. His team looked doomed to go the way of the 1998 Hibs side so wee Pat Fenlon was brought in to save the club from relegation. He achieved this and also flukily reached two Scottish Cup finals with very poor Hibs sides, but one of those finals was a 1-5 loss to a big-spending Hearts side and that, along with a 0-7 home reverse against Malmo in the Europa League, meant that Pat was gone by late 2013. In came Terry Butcher who started well but ended up on a long miserable winless run just like the one Jim Duffy's doomed side went on in 97/98. Butcher got Hibs relegated. Alan Stubbs came in and, though he failed to get Hibs promoted in two attempts, he won us the Scottish Cup for the first time in 114 years. The holy f*****g grail finally delivered!

Causality. Cause and effect. We looked at that in *Oblivion to Hampden* when discussing what life would have been like after 1990 had Hibs as we know Hibs ceased to be. It's just as relevant here. Alex Miller leaving in 1996 began a 20-year chain of events which ultimately led us to that glorious, beautiful sun-soaked day at Hampden against Rangers on 21 May 2016. Remember that joyous day and its aftermath, and even our brilliant return to the top flight in season 2017/18? Given that the events of the previous 20 years, however upsetting or annoying some of them were at the time, were the path that led us to Scottish Cup glory, would you go back and change them if you could? I'll wager the answer is 'no way'. We won the Scottish Cup in 2016 because our team was good and didn't dwell on the failings of their predecessors. The sequence of events leading up to that triumph, though at times arduous, was what created the conditions and circumstances that allowed Stubbs's good Hibs side a real opportunity to lift that holy grail. In short, in Hibs' modern history, all roads, no matter how potholed or arduous, lead to Hampden Park in May of 2016. All of the successive managers, comings and goings, financial crashes, TV deals falling apart, stadium development, good players, shite players, songs, stories, relegations, promotions, cup wins, Euro trips, scandals and legend, have made Hibernian FC what it is today. Anyway, I digress. So, with all that in mind, let's head back to the 90s together; after all, that's why you're here …

May your mind set you free
(Opened by the wonderful)
May your heart lead you on.

SAY SOMETHING

'Bill Shankly said to Bertie Mee, have you heard of the Northbank Highbury? Shanks said "No I don't think so but I've heard of the mental Hibees", anananananananana, we are the mental … Hibees!'

IT'S A Wednesday night match at Easter Road in the 1990s. Just over 8,000 fans are in attendance, despite the match being shown live on terrestrial TV. There are fewer than eight minutes remaining and the late summer sun has abated, the match continuing under the warm, powerful glow of Easter Road's lights. Alex Miller stands in a familiar spot on the touchline, his arms folded; his opposite number in the other technical area – an Aberdeen legend – is doing the same. It's a cup tie and a penalty kick has been awarded. The fans, red and green, had been expecting to go to extra time after what has been a hard-fought but not exactly entertaining tussle between two of Scotland's biggest football clubs.

Referee Stuart Dougal has awarded a penalty kick at the 'Hibs end' of the ground. Fans in the stands around anxiously await the outcome of the spot kick. Jim Leighton waits on his goal line like a cat waiting to pounce upon a mouse, in that trademark low crouching position of his that

Hibernian fans know all too well. Alex Miller has every confidence in his goalkeeper. Then, upon Mr Dougal's whistle, the striker charged with beating Leighton from the spot steps up and unleashes a near-perfect penalty strike, which flies into the corner of the net despite a valiant attempt by the goalie to keep it out. Jim Leighton hammers the turf with his fist in frustration. Alex Miller's head goes down momentarily, then he shouts instructions to his now demoralised team.

All around them, Easter Road erupts in sheer joy. That's because it had been a penalty to Hibernian. Striker Stevie Crawford has just beaten Jim Leighton from the spot to seal an unlikely victory for Hibernian over Aberdeen, who at the time, in August 1998, were managed by former Hibernian boss, Alex Miller. The No.9 striker, wearing the famous green jersey, sponsored by Le Coq Sportif and Carlsberg, celebrates with his team-mates and with the fans.

The match finishes 1-0 to Hibs and the Hibees, managed by ex-Dons legend Alex McLeish, are into the Scottish League Cup quarter-finals. The reason for the Hibs fans' joy at this narrow victory is simple – at the time Hibernian were playing in Division One, having been relegated in 1997/98, while Alex Miller's Aberdeen side topped the Scottish Premier League after making an excellent start to the season.

Hibernian FC's relegation in season 97/98 was not the fault of Alex Miller or Jim Leighton; by then neither was at Easter Road. Both men are iconic figures at Easter Road, especially Alex Miller. To most Hibs fans, they represent the 1990s just as much as Blur v Oasis, raves and *The Big Breakfast* do. Quite how Hibernian FC ended up in Division One and playing against these two former heroes of theirs in the cup isn't the real story; it's more of an ironic anecdote, especially given that in the next round of the cup McLeish's Hibs were thrashed 4-0 by St Johnstone up at McDiarmid Park.

But to understand how Hibernian FC got to where they were at the turn of the century, we should look at part of the final decade of that 20th century, when big changes at Hibs, in Scottish football and indeed in global football saw the birth of a truly modern Hibernian FC. To do that, we must look at the reign of Hibernian boss Alex Miller, or at least the second half of it. My 2016 book *From Oblivion to Hampden* already covered Hibernian FC's history from 1986 to 1992, so in this work we will look at Hibs between 1992 and 1999, but with most emphasis on the period 1992–1996, the final four-and-a-bit seasons of Alex Miller's decade in the Easter Rod hot seat. It is my hope that by writing about our beloved Hibs in this style, some of the other brilliant established or up and coming Hibby authors and historians will 'pick up the torch' and write similar books about other periods in our club's proud history. But if they don't, that's okay, let's just have a reminisce, a laugh, a cry and maybe even a debate as we go back to the 1990s and follow Alex Miller's green and white army on an epic journey. I assure you, even with no major trophy wins, following Hibernian in the mid to late 90s was certainly not boring …

Say something, say something, anything
I've shown you everything
Give me a sign …

BORN OF FRUSTRATION

'And now we've got a younger team, I dinnae want tae brag.
I only want to say the Scottish Cup is in the bag!
We're going to top the league next year and win the Scottish flag!
As we go marching on!'

IT'S AN unusually cold Saturday afternoon in March of 1992. An outright battle is underway on the pitch at that beautiful stadium which sits in the shadow of Arthur's Seat. On one side of this battle is Alex Miller's reborn Hibernian, resplendent in an iconic Adidas kit and looking to get back to Hampden for the third time in six months. On the other side is a dogged, physical yet frustratingly effective Airdrieonians side managed by ex-Hearts boss Alex MacDonald. The Diamonds, as they were known, are looking for a draw; a chance to drag their opponents back to Lanarkshire for a replay. Hibs, on the other hand, want this Scottish Cup quarter-final to be decided in 90 minutes; doing so successfully will give the green jerseys a chance not only to end the club's 90-year wait to lift the Scottish Cup but also to seal an historic cup double, Hibs having won the SKOL League Cup back in October 91. Hibs have laid siege to Airdrie's back line for most of the match, despite persistent fouling and time-wasting by the Lanarkshire side, yet for all their efforts a goal has eluded Alex Miller's men. Penalty specialist Tommy McIntyre has even had a second-half spot kick brilliantly saved by Airdrie keeper John Martin. Alex Miller has gone with the same starting XI which won the League Cup Final against Dunfermline.

John Burridge in goal, Miller, Mitchell, Hunter and McIntyre at the back, the 'magic square' in midfield of MacLeod, McGinlay, Hamilton and Weir, with Gareth Evans and Keith Wright up front. Heroes all – already immortal in the eyes of the Hibbies. Unfortunately for the men from Leith, Mickey Weir is cruelly fouled midway through the first half and has to be stretchered off. Hibs fans on the terracing are already making plans for a midweek trip to Broomfield when up pops Airdrie's young substitute Owen Coyle to score in the last ten minutes with Airdrie's first shot of the match. Hibs throw everyone forward; suddenly that replay doesn't seem like such a bad idea, but when the match's second goal comes it's not a green jersey who puts the ball into the net, it's a red and white-clad Sammy Conn, catching Hibs on the break deep into injury time and lobbing the exposed John Burridge to seal Airdrie's 2-0 victory and end Hibernian's double dream.

Despite the expletives and groans among the home support as they trudge out of the stadium, for their part the fans don't play the blame game – this time. Yes, everyone's scunnered at the loss, but no one really blames Budgie for conceding the goals, no one's blaming Tommy McIntyre – one of the finest defenders to wear the green in the modern era – for his penalty being saved, no one blames goal-machine Keith Wright and his strike partner Gareth Evans for not being able to breach the Diamonds' defence.

After all, Hibernian have already bagged one major trophy in season 91/92 and doing so has guaranteed them a place in the following season's UEFA Cup. Airdrie came to Easter Road intent on stopping Hibs from playing football and on this occasion, Hibs had no answer to such strategy. So goes the world – the smaller team with the game plan won the cup tie. Airdrie went on to knock Hearts out in the semi-finals then lost to Rangers in the final. Alex Miller's men puttered along until the end of the season, finishing fifth in the league after a final-day 2-1 victory over Celtic at Parkhead.

Considering that a year earlier there had been a real chance that there would be no more Hibernian FC in Scottish football's senior ranks, things were going well. The cup win had quietened many of the fans who had been calling for Alex Miller to be sacked. There was European football to look forward to in the coming 92/93 season and Hibernian were now safe from existential peril and financial mismanagement. Tom Farmer CBE (as was at the time) and the Hibs fans had saved the club in 1990 and 1991, now Douglas Cromb was club chairman. He was a safe pair of hands, a far cry from the ousted Duff/Gray regime which had almost caused the club's death. The future looked good for Hibernian; the youth team held the BP Scottish Youth Cup, the club had some excellent coaches like Martin Ferguson, brother of Manchester United's boss Alex. Two new sponsorship deals were in place, too. Both deals involved six-figure sums. Lanarkshire-based MacBean Protective Clothing – a firm specialising in outdoor wear and which people often confused with haulage firm JB Macbean – were now the club's main sponsor and, with the five-year Adidas deal having expired, a new kit sponsor was also in place. The name was familiar to many Hibs fans; it was Bukta, though by 1992 the Bukta brand actually belonged to French firm En Tout Cas. Bukta famously sponsored Hibernian's kit in the 1970s and their simple designs were remembered fondly by many Hibbies. The new Bukta kit was very different from both to the simple Adidas design of previous seasons and from earlier Bukta Hibs kits. It still featured a green jersey with white sleeves, white shorts and green socks, but now also had an innovative 'stand-up or button down' type of collar and large green chevrons on the shorts and upper sleeves. The new away kit was revolutionary – a purple shirt with a green collar, black shorts and socks. The 'beermat/egg' club badge brought in by the old Duff/Gray regime remained as the club's emblem. Ironically, it had been one of the few things pertaining to the old Edinburgh Hibernian PLC which had survived the club's restructuring intact. The new kits were popular with fans, though in the summer of 1992 most fans looked for a very different type of new arrival at Easter Road. Most agreed that an experienced striker was needed to partner Keith Wright up front. In this instance, the fans, Alex Miller, Douglas Cromb and the press all shared that view.

There were already other good strikers at Hibs. Gareth Evans was an established and well-liked player, while Hibs also had young hot-shot Mark McGraw, who had really stepped up to the plate in season 91/92 until an injury just before the SKOL Cup Final sadly interrupted his first long run in the first XI.

Nevertheless, Alex Miller set his sights on Dundee United's 26-year-old striker, Darren Jackson, who had bagged 31 goals for the Terrors in just over three years at Tannadice. He had also played for Newcastle United and Meadowbank Thistle. He had scored a last-minute equaliser for Dundee United in 1991's Scottish Cup Final, though

Motherwell went on to win that match 4-3 after extra time. By 1992 Jackson's contract had expired but under the old pre-Bosman transfer system Hibs would still have to pay Dundee United a transfer fee in order to secure his services and free up his registration. His transfer fee was thus to be decided by a transfer tribunal, a common way of settling such disputes before 1995. Hibs cheekily offered around £250,000 for the striker. Dundee United wanted almost £1m. The tribunal eventually decided that Jackson was worth £400,000 – an excellent bit of business by Hibernian as Jackson would go on to become a 90s icon at Easter Road and was to be worth every penny.

Asides the arrival of Jackson, Hibernian's squad was almost unchanged from 1991/92 … long-serving defender Alan Sneddon departed after making 372 appearances over 12 seasons in the green, leaving on a free transfer to join Motherwell, and goalkeeper Stevie Woods – now a coach at Celtic – joined Clydebank.

As July neared its end Alex Miller's men completed their pre-season matches. Danny McGrain's Arbroath, Gavin Murray's East Fife and Jimmy Nicholl's Raith Rovers all lost to Hibs by the same 3-0 scoreline, while Highland League outfit Deveronvale held a weakened Hibs team to a 3-3 draw up north.

Talk talk talkin 'bout who's to blame
But all that counts is how to change
Stop stop talkin 'bout who's to blame
When all that counts in how to change …

RING THE BELLS – SEASON 92/93 – PART ONE

'Hail, Hail, the Hibs are here, all for goals and glory, all for goals and glory
Hail, Hail, the Hibs are here, all for goals and glory now!'

THE FINAL match of Hibernian's pre-season campaign of 92/93 was played at Easter Road on Monday, 27 July 1992. As usual, a top English side provided the opposition for the big showpiece pre-season match; in that year it was Kenny Dalglish's Blackburn Rovers, who had been promoted to England's new Premier League in season 91/92 after beating Leicester 1-0 in the play-off final at Wembley. Though not yet the title winners they would later become, Rovers had spent a lot of money and had a talented squad which included Mike Newell, Tim Sherwood, Stuart Ripley, Stuart Munro, defenders David May and Colin Hendry and USA star Roy Wegerle. On the bench they also had a certain talented young midfielder whom the media down south were already dubbing 'the New Paul Gascoigne'. His name was, of course, Lee Makel. Blackburn's biggest name was Alan Shearer, whom they had just signed from Southampton for a then UK record £4m. The striker happily signed autographs for fans outside Easter Road's main stand before the match – little did he know that he was to be eclipsed on this occasion by a striker who had cost Hibernian a mere tenth of his big transfer fee. Shearer's appearance and the fact that it was a lovely warm July evening helped draw a crowd of around 8,000 to Easter Road for the encounter. Hibs usually had the edge over English teams in pre-season matches by virtue of the fact that Scotland's football season began two to three weeks before England's did, so Hibs were usually that little bit sharper. Blackburn's traditional home kit clashed with Hibs' so the Lancashire side wore their red and black striped away kit. Hibernian took the lead on 23 minutes when Tommy McIntyre beat Colin Hendry to Murdo MacLeod's corner to head the ball into the net. Brian Hamilton added a second for Hibs after 61 minutes, prodding home after a 'stramash' in the box. Seven minutes later Darren Jackson scored on his home debut, robbing David May then slotting the ball past Blackburn keeper Bobby Mimms. Alan Shearer had a decidedly quiet debut in contrast, Tommy McIntyre shackled him superbly and what few half chances the striker had never really troubled young Chris Reid in the Hibs goal. Shearer was substituted late on when Hibs were 3-0 up, to cries of 'what a waste of money' from the fans on the East Terracing. It came to pass that Shearer did go on to become a legend, but, like Wayne Rooney with Everton ten years later at Easter Road, he just couldn't defeat Hibs!

Four days later Alex Miller led his team up to Pittodrie to face Aberdeen in the Premier Division's opening fixture. As the season began, actor Jimmy Nail was number one in the UK charts with his song 'Ain't no doubt' and the original movie version of *Buffy the Vampire Slayer* was taking cinemas by storm. The Olympic Games in Barcelona had just finished, Slovakia had just seceded from Czechoslovakia and Colombian drug baron and mass-murderer Pablo Escobar had just escaped from his luxury prison, foiling attempts to extradite him to the USA.

The summer of 92 had seen Scotland do reasonably well at the European Championship finals in Sweden, losing narrowly to Germany and the Netherlands but beating the CIS (the former USSR) 3-0 to salvage some pride in the final group game. The tournament was won by Denmark, late entrants who replaced Yugoslavia after the Balkans civil war persuaded UEFA to bar Yugoslavia from the finals. Denmark had been the summer's surprise package – just as Hibs had been Scotland's surprise package in season 91/92. The question most Hibs fans asked themselves as the 92/93 season opener at Pittodrie loomed was simple – could we do as well or even a bit better in the coming campaign? A Hibs season ticket for the East Terrace in 1992 cost £150 for adults, £75 for youths.

* * *

Having vanquished Alan Shearer and his team during the week, Hibernian were up against his namesake Duncan, Aberdeen's new signing from Blackburn Rovers, when they faced the Dons away in the weekend's season opener. Duncan Shearer had actually been one of Alex Miller's signing targets but had ended up at Aberdeen. Dons legend and manager Willie Miller unleashed his new powerful strike force of Shearer and a certain Mixu Paatelainen in the match. Keith Wright and Mickey Weir both came close for Hibs in what was a pretty even first half but the second 45 minutes saw Chris Reid beaten three times, twice by Duncan Shearer and once by Scott Booth. The match, played in the shadow of the new stand which was being built to replace the old Pittodrie Beach End, finished Aberdeen 3 Hibernian 0. 'We didn't compete in midfield,' said Alex Miller afterwards.

Alex Miller gave the same starting XI another chance three days later at Fir Park against Motherwell, and this time the purple-clad Hibees took both points, winning 2-1 thanks to goals from Pat McGinlay and Keith Wright. Champions Rangers were then held to a goalless draw at Easter Road the following Saturday, ideal preparation for the beginning of Hibernian's defence of the SKOL League Cup against Raith Rovers at Easter Road on the Wednesday evening.

It was the last season in which the Scottish League Cup was sponsored by SKOL Lager and the cup holders blew away Jimmy Nicholl's side 4-1, Hibernian's goals coming courtesy of a double by Gareth Evans, a Pat McGinlay strike and a Brian Hamilton penalty. John McStay netted the Fife side's consolation. Just like in season 91/92, Hibs were drawn to play Kilmarnock at Rugby Park in round three of the tournament. Tommy Burns had replaced Jim Fleeting as Kilmarnock player-boss early in 1992 and Killie were out for revenge. They had given Hibs a real test at Rugby Park the previous season – a real fright – but the Hibees had dug deep and won 3-2 that time. Tommy Burns had missed that match because of suspension but was available for the 1992 rematch.

Hibs warmed up for the cup tie by losing 1-2 to Jim Jefferies' Falkirk side at crumbling Brockville in the league, Joe Tortolano scoring Hibs' goal. Eddie May and Tommy McQueen were on target for the Bairns, the latter with a penalty after Chris Reid had hauled down Falkirk's tricky little winger, Kevin McAllister. A crowd of just less than 8,000 then turned up at Rugby Park for the midweek SKOL

League Cup rematch between Kilmarnock and Hibernian. Hibs fans expected a tough game but were confident of victory, while Killie fans believed that their team could avenge the previous season's defeat. Kilmarnock scored first in this fiercely contested match, McSkimming scoring after 39 minutes, but Keith Wright equalised for Hibs on 67 minutes. The match then went to extra time and the Ayrshire side stunned Alex Miller's men, winning the match 3-1, with one of their extra-time goals being scored by ex-Hibs striker George McCluskey, the other by Calum Campbell, who had scored for Killie against Hibs a year earlier. To complete a frustrating evening, Bobby Geddes saved a late extra-time penalty from Tommy McIntyre. Alex Miller kept the players in the dressing room for a full hour after this defeat.

Kilmarnock, under Tommy Burns, were becoming a force to be reckoned with and that season would see them achieve promotion to the Premier Division, however, that didn't mean that this result wasn't still a sore one for the Hibs faithful. Hibernian's hold on the SKOL League Cup was relinquished. Killie were themselves beaten 3-1 in the next round by St Johnstone at Rugby Park. The last ever SKOL League Cup Final was eventually contested by Rangers and Aberdeen that October, Rangers winning 2-1 after extra time, thanks to an own goal by Aberdeen's Gary Smith, who would of course later play for Hibernian at the turn of the century. (SKOL sponsored the Scottish League Cup between 1984 and 1992.)

Later that season, Kilmarnock's youth team eliminated Hibs from the BP Scottish Youth Cup, which meant that the Ayrshire side had knocked the green jerseys out of both cups that they were the holders of. Alex Miller and his players didn't have much time to dwell on the League Cup exit, as the following Saturday Hearts were due at Easter Road for the season's first capital derby.

Hearts had gone 13 matches unbeaten against Hibs since Eddie May's goal had given Hibernian a 1-0 win at Easter Road in January of 1989. Banter between Edinburgh football fans at the time was fairly simplistic – Hibs fans sang 'No cups in Gorgie' and mocked the Jambos' 30-year trophyless run, while Hearts consoled themselves with their wee unbeaten run against their city rivals. Just fewer than 16,000 fans were at Easter Road on Saturday, 22 August to witness the first Edinburgh derby of season 92/93.

Joe Jordan was confident that his Hearts team would win, while Alex Miller seemed just as confident that the men in green would come out on top. As it turned out, the match-day programme played a hugely important role in the outcome of the match.

The fans saw Hibs make a bright start.

Keith Wright had a clever toe-poke brilliantly saved by Henry Smith. Then, a Graham Mitchell diagonal ball into the box found Darren Jackson, whose brilliant header was net-bound until Smith clawed it away, denying the striker his first competitive Hibs goal. Peter van de Ven then hauled down Gareth Evans in the box and referee David Syme pointed to the spot.

The derby was Hibernian's first home game since the 4-1 demolition of Raith Rovers in the League Cup. The match programme contained handy diagrams of the team's goals from the Raith match, including one showing exactly where Brian Hamilton had placed his penalty into the back of the net.

Hibernian's last spot kick against the Jambos had been on New Year's Day 1992 at Tynecastle. Tommy McIntyre had coolly sent Henry Smith the wrong way and flicked the ball into the bottom corner at the Gorgie Road end, right in front of the Hibs fans, to earn the Cabbage a 1-1 draw on that occasion. Big Tam was playing this time, too, but Brian Hamilton had taken and scored Hibs' most recent penalty against Raith so he was given the task from the spot once more. Hammy stepped up and blasted the ball towards the roof of the net. A huge roar engulfed Easter Road but it was a defiant roar from the Hearts fans on the Dunbar End, as Henry Smith brilliantly saved Hamilton's net-bound thunderbolt. Smith later admitted that he had read the match programme before the game like he usually did, and had seen the diagram of Hamilton's spot kick against Raith, so he knew exactly where the Hibs midfielder would place his shot! This simple act of sporting espionage kept the derby level and probably saved Hearts' unbeaten run in the fixture. (Hibernian ended up missing no fewer than seven penalties in season 92/93.)

The penalty incident seemed to awaken Hearts, who surged forward and were denied a penalty of their own when Neil Orr's last-ditch tackle sent John Robertson crashing to the turf, but Hibs remained in the ascendancy. Henry Smith denied Keith Wright once more, diving at the striker's feet to block the type of one-on-one situation which Keith usually scored from. Darren Jackson did beat Smith just before half-time, his wonderful flick sailing through the air into the net, but the goal was ruled out because Pat McGinlay, who had matched Jackson's run, was offside. Pat wasn't interfering with play but the rules were more simplistic back then so the goal didn't stand. Jackson tried again moments later with a shot from the edge of the box which Smith parried brilliantly. Gareth Evans was first to react to the loose ball and looked set to score, but collided with the onrushing Jackson at the crucial moment, letting Hearts off the hook once more.

The second half saw the onslaught continue but Hibs just couldn't find a way past Henry Smith, whose heroics denied Keith Wright and Mickey Weir certain goals. In contrast, John Burridge was virtually a spectator for the whole 90 minutes. The match finished 0-0 and the Hibees had missed out on their best chance of beating their city rivals since 1989. Of all the matches in what would become a 22-match winless run in the fixture, this was the one Hibs really should have won and won convincingly. Over the years some Hibs fans have accused Alex Miller of using negative tactics, particularly in matches against Hearts. Yet this derby saw Hibs' starting XI include Wright, Jackson, Evans, McGinlay and Weir – three strikers and two attacking midfielders – not exactly Catenaccio, was it?

The 12-team Scottish Premier Division set-up, with sides playing each other four times a season, amounted to a gruelling 44-match league season which saw clubs play Saturday and midweek most of the time. Teams still earned two points for a win, one point for a draw, as in most other world leagues, though England's leagues had changed to three points for a win in the early 80s. Hibs were back in action a week after the Edinburgh derby, away to St Johnstone at McDiarmid Park. Tommy McIntyre was saint turned sinner, brilliantly heading the green jerseys into the lead in the second half, only to later be red-carded for hauling down Paul Wright in the box at the other end. The ex-Hibs striker took the resultant penalty himself and had the ball in the net before Budgie had even moved his feet. The match ended 1-1. Darren Jackson hit the post twice in this match. Strangely, some elements of Scotland's press were by then referring to the fact that Jackson hadn't yet scored a competitive goal in the green as 'a crisis', despite the season being only a few matches in. He didn't have to wait long to silence his critics.

Next up Hibernian faced Dundee United at Easter Road in a midweek fixture. Paddy Connolly gave the Terrors the lead just after half-time, 'skinning' defender Dave Beaumont before rounding John Burridge. With 18 minutes remaining, Hibs beat Dundee United's offside trap right on the halfway line. As the Tangerine defenders waved their arms in vain, Mickey Weir and Joe Tortolano raced through on goal with only Alan Main to beat. Mickey simply waited until Main advanced from his line then rolled the ball to Tortolano, who tapped in the equaliser. A minute later Maurice Malpas hauled down Keith Wright in the box and up stepped Jackson to score from the spot, sending Main the wrong way and ending his mini goal drought, as well as putting his old club to the sword – and not for the last time. Hibernian won 2-1 which set the team and fans up nicely for the weekend trip to Celtic Park.

In the early 90s Celtic were nothing like the dominant force that they are today or were in bygone years. Their club business model was flawed and outdated and their team was really no better than Hearts, Hibs or Aberdeen. Off the field they were in turmoil, on the field they were mediocre and, though capable of beating Rangers in a match, they had no chance of matching them when it came to a title challenge. That said, they still had some fine players in the early 90s and a fiercely loyal support. Parkhead was a good 'away day' back then. As Hibs fans we got a huge terrace behind the goal all to ourselves, at the same end of the ground where away fans are housed today. It was also a generally nicer place to watch football, a far cry from the hostile match-day experience that watching Hibs at Ibrox could be. Hibs had of course won on their last visit to Parkhead, triumphing

2-1 on the last day of season 91/92, thanks to a Derek Whyte own goal and a goal by Pat McGinlay. Alex Miller's men were looking for back-to-back wins at Celtic Park for Hibernian FC for the first time since the mid-50s.

Hibs took to the field wearing the new purple away kit and with a new combination in central defence, Dave Beaumont teaming up with Neil Orr. Most Hibs fans agreed that Hibernian's best pairing in that position at the time was the McIntyre/Hunter duo and some fans found it puzzling that the manager seemed so keen on tinkering at the back so often. In many eyes the ideal defensive partnership had been found in season 91/92, only to be discarded. Nowadays it's called squad rotation and all managers do it to a certain degree. Nevertheless, Orr and Beaumont got the nod at Celtic Park. There was a big European match coming up in midweek so every Hibs player was out to impress that day.

Two future Hibernian managers were in the Celtic line-up, defender Tony Mowbray and midfielder John Collins. Stuart Slater had the first attempt on goal, his top-corner-bound effort being brilliantly saved by John Burridge. Eleven minutes in, Celtic left-back Dariusz Wdowczyk curled an excellent low free kick past Budgie, giving Celtic the lead. Alex Miller's men came roaring back, Darren Jackson seeing a fine shot from a tight angle saved well by Celtic keeper Gordon Marshall at the near post, up at the Celtic end. Keith Wright equalised for Hibs just before half-time with a superb volley from 14 yards and the 29,000-strong crowd looked forward to an even better second half. Celtic had dominated the first 20 minutes but Hibs had ended the first 45 in the ascendancy. Hoops manager Liam Brady sent his team out to attack, like he always did. His side regained the advantage on 57 minutes when Paul McStay scored with an acrobatic volley, but Hibs fought back again and Celtic's lead lasted for only seven minutes. A long ball punted forward by Graham Mitchell reached Celtic right-back Tom Boyd, who kicked the ball back to his goalkeeper. Darren Jackson had anticipated Boyd's pass and rushed on to face Gordon Marshall, who of course couldn't pick the back pass up with his hands because of the newly introduced 'passback rule'. Marshall hesitated, took a fresh-air swipe at the ball, then panicked and hauled Jackson to the ground. The keeper should have been sent off, but escaped with a booking.

Darren Jackson took the kick himself and blasted it into Marshall's top right-hand corner to level the match at 2-2 with 25 minutes remaining. Both sides had chances to win what was a thrilling match. On 83 minutes Willie Miller launched a long diagonal ball forward to Keith Wright, who left Tony Mowbray for dead and bore down on goal. Gordon Marshall rushed from his penalty area to close Wright down but Wright 'dummied' him then squared the ball to substitute Gareth Evans. From eight yards 'Gazzer' still had a lot to do as there were two Celtic defenders on the line. His first shot was blocked by Gary Gillespie but he smashed the rebound into the net, putting Hibs 3-2 up and sending the large travelling support behind the goal into joyous rapture. John Burridge held firm at the very end, thwarting Andy Payton's late header, so Hibs won the match by three goals to two. The home fans left their stadium with the chant of 'Hibees Hibees Hibees' ringing in their ears. The victory was ideal preparation for the upcoming midweek UEFA Cup match against Belgian cracks Anderlecht. Alex Miller said this after the match: 'To have come through to Glasgow and to win 3-2 while having to come from behind twice does my players enormous credit. The strikers played very well indeed.' He was right. All three strikers had scored and in this match the usefulness of the Jackson/Wright partnership had at last become apparent. It wasn't just two points. It wasn't just Hibernian's first back-to-back wins at Celtic Park since the 50s, it was also the first time since the 60s that Hibs had scored more than two goals at Celtic Park. Hibs wouldn't beat Celtic at Celtic Park again until 2005, 13 years later.

Break, break the code
Concentrate
Let the doors swing open
See through all your walls
All your floors
Now you're in deeper than sleep.

RUNAGROUND – SEASON 92/93 – PART TWO

'For it's a grand old team to play for, and it's a grand old team to see
And if you know your history, it's enough to make your heart go oOoOoOo'

WHEN HIBS were drawn to play Belgian side Anderlecht in the 1992 UEFA Cup, many predicted that Alex Miller's men would be easily defeated by former Yugoslavia internationalist Luka Peruzović's experienced side. For Hibernian's part, the place in Europe had been a reward for winning the 1991 SKOL League Cup and everyone at the club, players, fans and staff alike, was just delighted to be in the competition with such a glamour tie, so soon after the club had almost died.

Nowadays the Belgian league has suffered as much as the Scottish one from being marginalised by bigger leagues who cherry-pick its better players, but in the 80s and 90s Belgium boasted some of Europe's top clubs. If you drew KV Mechelen, Brugge or Royal Antwerp in Europe you knew your team was in for a tough match. These clubs, including Anderlecht, regularly reached the later stages of and even sometimes won Europe's top competitions.

Anderlecht themselves had already won the UEFA Cup three times and even won the European Super Cup, and had also been beaten finalists, as well as having a very impressive domestic trophy haul. Anderlecht's squad in 1992 featured both established and future stars of European football. They had guys like Philippe Albert, Peter van Vossen, Luc Nilis, Marc Degryse and Danny Boffin, as well as Belgium's goalie Filip De Wilde. Also in their squad was a certain Jean-Francois De Sart, the man whose extra-time long-range pile-driver for Royal Liege had so cruelly knocked Hibernian out in round two of 1989's UEFA Cup.

Hibs' 1989 UEFA Cup campaign had begun against Hungarian side Videoton. Hibs had narrowly won the home leg 1-0 but had romped to victory in the second leg in Hungary, winning 3-0 to take the tie 4-0 on aggregate. That 3-0 win in Hungary had been a textbook example of how to win an away tie in Europe; a tactical masterclass by Alex Miller and his assistant Martin Ferguson. Everything had gone well – tactics, strategy, performance, fitness, fans' vocal backing, a bit of luck and the opposition even had a slight off day. Hibs didn't win an away match in a major European competition after that until July of 2016, when Neil Lennon's men beat Brondby 1-0 in Copenhagen, only to lose the resultant penalty shoot-out.

Of course, in 1989 Alex Miller's men had been knocked out by a Belgian side, RFC (Royal) Liege, after a 0-0 draw at Easter Road and then that 0-1 defeat after extra time in Belgium. All who wore the green hoped that Belgian lightning wouldn't strike twice. On Tuesday, 15 September 1992 Hibs took on Anderlecht in the UEFA Cup first round, first leg at Easter Road. The crowd was fewer than 15,000 because UEFA had started to severely restrict the stadium capacity of teams without all-seater stadiums for the matches in their own tournaments. Nevertheless, the atmosphere inside Easter Road was to be electric, improved by the fact that Hibs fans, for one night only, occupied the Dunbar End terracing as well as the other three sides of the stadium. A terracing ticket for that night cost £8. A few hundred Anderlecht fans were also in the stadium, to spice up the atmosphere and cheer on their beloved 'Purple and Whites'. A confrontation of epic proportions was on the cards …

The chant of the evening around the stadium before and during the match was 'Alex Miller's green and white army'. Fans today will recognise it as it's now sung about most Hibernian managers, often before they've even earned a song. In 1992 when the Hibbies sang the chant it was sung more slowly than it is today and could be akin to the warrior chanting in the movie *Zulu*. Hibs started with the same XI who had beaten Celtic: Burridge, Miller, Mitchell, Orr, Beaumont, MacLeod, Weir, Hamilton, Wright, Jackson, McGinlay. Alex Miller had made it clear that he wasn't sending his players out to stop Anderlecht from playing; he wanted his team to do the attacking. Before the game, the boss told the media, 'We know that Anderlecht are a top side, but we do not fear them. We only get one chance at home so we must make the most of it.' Hibs got off to the ideal start, pinning the Belgians back from the off. Murdo MacLeod looped a high ball into the box at the Dunbar End, which Keith Wright knocked down to Darren Jackson. With his weaker left foot Jackson hit a shot on goal from ten yards which was brilliantly saved by De Wilde, but the rebound was stabbed into the net by the onrushing Dave Beaumont. Hibs had the lead after just four minutes, 1-0.

Stunned, it took the Belgians ten more minutes to finally get their slick passing game going, yet Hibs dealt with the

Belgian attacks adequately. Then, just before half-time, Peter van Vossen, clean through on goal, collapsed to the ground when John Burridge dived at his feet. The German referee pointed to the spot and the ball was given to Marc Degryse, Anderlecht's playmaker. Degryse sent Burridge the wrong way from the spot and Anderlecht were level. The equaliser was greeted with a huge roar of encouragement from the home support, who were clearly confident that the green jerseys could win the match. Hibs went straight back onto the offensive and were denied a penalty of their own at the other end when Albert blatantly handled the ball in the box. Herr Weber, the referee, waved away the claims and protests and the teams went in at half-time level at 1-1.

The two sides went at each other from the off in the second half, with neither side gaining the advantage. It was hard to tell which side were the European cracks and which were the relative novices. That says more about how well the green jerseys were playing than it does about Anderlecht.

Disaster struck for the Hibees on 67 minutes. The highly impressive Degryse played a world-class 40-yard lob towards the Dunbar End. The ball bounced just outside the box and John Burridge rushed from his line to narrow the angle, but Peter van Vossen got there first and coolly lobbed the ball over Burridge and into the net. It was an exquisite finish; 2-1 in Anderlecht's favour.

Hibernian now faced having to travel to Brussels for the second leg having conceded two away goals and being a goal behind. It was a daunting prospect and one which Alex Miller resolved to avert.

Gareth Evans was thrown on up front. Hibs tried to hit back but things appeared to go from bad to worse when Mickey Weir was sent off for a second bookable offence, after showing his studs in a challenge just after a Hibs corner. The home fans' reaction to the sending off was a deafening chorus of 'He's here, he's there …', Mickey's song.

The red card seemed to galvanise the Cabbage, and shortly after Mickey's dismissal Pat McGinlay's lofted ball into the box was thunderously volleyed goalward by Keith Wright. The ball beat De Wilde all ends up, hitting the underside of the crossbar, bouncing over the goal line then back outwards. A roar engulfed Easter Road but the fans' celebrations turned to annoyance when the referee Weber waved play on, refusing to give the goal. Denied a clear equaliser by refereeing ineptitude, Hibs fans began to think that it just wasn't their night.

Then, with just 15 minutes remaining, Darren Jackson played a clever pass inside the box to Pat McGinlay, who from ten yards brilliantly lofted the ball over De Wilde at a tight angle. Philippe Albert had a chance to clear the net-bound effort off the goal line but in came the onrushing Gareth Evans to bravely risk injury by sliding in head first to ensure the ball crossed the line. The goal was credited to McGinlay, a player who just seemed to get better and better with each passing season. Easter Road erupted in a frenzy, both of joy and defiance – joy at having scored, defiance at having squared the tie despite the ineptitude of the match officials.

Hibs had three more chances to score, the best of them being a Pat McGinlay shot which bruised the crossbar, but the match finished 2-2. Though two away goals had been conceded, Alex Miller's men left the field to passionate applause and singing from the East Terrace and still had a chance of progressing to the next round, if they could beat the Belgian cracks on their home turf. Whatever Hibs did in Brussels, though, they would have to do it without fans' favourite Mickey Weir, who was suspended for the away leg.

Two league matches were played before the Hibees got another chance to shine in the UEFA Cup. After the home tie against Anderlecht, Hibs played host to the somewhat less glamorous opposition that was Airdrieonians FC. Jimmy Boyle put the Diamonds one up from the penalty spot early in the first half after Graham Mitchell had deliberately handled one of the Lanarkshire side's seemingly endless high balls in the box. Hibs equalised before half-time when Airdrie's Chris Honor deflected a Pat McGinlay shot past his own goalie, John Martin. A stunning bullet header from 14 yards by Mickey Weir gave Hibs the lead in the second half on what was largely a frustrating afternoon against Airdrie's hatchet men, but it was to no avail. Prior to the match, Jimmy Boyle had asked the referee if it was okay to take quick free kicks and the referee had said yes, so he took advantage of the referee's consent and slammed a fine shot past Burridge from the edge of the box to ensure the match finished 2-2. Burridge had still been arranging his wall when the ball hit the net.

Airdrie were fast becoming Hibernian's bogey team and would remain so for the next five years. Asides the Diamonds' ruthless physical style of play, their manager Alex MacDonald used to manage Hearts and was a playing legend for Rangers. Add to this the fact that half of Airdrie's team was made up of either ex-Hearts players or guys with known Hearts or Rangers sympathies plus the obvious dislike that both teams' fans had for each other and it's clear why, coupled with Airdrie's good record against Hibs at that time, there was always such a uniquely poisonous atmosphere when these teams met.

The following week Hibs drew 0-0 against Dundee at Easter Road, in a tight encounter which saw Stevie Raynes make his first competitive start for Hibs.

Tuesday, 29 September 1992 saw Hibs once again face off against Anderlecht, this time at the Constant Vanden Stock Stadium in Brussels, the stadium having been renamed after the club's chairman back in 1983. Around 25,000 fans were in attendance including a sizeable Hibs contingent. Hibs were officially allocated 2,000 tickets for the match, 1,000 standing tickets costing £7.50 each and the same number of seated tickets, which were £14.50 each (the number of Hibs fans who went to Belgium exceeded our official match ticket allocation by about 600). A small number of Hibs fans were deported after disturbances in the Belgian capital and thus missed the match but of much greater concern to the Hibs family at the time were two Hibs fans that tragically didn't even make it to Belgium. Two young men, John McTigue and George Crook, were killed in an accident on board a train that was taking them and other Hibs fans down to the coast to catch the ferry to Belgium. The tragedy occurred on the Sunday before the match and deeply saddened many Hibs fans, adding a sombre aspect to what was supposed to be an exciting away trip.

With Weir suspended, Joe Tortolano and Callum Milne were drafted into the first XI, with Graham Mitchell also missing out because of injury. Anderlecht had recently been thrashed 2-5 at home by struggling Waregem so Hibby hopes were high, despite carrying the burden of the two away goals conceded at Easter Road. To qualify would require an outstanding performance from Hibernian and a sub-standard one from the Belgians.

As in the first leg, the match saw a goal after just four minutes; sadly for Hibs it came at the wrong end of the pitch, Luc Nilis, the Belgian international striker, firing a low shot past Burridge from the edge of the box, following an assist from Van Vossen. That goal didn't actually change the match's dynamic too much, as Hibs needed to score anyway, but it did give the Belgians a welcome cushion – they would need it.

Many teams 3-2 down on aggregate with two away goals against them might despair, yet Alex Miller's men rallied, roared on by a loud green legion in the stadium. A free kick some 45 yards from goal was thumped high into the box by Callum Milne on 15 minutes. After a brief stramash in the box Darren Jackson reacted quickest to McGinlay's lay-off and, despite the attention of three Anderlecht defenders, planted a sweet left-foot strike beyond De Wilde into the bottom left-hand corner of the net to level the match and the tie. Against all odds, Hibs had a great chance to knock out a top European side. One more Hibs goal would see them through and nullify Anderlecht's precious away goals.

Unfortunately for the green jerseys, Anderlecht's home drubbing a few days earlier brought out a professional if not very dangerous performance from their players. Burridge saved well from Degryse and Albert. Hibs had chances to score but didn't take them. Without Mickey Weir to link the midfield and the strikers, there were relatively few opportunities to be had for Wright and Jackson. Hibs' best chances fell to MacLeod, Jackson and Gareth Evans, the latter being brought on far too late to have any real impact on the match – and not for the first time. The standout performance from Hibs was by Callum Milne. Alex Miller deployed him in a defensive midfield role to counter Anderlecht's technically brilliant and highly dangerous short-passing game, and in essence it worked, Milne breaking up much of the Belgian cracks' attacking play. It was probably Milne's best performance in the famous green jersey.

The match finished 1-1 and Hibs were eliminated on away goals, 3-3 on aggregate. Hibs could easily have won the tie but fans were able to console themselves; they hadn't lost a match and had fought one of Europe's top sides to a standstill. Had Keith Wright's thunderbolt off the bar in the first leg been given, things could have been very different. Alex Miller said that he was proud of his players. Hibs were out of Europe but not disgraced. As for Anderlecht, they reached the tournament's last 16, where they lost on away goals to Paris St Germain, and they completed yet another domestic league and cup double in Belgium. Scotland's other representatives in Europe that season, with one exception, fared little better. Airdrie fell at the first hurdle in the Cup Winners' Cup to Sparta Prague. Hearts eliminated Slavia Prague then lost to Belgian side Standard Liege, while Celtic beat Cologne but were then knocked out by Borussia Dortmund. Glasgow Rangers reached the new Champions League phase of the European Cup and narrowly failed to qualify from their semi-final group, losing out to Marseille, the tournament's eventual winners. The Govan side – whose European campaign that season was impressive – drew twice with Marseille in the group. Their 1-1 draw in Marseille, the match which deprived Rangers of a place in the European Cup Final, saw Marseille's goal scored by a midfielder. His name was Franck Sauzee.

Dear reader, we will now take a short break from the wider season 92/93 overview and I once again hand you over to that good Hibby Matthew Kane, for a wonderful tale of that 1992 Hibs away trip to Belgium from someone who was there on the ground. You're about to read what's probably the best part of the book …

You say there's nothing you can do
You tried your best but you were only being you.

SHE'S A STAR – ANDERLECHT AWAY – BY MATTHEW KANE

'We don't care what the animals say, what the hell do we care?
For we only know that there's gonna be a show and the Embra Hibees will be there!'

NUMBER 12 Montgomery Street was the home of Sphere Travel, a small travel agency that specialised in sunny bargain trips abroad and, *crucially*, coach tours.

When Hibs' SKOL Cup win in 1991 brought with it the Brucie bonus of qualification for the 1992–93 UEFA Cup, Sphere were appointed the convenient, inexpensive, local partners for the club in providing away trip tours to the second leg of the tie in Brussels. Forget your modern-day budget airline DIY European trips, courtesy of every provincial airport known to man. Or the more costly charter flights with the first-team squad generally frequented only by those who could afford them.

Whilst there was an option to fly with Sphere, most fans travelled using the most economical option. This tour, my friends, was proper old school: by single decker bus from Easter Road all the way to the capital of Europe with one smelly bog. *Overnight*. Aye, it doesn't get any more old school than that. Like a Flintstones mobile away day to Aberdeen on steroids.

We'd all been desperate to go, our wee posse of Hibees. Desperate enough to contemplate sitting cross-legged all the way to Dover. Desperate enough to do without nights out for a month beforehand and desperate enough to find the money to fund it by any legal means possible. None of our group wanted to miss out on a visit to one of European football's (then) truly big names. Or miss out on a few days on the Belgian beer. The tie was glamorous, the trip accessible and the excitement palpable as we waited for our late-night coach departure time to slowly approach …

Now, we're not talking luxury liner coaches like the ones you see the giants of the game taking, in advance, to their away legs. Driven all the way from their homeland regardless of where they are playing. Nope, not those towering, imposing, glistening technological masterpieces with blackened-out windows for privacy. Ours were buses you'd see doing the school run in the countryside, in 1977. With the comfort factor not really a major factor.

You can imagine the synthetic, almost nylon carpet-like, seat coverings of a certain vintage. They were sticky and stinky and contained the stains of a million previous outings. Beer, juice, coffee, hardened chewing gum, stale sweat and Sauzee knows what else. Minging – and likely to be even more so by the time they had been to Brussels and back.

Our party comprised a mixture of folk. Old, young and everything in between. Grumpy auld gits looking for a quiet snooze with the lights out as soon as we'd left the Edinburgh city limits and pissed auld farts looking to keep them awake with their Wolfe Tones and UB40 on an irritating ear-worm loop. Young 'uns on their first-ever away trip, wide-eyed and bushy-tailed, about to get the kind of education that school could never bring. The weak-bladdered, who didn't seem to make the connection between the copious amounts of Tennents they'd scooped and the unrelenting need for their stuttering visits to the slosh pit of a loo.

At the front of the bus (let's really not call it a coach) was a simple, low-quality video player and television that could just about be seen if you were midway up the bus. Someone had brought a homemade recording of *Sportscene* (or maybe *Scotsport*) showing Hibs' goals from the last season whilst another had a video of the SKOL Cup Final and *The Team That Wouldn't Die.* There was a constant competition between the grumpy auld gits looking for a quiet life, quite happy with Keef goals on a loop in the background, and the pished desire for a wee singsong by the other mob. The driver, who was probably dreading the middle of the night on the motorway as it was, was leaning towards the football videos. For the dark hours of the overnight trip, the driver (and Keef) won.

At the first stopover at a service station though, the bus choir got their own back …

At every stop-off point, the driver would be clear.

'Here's the time you've got here at this stop. This is the time you have to be back on the bus. If yer no' back by then, we run the risk of missing our slot at the ferry terminal. Dinnae be late.'

Aye, you can guess the rest. The Wolfie Gang were late back to the bus having used the stopover to … have pish, get mair pished. The driver really wisnae happy. The grumpy auld guys looking for a quiet time really wurnae happy. One of the younger lads on the bus who was operating strategically somewhere in between these two factions (like some bus convener Henry Kissinger) offered to go and find them. With the driver's words 'five minutes or I leave without you all' ringing in his ears …

This routine was to play itself out at every service station we were subsequently to stop at. At least on the trip down south, folk were still on the excited side of the trip and fairly tolerant of the shenanigans. Later on, this was not going to be the case. But more of that, later.

The bus was to arrive in Dover just before breakfast time. Nobody had slept and even the Wolfies were looking for something other than a can and the Black and Tans for breakfast. The driver had advised everyone that we might need to stay on the bus until we got on our ferry. There were seemingly busloads of Rangers fans already at the port waiting to board ferries to the continent en route to Lyngby in Denmark for a UCL qualifying tie. In addition, and here's something you'll not hear very often, there were minibuses of Airdrie fans waiting to board ferries en route to Czechoslovakia to play Sparta Prague in the Cup Winners' Cup. There's more chance of Prague being back in a country called Czechoslovakia again than Airdrie being back in Europe. But enough bitching about our hammer-throwing nemesis of the 80s and 90s.

There was going to be no way that the police were going to let us off our buses now, was there? The other two motley crews were at that point being kept hostage on their buses, so we would be the same, right?

Erm, naw …

The driver parked the bus and spoke to some guy in an official uniform carrying a clipboard. A few minutes later, he said, 'Right, you lot! You are getting off the bus. You've to go for a pee. You can buy something to eat – you lot up the back might want to consider that! – and you can get some fresh air. What you cannae do is go looking for bother or we'll all get it. Understand?' We couldn't believe our luck. After hours stuck, literally, to nylon seats from another decade, we were so grateful, there was never any question of even the Wolfie Gang not playing ball. In fact, that's exactly what was about to happen. Everyone was about to play ball …

I've no idea where the ball came from. However, suddenly everyone was taking part in the biggest kick-about possible in a car park in Dover. Aware, only too well, that our compatriots with poor taste and nae sense were being supervised closely by the other boys in blue, this was the most enthusiastic game of fitba' imaginable. *Getitrightupyees!*

It brought laughter where there may have otherwise been tired frustration. It brought gloating as only football fans know how to gloat. It was better than any alternative confrontation with the other lot. There was nothing they could do about it and they knew it. For once, it was *them* being kept in at the end of a game.

We were headed to one ferry, the Airdrie minibuses another and the other lot, yet another. All three ferries were docked in adjacent moorings though. To our right, the forces of darkness. To our left, their central belt wee pals. As the seagull flies, there was not too much distance between the sets of supporters across the docks … horizontally speaking. Vertically speaking, there was a massive drop. To our right, some of the Rangers horde started dropping their breeks and mooning at us over the railing of their ferry. It brought howls of derision and mockery from the Hibernian supporters, still buoyed by their League Cup semi-final triumph last year. Every expected insult that could have been directed at the erses in blue were delivered, landing firmly and accurately on their nappy-rashed bahookies. They were both landing and triggering the Y-front droppers at the same time.

Then, suddenly, their ferry began moving off towards the continent and the unexpected forward thrust of said vessel took the mooners and moon howlers by surprise, with one of them nearly losing their grip of the handrail and falling into the water. Somehow, some of his fellow travellers managed to haul him up by the armpits, saving him from more than just the absolute embarrassment he was enduring right there and then. Howls of derision and laughter from our deck turned his cheeks bright red – all four of them. The story was to endure for the remainder of the trip, growing arms and legs with every hour.

'Did ye hear about that Rangers diddy that was nearly drowned in the Channel/eaten by a shark/died of hypothermia/got run over by the ferry?'

* * *

The remainder of the Channel trip was spent in the bars on board. Chat of the near drowning on everyone's lips when a pint of Tennents wasn't there instead. Things were good-natured, enjoyable and it was brilliant just to be able to stretch the legs, speak to new people and take in some fresh air. Before long, we would be back on the bus and heading to the capital of Belgium, so it was important to make the best of this opportunity. Only, as you can probably by now predict, some took more of the opportunity than others ...

The tannoy announcement to return to our vehicles saw most folk head happily back to their buses and cars. On board the Fred and Wilma Bus, the driver did a head count. Everyone was back bar the Wolfies. Of course.

'They'll be getting left if they're not back on here by the time those doors open on the ferry,' said the driver. 'If any of you lot ken where they are, get them telt ... and get them telt now.' Up from his seat, wee Henry Kissinger jumped.

'Nae bother, boss! I'll find them. I'll be back in five!' And off he went, running like Keef in a one-on-one with Andy Rhodes – looking for his target and confident he was going to find it. The auld brigade grumbled something down the front of the bus. The driver checked his paperwork, ready to depart. The rest of us just hoped that wee Henry would get the Wolfies back in time to avoid further tension. Staring out the bus windows at the walls of the ferry, trying not to get too uptight at the moaning going on and hoping everything would come good in the end, we heard the engine start up.

And then onto the bus bounced Henry and the Wolfies.

'Hiya, pals!' shouted one of them. 'Sorry, lads! Needed a pish!' 'Sit doon, shut up – we're moving!' And with that we were off on our way to Brussels.

By the time we arrived in the capital city, we were getting weary. Some folk couldn't wait to get off the bus and just have some time to themselves. Others had finally begun to run out of rocket fuel in a dark green bottle and some were simply flagging through lack of sleep. However, once departed from our bus outside the hotel we were due to spend two nights in, a second wind benefitted everyone and people were soon plotting their night out with renewed vigour.

'Where are folk meetin' up? Is it that big square?' asked one of the Wolfies, referring to the Grand Place.

'No sure, pal,' came the response from one of the Auld Yins.

'Where is everyone headed, like?' The Wolfie was persistent.

'No sure, pal,' came the response again from another Auld Yin. He was equally evasive.

'Aww right, cheers.'

We all went our own way into the evening, looking for pints of Leffe or Duvel and portions of chips with that very Belgian of dressings – mayonnaise. Let's face it, at home it's salt and sauce. Or maybe just salt. Never salt and vinegar. Ketchup if you're eight years old. No mayonnaise though, eh? I mean, you just dinnae. You just widnae. But put a stretch of salty water between yourself and Old Blighty and before you know it, you're on the mayo and raving about it.

There were pockets of supporters round every corner and we had been warned to look out for each other, wary of reports of the extremes the local North African contingent in the Anderlecht support could extend to. There had been rumours of such nonsense and we were on our guard. Tired from the journey and wanting to make the most of match day, we went to bed at an earthly hour. The shenanigans could wait until morning.

* * *

The morning of 30 September saw a continental breakfast being pushed round the plate as the lure of black coffee was stronger than any solid sustenance. The plan of attack for the day went something like this ...

- Find the *Manneken Pis* and get a photie
- Find Heysel and get a photie
- Find the Atomium and get a photie
- Find the main square again by lunchtime, pull up a chair and enjoy the atmosphere. Drink it, and everything else, in.

First up, the wee gadgie with the pishy fountain. We found it on the map. It seemed quite straightforward a mission on paper. In reality, we went round and round in circles without finding it. Or so we thought. We'd probably passed the wee beggar about four times before we realised that he was the size of tuppence ha'penny and stuck up in a corner that you could easily walk past depending on the angle of your approach. Talk about an anti-climax.

Okay, next – Heysel. Venue of one of the darkest days in recent football history and the reason that English clubs were not competing in Europe that season. As sombre a 'ground-bagging' experience as you could imagine, we wondered how many people might just give it the body swerve. However, we most certainly were not on our own and, on arrival, we found ourselves at the stadium alongside a number of Hibs non-playing staff and other ground-baggers, all paying our respects. The state of the stadium was poor and we contemplated how UEFA could have ever given a major cup final to such a hapless venue. The thought processes in the corridors of power in Geneva were consistently and continuously a mystery.

Sombre and sober after Heysel, we were determined to make the visit to the Atomium short and sweet so that we could get on to the main event. No more than five minutes at the tourist attraction, we were on our way back towards the Grand Place – chips, mayonnaise, Leffe and Duvel were calling.

We were going to be escorted by coach from our hotel to the ground and had a specific time by which to be at our accommodation to catch said transport … but in the hours between lunchtime and then we were able to take in proceedings and get a sense of what was to come. There were certainly tensions in the local community. It was a different time in football, the authorities were toiling with how to manage the various elements of support who enjoyed more than just simply going to the game. It was the height of the 'casual' movement and we were not without our own. The

Belgian police were well aware and, combined with their own issues managing the North African group of supporters who followed Anderlecht, who had their own reputation to live up to, well, let's just say they were wary. Wary as in big doberdug wary, water cannon wary, firearms wary.

They weren't comfortable with the main gathering of supporters in the Grand Place. They really weren't.

Gathered under the red and blue striped canopy of a café bar next to the Town Hall, there seemed to be a million green and white bucket hats and Saturn-badged strips protecting giant pints of Jupiler. Up high on the edge of a container, some fans were happily parading a London Hibs banner whilst others tried to unravel and unveil even bigger Hibernian flags. Some gadgie commemorated in statue form was wearing a green and white hat and Hibs scarf as a nod to Sherlock Holmes of Picardy Place circa 1991. A clown-faced Hibs fan wandered by, completing the sense that we were in the middle of the greatest show on earth. And the Edinburgh Hibees, they were there, too.

In the middle of all of this, the copious baskets of flowers, canopied stalls and tourist outlets tried to act as if it were simply any other day. The police acted as if they were waiting for a day like no other.

We were in the middle of an addled blether with some laddies from West Lothian when someone suggested going to another place Hibs fans were congregated, away from the square. Le Pigeon Noir de Bruxelles was the new *place to be* and we went with everyone else to this new venue until it was time to head for our bus.

Anderlecht was not just the name of our football opponents that evening, it is also the area of Brussels in which the club reside. A Belgian equivalent of Queen's Park. The stadium sat on the edge of Astrid Park, an expanse of greenery with a lake in the middle and, at that time, the stadium was called the Parc Marie Astrid, before it would later become the Constant Vanden Stock Stadion. Hibs had been rumoured to be considering the design of the Belgian's stadium upgrade as a prototype for the renovation of Easter Road with Dougie Cromb very vocal in his praise for said architecture.

Our bus left from the front of our hotel to take us to the ground. It was meant to be a door-to-door service through a police corridor, designed to prevent any outbreaks of violence involving the local North African contingent who were renowned for their efforts on that front and who would inhabit the area behind the goals in the home end during matches.

The excitement aboard the vehicle was palpable. Everyone was determined to make the most of the evening and give as much support as possible to the team. Whilst the diving and goal of a certain Peter van Vossen had put Hibs' chances of progressing in the balance, nobody travelled to the Belgian capital prepared to simply capitulate to European footballing royalty. There was a sense of defiance and hope in the air … until we were dropped by the bus on the wrong side of the park and stadium. Suddenly, we found ourselves abandoned in the territory of the local mob. The bus was full of a range of fans – young, old, male, female – and would most certainly be described, as they were then, as 'scarfers' – Hibernian fans not interested in the ongoing casual movement of the time. So, nobody was particularly happy at being left where they had been and many were concerned for the safety of our more vulnerable co-travellers.

There had been stories of the local group ambushing opposition fans in and around the area of the park but this was also the most direct and obvious route to the stadium.

Some fans immediately headed off round the perimeter of the park, following the railings and the glow of the floodlights over the top of the trees … hoping for the best. Others stood debating what to do, which route to follow in an era where there was no Google Maps to consult and no sense of which way to go in this walk of Russian Roulette. We stood wondering if it really was mental to try and cut through the park. Oscillating between a gung-ho 'aye, let's do it' and a more cautious 'naw, let's follow the crowd', we were approached by a solitary gendarme armed with a machine gun. What the hell was he wanting?

Putting on our best 'we come in peace' faces, we smiled helplessly at his firearm and hoped he could speak English.

Of course he didn't. However, he did speak some pidgin French and so did we. After much grovelling and frantic recall of Conversational French O Grade circa 1982, it became apparent that he was wanting to help us. *Merci bien!* The heart rate lowered a few beats per minute from the first moment he approached but would soon accelerate again when he beckoned us to go with him through a shortcut in the park. What the hell was he doing?

Looking frantically at each other behind his back, we had little choice but to follow him. What the hell else were we really going to do? Every creak in the darkness, every sudden glimpse of light from the distant stadium and every sudden movement in the foliage had us sphincter twitching. We had to trust him and his judgement. And he had a big gun, anyway. *Dae as yer telt.*

After what seemed like an age, our police-escorted shortcut brought us out into the light and the stadium in full view. The gendarme pointed towards the gates by which we would enter the arena and then said, 'Good luck, stay safe. I hate Anderlecht!' and off he disappeared into the night.

The array of hardware at the disposal of the match police struck us as soon as our attention returned to getting on our way. Water cannons. Great big sod-off water cannons we had never before encountered at a game of football. A multitude of armed uniforms and a kennel full of Doberdugs and Rotties with no muzzles. Armed riot vehicles with more plating than an armadillo on steroids. It felt like we'd arrived into the light and into a war zone. That 'Dae as yer telt' inner voice was screaming, loud and clear, between our lugs. Our tickets were for the upper tier of the Hibs' end, which was a seated area that would provide greater protection from the mosh pit of the enclosure behind the goals, which was fenced in like so many other grounds at that time – the full effect of Heysel and Hillsborough had yet to filter fully into the architecture and management of many stadiums. We were all to stand for the duration of the game but there is no doubting that the upper tier had a better view of the game and a safer distribution of bodies.

We negotiated entry to the ground with trepidation but, once in our vantage point, we were able to sort of relax and begin to take in proceedings for what really mattered. The game. A pipe band was on the pitch bringing a sense of home and twee to the stadium. Hibs players were warming up in the glow of the floodlights, laughing and joking but looking like they meant business. And they did.

After less than a minute of the game, Super Joe Tortolano was booked for a card-marking challenge on Anderlecht's Degryse. It was a sign of intent but also of anxiety. It took a wee while for the team to settle well and, before we had been allowed this privilege, that Van Vossen person set up Luc Nilis to score an opening goal for Anderlecht within the first five minutes. The fans had been noisy from the moment they had entered the stadium and singing had, up to this point, been incessant. You'd have thought that the setback of the goal might have knocked this on the head for a few moments but this was not to be the case. The Hibernian support were about to sing non-stop for a full 90 minutes, a key aspect of the team's ability to get back into the game. And the one thing everyone who was there still talks about to this day.

Then, 18 minutes into the game, Darren Jackson was going to provide us with even more reason to keep on going.

A great ball from the Marmite Brian Hamilton found Jackson, whose strike from within the penalty area beat the goalkeeper and our end of the ground went absolutely nuts. Those in the enclosure mosh pit found themselves under bodies, sweaty oxters and hugging folk they'd never met in their lives before. It's a scenario that has played out a few times in the club history but it's not often it has happened in such an illustrious venue as European royalty's back yard. Once the initial euphoria and disbelief died down, it was back to the song book …

Captain Murdo MacLeod was running the show, his European pedigree to the fore, and he came close with another chance in the first half along with club talisman, Keith Wright.

In the second half, the mighty Super Tortolano put in a cross from the left wing that was met by Jackson, but sadly his header went wide.

About ten minutes from the end Gareth Evans was brought on as a substitute to try and force the elusive strike that would see Hibs progress but it wasn't to be. The away-goals rule determined the winner after the tie remained all square.

The Hibernian players were disappointed after such a monumental effort but they remained unbowed. The fans were likewise proud and gave the side a standing ovation at full time – then refused to move from the arena, chanting relentlessly for them to return to the pitch for an encore. A flag debate (for which online Hibees are renowned) ensued after Callum Milne displayed the green and black Union Flag associated with one faction of the Hibees support. For a nanosecond the old scarfer v casual differentiation resurfaced but even that didn't last long. At the other end of the stadium, the home support watched on impressed and showed their appreciation of the magnitude and relenting nature of the Hibees' backing with some applause of their own. It was a compliment I suppose but we still had the local mob to negotiate on the way back to our hotel …

The big doberdugs, the armed uniforms, the water cannons and the mad locals were all still present and correct as we finally made our way out of the ground in search of our coaches. The local constabulary were somewhat less anxious about what our support might be capable of and some even smiled in our direction as we descended into the darkness of the night outside the ground. Our coaches had been brought round to near the exit doors and we were soon able to board our vehicles, relatively safe in the comfort of a police escort back to the hotel … though our friendly neighbourhood nutters were very much lurking and looking for an opportunity to pounce.

It was hard to even consider sleeping that night. The adrenaline was still pumping through our veins and the alcohol was flowing freely. Who would have possibly thought that we might have taken these giants of the game all the way to the away-goals rule deciding factor? Who could switch off after such an unrelenting show of support from start to finish – 90 mins plus of unparalleled non-stop singing? A sense of support, club and manager being completely at one. A moment of genuine pride for the support of a club whose very existence had been threatened only months earlier. So, we didn't give sleep much chance and the evening descended into an alcohol-accompanied blur.

* * *

The next morning we were headed back across the Channel to Blighty and an unforgiving early start was going to prove too much for some. Yep, the Wolfies didn't turn up for the coach at the time they ought to and their now well-rehearsed and obliging minder was despatched to kick their door in and their erses out their beds. Stinking like the whiff of a Gorgie brewery on the Western Approach Road, they came tumbling onto the bus, in their role as the friendly drunks, but were met with the tired snash of the now less tolerant among us. It wisnae funny any more for the majority of folk. It's always that way on any trip though, the going home bit is always the bit you just want over and done with. If they had any self-awareness, they might realise …

The journey to Calais was a quiet one. Most folk slept soundly en route and only found themselves back in the land of the living when they realised they were just minutes from the ferry bar again and got a second wind. Hair o' the dug an' a' that.

The bars were filled with tired, happy, slightly queasy Hibbies reminiscing about the night before and the trip in general. Like a floating local boozer with yer mates, tales were regaled and eyes glazed over just thinking of the time we had shared.

When we arrived back in port at Dover, we piled onto the bus as instructed. All bar the Wolfies, of course. You'd have thought they'd have learned by now. You'd be wrong.

And the usual routine played itself out against the backdrop of tired grump. C'est la vie …

It's a long road
It's a great cause
It's a long road
It's a good call
You got it
You got it
She's a Star.

HYMN FROM A VILLAGE – SEASON 92/93 – PART THREE

'Ooh to, Ooh to be, Ooh to be a Hibby, Ooh to, Ooh to be, Ooh to be a Hibby'

HIBS' EUROPEAN exit, for some fans, brought to an end a euphoric period which had lasted since the SKOL League Cup win of October 1991. Though by no means disheartened, Hibbies now faced the reality of the Premier Division, that endless yet compulsive routine.

Having almost conquered a European giant midweek, Hibs, typically, then found themselves 1-0 down to Partick Thistle at Firhill the following Saturday. The growing brilliance of the Jackson-Wright partnership, supported by Mickey Weir, enabled Hibs to grab a 2-1 lead in the second half, but Ray Farningham's second goal of the match earned the Jags a 2-2 draw. There then followed another drubbing from Aberdeen on Wednesday, 7 October, this time a 1-3 reverse at Easter Road, in which Wright scored for Hibs but the Dons scored more with a double from Jess and one from Shearer. After that came a narrow 1-0 defeat at Ibrox ten days later.

Hibs got back to winning ways against St Johnstone at Easter Road on Saturday, 24 October, beating Alex Totten's side 3-1 thanks to a double by Darren Jackson and a Mickey

Weir goal – Vinnie Arkins netting for Saints. Once again the Wright/Jackson/Weir combination was effective. Two 0-1 defeats followed, one to Dundee Utd up at Tannadice, the other coming in the season's second Edinburgh derby.

Almost 18,000 fans were at Tynecastle on Saturday, 7 November to see a dull affair. Hearts triumphed 1-0 thanks to a headed goal at the School End by towering English striker Ian Baird. Hibs offered virtually nothing in the way of invention in the match and were limited to thumping high balls up to Keith Wright, which were easily dealt with by Hearts' defence. The match is best remembered for Darren Jackson being stamped on by Hearts defender Ali Mauchlen.

It was back to winning ways the next week for Hibs though, as they defeated Jim Jefferies's Falkirk side 3-1 at Easter Road. The Bairns actually scored first through Gary Lennox but the Cabbage eased to victory thanks to goals from Tortolano, Hamilton and Evans.

Late November brought two more defeats, a miserable 0-2 reverse to Airdrie at Broomfield and then a narrow 1-2 defeat at home to Celtic, Darren Jackson scoring again, Brian O'Neill bagging a brace for Celtic. During the Airdrie match at Broomfield, opposing fans pelted each other in a snowball fight on the terraces. On the same day that Hibs lost 1-2 to Celtic, Hearts were murdered 6-2 by Aberdeen up at Pittodrie. The defeat at home to Celtic left Hibs in eighth place in the table as December dawned.

Hibernian began December by drawing a thrilling match at Easter Road with Motherwell, 2-2. Keith Wright put Hibs in front but Steve Kirk and Iain Ferguson struck for the Steelmen. Only a late Brian Martin own goal spared Alex Miller's blushes. This was followed by another draw, this time at Dens Park, a 1-1 draw in which Darren Jackson was again on target. John Burridge was dropped after this match, in which Dundee's player-manager Simon Stainrod scored directly from a corner. Chris Reid took over in goal for a time.

The inconsistent form following the European exit saw home crowds fall a little and fewer than 6,000 fans were at a freezing Easter Road on 12 December to see the Hibees take on Partick Thistle. The song 'Hibs Heroes' claims that fans don't feel the cold when watching Hibs, yet many were doubtless numbed both by the freezing temperatures and the mind-numbing soccer on display that day. Hibs had but one shot from open play, a Murdo MacLeod effort straight at Craig Nelson. Partick weren't much better. It was the most stereotypical Scottish 0-0 draw one could imagine, with one difference: Hibs won! Late on, with the match heading to a goalless draw, Hibs were awarded a very soft penalty at the home end. Darren Jackson duly stepped up and slammed the ball into the top corner, giving the green jerseys possibly their most undeserved victory of the 1990s. Partick boss John Lambie gave but a three-word press conference afterwards, saying simply 'we were robbed!' The next week saw Hibernian lose to Aberdeen for the third time that season, slumping 0-2 up at Pittodrie, Booth and Richardson scoring for the Reds against a threadbare, injury-hit Hibs team.

Boxing Day in 1992 fell on a Saturday and saw Edinburgh's green and white make the short trip to crumbling Brockville to take on Falkirk. Though the two sides managed to cook up a Christmas cracker for the fans, it was definitely a case of a point dropped for Alex Miller's men. Fans were, however, treated to a thrilling 3-3 draw, with Hibernian's goals coming from Gareth Evans and a brace from David Fellenger – his only other two goals for

Hibs had been scored in two separate games against Dundee Utd. Callum Milne saw red in this match and would only start one more match for Hibernian thereafter. Falkirk's goals came from Kevin Drinkell, Richard Cadette and Ian McCall. Hibs could've won 4-3 but Neil Orr had a penalty saved by Ian Westwater.

The 92/93 New Year derby was played on 2 January 1993. Almost 22,000 fans were at Easter Road to see what can only be described as a bruising encounter. For the second New Year in a row, Hibs were largely saved from derby defeat by Tommy McIntyre. A year earlier his late penalty at Tynecastle on New Year's Day had saved a point for Hibs. This time, big Tam – whose first-team appearances had been limited since his red card against St Johnstone the previous August – was recalled to bolster the team's struggling defence and specifically to counter Hearts' huge striker Ian Baird. Tam marked the big Englishman out of the game and the match ended 0-0. It was a fair result on the day but it meant that Hibs now hadn't beaten Hearts in 16 attempts over exactly four years.

With the team languishing in mid-table mediocrity, many Hibs fans were delighted when the Scottish Cup began for them at the usual third-round phase. Jimmy Bone's St Mirren were the opposition on 9 January. Just fewer than 8,000 fans were at Easter Road for the tie. The Buddies, recently relegated, gave an excellent account of themselves and showed no fear. They managed two goals, one scored by and the other made by their teenage striker Barry Lavety. Lavety and St Mirren would have had more goals were it not for the heroics of Chris Reid in the Hibs goal. Young Lavety impressed everyone watching, including Hibs boss Alex Miller. Of course, St Mirren's two goals and pluckiness shown ended up mattering little, as Hibs also played very well and hammered five goals past the Paisley side in reply, and could have had many more. Mickey Weir scored twice; the other three goals came from Wright, Jackson and McGinlay.

The following week in the league at Easter Road, Dundee United were the visitors. Darren Jackson scored a wonderful 25-yard screamer, following good link-up play with Keith Wright. Dundee United equalised through Jim McInally in the second half after Chris Reid made a mess of a clearance kick, but the Hibees triumphed 2-1, the winner coming courtesy of a Freddy van der Hoorn own-goal 12 minutes from full time. Many Hibbies remember this match because of Jackson's wonderful opening goal.

Season 92/93 had seen Eric Cantona join Manchester United from Leeds. The Red faithful had been so impressed with the French forward that he had quickly earned a new song:

'Ooh ah Cantona, say ooh ah Cantona!'

Actually, the Red Devils probably nicked the chant from Leeds, like they nicked the player. No matter.

Cantona played with his shirt collar stood up. So did Darren Jackson. Jackson's goal against Dundee United in January 1993 saw the first mass rendition of a new Hibs chant, bellowed from the East Terracing after his goal.

'Ooh ah Jacksona, say ooh ah Jacksona!'

The striker seemed to revel in the song and in the acclaim. The chant would be a mainstay of the Hibs support right up until Jacko's last match for Hibernian in 1997.

A trip to Perth was next for Alex Miller's men, to face St Johnstone. Terrible weather ruined the fixture – which should really have been abandoned as the white lines of the pitch weren't visible and mist reduced visibility, but the match, played on a swampy pitch, was concluded. The

Saintees won 2-0 and could have had more but for some excellent goalkeeping from Chris Reid. So bad were the conditions that the match had to be played using a bright orange ball.

The last-ever Tennents' Sixes indoor tournament was held at the SECC in late January 1993. Hibs had won it in 1990. Rangers didn't participate in the last few tournaments as they were sponsored by McEwan's Lager. The sixes were a great winter distraction; one can only imagine the hairy fits that club doctors and managers would have nowadays if asked to field a strong team in such a physically dangerous version of football. Hibs were in group one in 1993, and beat Aberdeen 4-3, defeated Falkirk 5-4, lost 2-3 to St Johnstone and in our final group match were leading Celtic 2-0. That scoreline was enough to get us into the semi-finals, so we kept possession, passing the ball around to run down the clock. Referee and Hearts fan Bill Crombie stopped play and gave Celtic a free kick for no apparent reason, Celtic then scored. We won that match 2-1 but the goal conceded meant that St Johnstone rather than us progressed to the semis. Revisionists later claimed that Mr Crombie had awarded the free kick because Hibs had broken the tournament's three-line rule, which we hadn't. The tournament was won by Partick Thistle. So ended the lifespan of one of Scottish football's most interesting and fun competitions.

January 30 saw league leaders and reigning champions Rangers visit Easter Road. The Gers were without skipper Richard Gough and midfield hardman Ian Ferguson. Injuries meant that our own midfield powerhouse Pat McGinlay joined Gordon Hunter in central defence for this match.

Mickey Weir and Ally McCoist both missed good chances to open the scoring in the first half, amid a white-hot atmosphere. Rangers went 1-0 up just before the interval through Mark Hateley. Hibs came out fighting in the second half, Keith Wright hitting the post with a header and Darren Jackson putting a golden chance wide when it looked easier to score. The Hibees scented blood in the water and kept pressing forward, shooting down the slope with a strong icy wind at their backs. Jackson again had a great chance to equalise but volleyed wide from around the penalty spot. Chants of 'Hibees' echoed around Easter Road. Gareth Evans then had a good effort saved by Andy Goram. The green jerseys were giving the Rangers back line a torrid time, especially their defender John Brown, who was having a nightmare. With 67 minutes gone, Hibs finally got their reward when Pat McGinlay headed in an equaliser from a corner. Easter Road erupted in rapture; Hibs had been all over the Gers.

The Rangers team of the early to mid 1990s was an exceptional side, unparalleled domestically at that time. The best Scottish players supplemented by foreign superstars made for a lethal footballing cocktail, and Hibs were about to receive an unwanted dose of that cocktail. The Ibrox side were 2-1 up within two minutes, Trevor Steven firing low past Chris Reid, to the delight of the Rangers fans behind the goal on the mobbed Dunbar End. Three minutes later the Ibrox side went 3-1 up, Mark Hateley heading in from a corner. The infamous 'party songs' now boomed out of the away end.

They were silenced a few minutes later when Darren Jackson smashed the ball past Andy Goram into the net to make it 2-3. Keith Wright had mis-kicked a much easier chance to score with his right foot but Jacko made no mistake with the follow-up. Now that old Hibee anthem 'Forever and Ever', always sung loudest against Rangers, reverberated around the stadium. Hibs kept battling, desperate to reward the fans for their support by salvaging a point, but then up popped Ally McCoist with five minutes remaining to nutmeg Chris Reid and put the Govan side 4-2 up. The green jerseys didn't give up and scored a last consolation goal in the 89th minute through Pat McGinlay. Alex Miller's men had hurled everything that they had at the champions but it hadn't been enough. Rangers won 4-3 but the Hibs fans stayed behind to applaud and chant their brave heroes off the park at the end. Fans that day had thus seen six goals in just 21 minutes. McGinlay's brace once again showed fans why he was one of the best young midfielders in Scotland. Rumours were already rife among the Hibs fans that Pat was to be sold to Celtic in the summer.

Hibernian's performance against Rangers in that game belied their otherwise indifferent league form. Some fans scratched their heads at how the same group of players could do so well against the champions yet falter against supposedly lesser sides. That bemusement would only increase during the next round of the Scottish Cup.

February 6 saw Hibs travel over the Forth to take on Cowdenbeath at Central Park in round four of the Scottish Cup. The Blue Brazil, managed by ex-Aberdeen and Motherwell man Andy Harrow, were at the time propping up the old First Division. A certain Nicky Henderson played for Cowdenbeath at the time; you may have heard of his son who is also a footballer, his name is Liam and he specialises in 'deliveries'.

Just over 4,000 fans watched Hibs achieve an embarrassing goalless draw that afternoon. At the time, the Blue Brazil had Europe's leakiest defence. The replay was just four days later at Easter Road. Much to the surprise of many Hibs fans, the Fife side were just as stubborn in the rematch,

Hibs only winning 1-0 thanks to a Pat McGinlay goal. Nevertheless, the quarter-finals of the cup had been reached once more. Hibs were drawn to play either Kilmarnock or St Johnstone at Easter Road. This cup draw was discussed in Irvine Welsh's hilarious, brilliant novella *A Soft Touch*, part of the book and movie *The Acid House*, in a scene where crazy Larry torments loser Johnny. St Johnstone won their replay against Kilmarnock.

Back to league business and 13 February saw Hibs go along the M8 to draw 0-0 with Motherwell. Young defender Steven Tweed, who had made his debut a year earlier against St Mirren, got his second chance in a first-team shirt during this dull match. Without Darren Jackson for three matches because of suspension – thanks mostly to bookings for giving referees cheek – the Hibees then easily beat Partick Thistle 3-0 at Firhill on Tuesday, 16 February, a brace from Pat McGinlay and a goal by Mickey Weir securing the two points. The following Saturday saw Dundee visit Easter Road. Chris Reid seriously injured his leg after 37 mins and, since in those days there were only two substitutes and no team ever included a substitute goalkeeper among those two, an outfield player had to take over. Stalwart left-back Graham Mitchell went in goal and Hibs did well and were tied at 1-1 with 15 minutes remaining. Mitchell made some good saves but Dundee went 2-1 up after 76 minutes through their young flying winger, Andy Dow. The impressive Dow then set up Andy Kiwomya – brother of the more famous striker Chris – who made it 1-3 in the Dees' favour. In between those two Dundee goals, Mickey Weir had blasted a penalty kick wide of the post. The 1-3 defeat for Hibs was largely thanks to the impact of Andy Dow, who, like Barry Lavety, had now been noticed by Alex Miller. Dow's form soon earned him a move to Chelsea.

The Easter Road scoreline the following week was again 3-1, this time in the Cabbage's favour as they easily put Airdrie to the sword, thanks to a double from Darren Jackson and a Pat McGinlay penalty. The Diamonds had initially led thanks to a deflected 30-yarder from Kenny Black. That victory moved Hibs up to sixth in the table, and 5,000 fans were at that match.

One week later, more than double that amount came out to watch Hibs take on St Johnstone in the Scottish Cup quarter-final at Easter Road. The Hibees easily brushed aside John McClelland's men, winning 2-0, with goals coming from Keith Wright and towering youngster Steven Tweed. Hibs were in another semi-final. The other teams in the hat were Rangers, Hearts and Aberdeen. Hampden Park had closed for a long refurbishment after the 1992 SKOL Cup Final so the later stages of the 1992/93 Scottish Cup would be contested at neutral venues. Fans hoped in vain for an all-Edinburgh affair but those hopes were dashed when Rangers drew Hearts, meaning that Hibs would play Aberdeen. Hibs' tie would be played at neutral Tynecastle, a ground where no Hibs side had won in four years. The other semi-final would be contested at Celtic Park. The location of the final depended on whether or not Rangers were in it; if they were in the final it would be held at Celtic Park, if they weren't it would be held at Ibrox.

After the cup quarter-final triumph and all of the excitement over the draw, Hibernian's next league fixture was actually a cup semi-final dress rehearsal, with Aberdeen visiting Easter Road on Saturday, 9 March. The Dons won yet again but in this match Alex Miller's men actually gave a much better account of themselves than in previous meetings with the Dons that season. Aberdeen won 2-1 with their goals coming late from Paatelainen and Paul Kane, Pat

McGinlay netting for the Cabbage. The performance gave Hibs fans some hope for the semi-final.

Next up came three away league encounters against the three teams whom Hibs fans most revel in doing well against. On 13 March the Hibees were blown away by the mighty Rangers at Ibrox, losing 0-3, the Govan side's goals coming from Hateley, McCoist and young David Hagen. A ticket to watch Hibs that day cost £8. Hibs fans occupied the whole lower tier of the Broomloan stand at Ibrox for this match, and were showered with missiles from the home fans in the upper tier throughout: a common occurrence back then, with police more likely to arrest the away fan who complained about it rather than the missile thrower. The missiles usually comprised lighters, cups of Bovril or urine, pies and coins.

A few days later on the Tuesday night the Hibernian faithful made the trip to Parkhead to take on Liam Brady's Celtic. Celtic were in financial turmoil off the pitch at the time and lived in the shadow of Rangers and their seemingly limitless supply of money. This was reflected in this match's relatively pathetic attendance of barely 12,000. The Celts came out on top 2-1 thanks to two goals in three minutes from their English striker Andy Payton, but it was a close-run thing. Keith Wright scored a great team goal for the green jerseys (wearing purple on this occasion) late on to give the home fans the jitters.

The last of this trio of big away matches saw Hibs travel to Tynecastle for the season's final Edinburgh derby on Saturday, 20 March. Around 13,700 fans turned up for this match, including, bizarrely, a fan wearing a full Pink Panther costume. Entry for the ground was £7.

Alex Miller started with Evans, Wright and Jackson up front, but that didn't stop Hibernian from turning in one of their worst performances at Tynecastle in a long time. Hearts did only win 1-0 but the large home support spent much of the match sarcastically cheering Hibs' laughable efforts to attack. With 61 minutes gone, John Robertson fired a zipping cross-come-shot into the box at the Gorgie Road end, which missed everybody then smacked off John Burridge's shoulder and into the net. As the Jambos erupted into a chorus of 'There's only one John Burridge', then carried on with their usual orange anthems interspersed with songs about how easy it was to beat Hibs, the Hibs players on the pitch could do little about it. Hearts by no means played well but once again a very average Hearts side had beaten Hibernian. This was the 17th match of Hibernian's annoying 22-match winless run in the fixture.

Bigotry in Scottish football is said by some to be a 'west coast' problem – except that's not always been the case, nor is it the case now. Atmosphere at Edinburgh derbies in the 80s and early 90s could be very different than in today's matches, particularly at Tynecastle. The civil war in the north of Ireland which had raged since the late 60s had polarised Scotland's working class. Add in the fact that Hearts were traditionally viewed as Edinburgh's staunchly pro-British, pro-protestant and 'establishment' team (despite having many Catholic fans) and that far-right groups sometimes tried to gain recruits at Tynecastle back then and it's understandable why the atmosphere was quite so different. Hearts' most boisterous and vocal element of fans occupied their terraced 'shed' in the corner of the School End, and from there, during Edinburgh derbies and when Hearts played Celtic, thousands of fans would belt out 'The Sash', 'Derry's Walls', 'I Was Born Under an Orange Scarf' and even a bastardised version of 'Glory Glory to the

Hibees', adapted from the US Army paratrooper anthem 'Blood on the risers', which went like this:

> 'Glory, Glory what a terrible way to die
> To die a fenian bastard!'

Hibs fans, on the other hand, didn't respond to such songs with Irish rebel songs – singing such songs had largely gone out of fashion at Easter Road in the early 1980s, and even then not everyone used to do it and whether or not those songs were sung depended on who we were playing against. We did, however, sing songs like 'You'll Never Walk Alone' and 'Forever and Ever' quite regularly in the 90s against Hearts and Rangers and our support did contain a fair portion of people from the very demographic those Hearts songs were aimed at, but Hibs fans simply booed or sneered at the 'party songs' emanating from the Hearts end when we played them. Not that the type of songs sung at a derby in the early 1990s made any difference to the results; Hearts would've strolled through these fixtures even if their fans were singing 'Ave Maria' or 'Ernie, the Fastest Milkman in the West'! In any case, that was a long time ago, times and people have changed. Supports, by and large, like wider society, evolve and move on. The sectarian nonsense at Tynecastle died down substantially after their stadium was redeveloped from 1994 onwards.

Having lost three difficult away matches on the trot, the Hibees' last warm-up for the upcoming semi-final against Aberdeen was a home match against Falkirk in the league on Saturday, 27 March. Again, around 5,000 fans were in attendance. Scott Sloan gave Falkirk the lead after 13 minutes, aided by an error from John Burridge. Pat McGinlay equalised a few minutes later and the match finished 1-1. Falkirk's wee winger Kevin McAllister tormented Hibs' makeshift defence during this match, and not for the first time. Callum Milne made his final Hibs appearance.

So, on Saturday, 3 April 1993 Hibernian faced Aberdeen at Tynecastle in the semi-final of the Scottish Cup, looking to take a step towards ending the 91-year gap since Hibs had last won that trophy in 1902. A terracing or ground ticket for this tie would set you back £7 if you were an adult. Prior to this match, Hibs had played six semi-finals at Tynecastle. We had bested St Mirren there in 1914 and Third Lanark in 1923, but had lost our last four semis there over the years, to Rangers, Clyde, Motherwell and Dunfermline. Had the Aberdeen semi ended in a draw, it was to be replayed at Tannadice on 13 April.

John Burridge was in goal, Miller, Mitchell, Hunter and Tweed in defence, MacLeod, Hamilton, McGinlay and Danny Lennon in midfield (the latter replacing an injured Mickey Weir), with Jackson and Wright up front. Over 21,000 fans were at Tynecastle, with a large Hibs support rammed into what were traditionally the Hearts areas of the ground. The Jambo 'shed' echoed to unfamiliar chants such as club anthems 'Hail, Hail', 'Glory, Glory' and the usual other terrace chants.

Aberdeen in season 92/93 had a somewhat excellent side that were providing the only real title challenge to Rangers.

The Dons had bested Hibs in their last two encounters at neutral venues, both of those matches coming in season 1985/86. Aberdeen had defeated John Blackley's Hibs team in both the 1985 SKOL League Cup Final at Hampden and the 1986 Scottish Cup semi-final at Dens Park by the same 3-0 scoreline.

This match was to prove no drubbing, yet still yielded the same outcome for the men from Leith. The first half was a tight affair; Hibs coped well with Aberdeen's excellent forward line. Wright and Jackson looked sharp but, without Mickey Weir to link them to the midfield, they largely fed off scraps in the first half. Keith Wright had Hibs' best chance of that first half, which brought out a superb save from Theo Snelders. Both sides matched each other well and the game remained all square until the 54th minute. With the Dons attacking the School End which housed the Hibs support, Gary Smith played a clever pass down the left wing to former Hibs player Paul Kane, who brilliantly slipped into a gaping hole on the right of the Hibs back line and squared the ball to Scott Booth at the front post, who stabbed the ball past Burridge and into the net: 1-0 to Aberdeen.

Hibs rallied well, roared on by that noisy support in the shed. Gareth Evans was brought on and Hibs gained the ascendancy in the second half. Aberdeen weathered the storm, largely thanks to a superhero-esque performance by a certain Alex McLeish at centre-back. The experienced defender seemed to be everywhere, thwarting Hibs' desperate attacks. Time and again Hibs knocked on Aberdeen's door, yet time and again McLeish was there to bar the entrance. When Hibs did find a way past the big stopper, Aberdeen keeper Theo Snelders was there to break Hibs' hearts at Tynecastle. The pick of his saves came in the dying minutes, when a Gareth Evans thunderbolt went through a forest of legs and looked net-bound until the big Dutchman brilliantly reacted and managed to tip the ball away. Aberdeen won the match 1-0. Alex Miller's men put in a good effort but were punished harshly, their one defensive mistake giving the Dons the winning goal.

At the same time as this Tynecastle showdown, Hearts were taking on Rangers in the other semi-final at Celtic

Park. The Gers won 2-1 and would go on to beat Aberdeen in the final at the same venue in May, winning 2-1.

The cup exit was a sickener to Hibs fans but at least the side had made it to the 'crunch' phase of a tournament for the second season running, and had gone one round further in the Scottish Cup than in the previous three seasons. Now the fans had the late season to look forward to, safe from relegation but with no chance of achieving anything else.

Three days after the semi-final defeat, Hibs welcomed St Johnstone back to Edinburgh. Only around 3,500 fans turned up for the match – Hibs' lowest crowd that season – which ended in a 2-2 draw, Keith Wright and Gareth Evans being on target, with Jackson missing a last-minute penalty. Allan Moore and Martin Buglione had put the visitors 2-0 up at one point. On the Saturday Hibs travelled to Tannadice to take on Dundee United and beat the Terrors 3-0, Keith Wright bagging an impressive hat-trick, the third of his Hibs career thus far, having previously netted trebles against Dunfermline and Nairn County in season 91/92, the latter in a pre-season match.

* * *

Celtic visited Easter Road on 17 April, sporting a black and jade away kit. The 11,000 fans at Easter Road witnessed something rarely seen in this fixture: a Hibs team annihilating a Celtic one. For the second time in a match in season 92/93, all three Hibernian strikers got on the scoresheet against the Hoops. Alex Miller's side blew away Liam Brady's men with a dazzling first-half performance which saw the Hibees lead 3-0 at the interval, thanks to goals from Keith Wright, Gareth Evans and a Darren Jackson penalty. The chant of the day from the Hibbies on the terracing was crude but clear.

'Celtic are shite, Celtic are shite, wooah, wooah.'

The visitors did put up more of a fight in the second half and even pulled one back through Charlie Nicholas, but Hibs were in the driving seat throughout. The result brought much-needed cheer to the Hibernian faithful and brightened up what was otherwise a dull run-in to the campaign's end.

Having beaten Celtic on the Saturday, the Hibees, almost typically, followed up that great result with a poor one, being thumped 1-3 by Airdrie at Broomfield on the Tuesday evening. Pat McGinlay scored again for Hibs and big Justin Fashanu scored two for the home side. Saturday, 1 May saw the Hibees defeat Motherwell 1-0 at Easter Road, Mickey Weir marking his return from injury with a goal. On the same day, Falkirk thrashed Hearts 6-0 at crumbling Brockville. The Bairns' dazzling performance was inspired by their winger, Kevin McAllister, who tore Hearts to pieces that day.

Dundee thrashed the green jerseys 3-1 up at Dens Park a week later, Gareth Evans bagging the side's late consolation after Ritchie, Wieghorst and Gilzean had netted for the Dees. Season 92/93 ended for Hibernian with a 0-1 defeat at home to Partick Thistle, Gerry Britton netting for the Jags just before half-time. Gareth Evans was red-carded.

There was a small protest at this match by home fans who didn't want the club to sell prize asset Pat McGinlay to Celtic, as by then it was common knowledge that that's where the player was headed. The protest took the simple form of a few hundred Hibbies on the East Terrace during the game periodically chanting 'Paddy must stay, Paddy must stay'.

And so, season 1992/93 came to an end. Hibs had suffered an early KO in the League Cup and had reached the semi-finals of the Scottish Cup. They had faced off twice against one of Europe's top sides in what was then UEFA's toughest competition, and not lost either match. Seventh place had been the club's final league placing, with 37 points won out of a possible 88. There were many positives but also some negatives. Unlike the previous season, the goals for and against tally was in the red, 54 league goals scored with ten more than that conceded. They had 12 wins, 13 draws and 19 defeats. The Wright-Jackson partnership had proved excellent, bagging 29 goals between them in all competitions. Pat McGinlay had scored 14 goals from midfield, bettering his tally from the previous season by two. Our football that season had been, well, a bit hit and miss – typical Hibs really. Sometimes good, sometimes mediocre. Our best performances had come in the two wins over Celtic, the 3-4 loss at home to Rangers and in both matches against Anderlecht. Our two worst performances were in the two derbies at Tynecastle. Paddy was our best player over the season.

It had been an inconsistent season. Matches against our 'big four' opponents of Aberdeen, Celtic, Hearts and Rangers, 17 in total, had yielded just two victories – both against Celtic. Hibernian had used the same squad as season 91/92 with the addition of Darren Jackson. It was obvious to fans and manager alike that the midfield needed strengthening, particularly on the flanks. Alex Miller had tinkered with his defensive line-up all season, particularly in central defence, where various combinations were used, with Hunter, McIntyre, Orr, Beaumont, Farrell and Tweed all taking turns. The goalkeeping situation needed rectifying. John Burridge was a cult hero and an excellent goalkeeper, but had been error-prone in his second season, while Scotland under-21 goalkeeper Chris Reid was more agile but had also cost the team a few points, more due to naivety than anything else. The most urgent thing that the team needed was additional players who could link the midfield to the strikers – for that role we only had Mickey Weir, and though Mickey was superb, if he wasn't playing or was effectively man-marked, Hibs lacked a cutting edge.

Six first-team players left Easter Road at the season's end. Murdo MacLeod departed to take over as Dumbarton manager. Murdo had played 95 times and netted three times in the famous green jersey. He departed as an iconic cup-winning captain. Another cup-winning hero who left Easter Road was John Burridge, returning to England, having played 77 matches for Hibs. Callum Milne had made 87 appearances in his decade as a fringe player, scoring one goal in a friendly against Millwall in 1990, but left to join Partick Thistle. Neil Orr also made for pastures new, joining St Mirren, ending a six-year stint at Hibernian in which he made 203 appearances and scored six goals. Davy Fellenger moved to Cowdenbeath, having played 41 times for Hibs and having bagged four goals in a four-year first-team career. The close season brought the news that Hibs fans had expected but were nevertheless sad about: Pat McGinlay being sold to Celtic. The fee was around £500,000 (via a tribunal) and Hibs chairman Dougie Cromb told fans that the funds raised would be spent solely on squad strengthening. After such a mediocre season and with players leaving the club, that £500,000 was going to be sorely needed if season 93/94 was to be any better.

In other news, Falkirk and Airdrieonians were both relegated from the Premier Division, replaced by Division One champions Raith Rovers and runners-up Kilmarnock. Glasgow Rangers won all three of Scotland's major competitions, including their fifth consecutive domestic title, finishing nine points above nearest challengers Aberdeen. Rangers qualified for the European Champions Cup, Aberdeen got the Cup Winners' Cup slot, while Celtic, Hearts and Dundee United qualified for the UEFA Cup. The 1992/93 European Champions Cup, which had included the Champions League group stage, was won by French cracks Marseille, with Franck Sauzee among their ranks.

If Hibernian's season 92/93 had been a school report card, it would have read 'talented, but could do better'.

Scream, shout, and dance about the campfire
You can hear the question, can you feel the reply?

JUST LIKE FRED ASTAIRE – OFF-FIELD STUFF

'When the Hibs, went up, to lift the Scottish Cup, we were there, we were there ...'

FOOTBALL FINANCE really bores me. I'm a terracing lad and I'm interested primarily in actual football, not off-field stuff. The basics of the background at Hibs throughout the 90s and thereafter are thus. When those great Hibs men Dougie Cromb and Kenny McLean went to see Tom Farmer CBE (as was) in 1990 to ask him to get involved with Hibs and saving the club from Wallace Mercer, their actions safeguarded the Hibs that we know and love today. When Tom first took an interest in Hibernian our club was skint and played in a charming but antiquated old stadium, unfit for the modern era. We had no training facilities and we hadn't won a trophy in almost 20 years. The team wasn't doing well at all. When Hibernian Football Club was rescued from the ashes of the old PLC in 1991 it wasn't just a sports club which was saved, it was a great Edinburgh institution, as much a part of the capital as the castle or Arthur's Seat is.

Since 1991 the club has won three major trophies, built an impressive training facility and has upgraded its stadium to an impressive 20,000-seat modern arena. It has also weathered the storm of the 2008 crash and half a dozen other big shocks in global finance. During that time, most Scottish clubs have faced a degree of financial hardship, some frequently. Some clubs have been in administration, often more than once. Others have been liquidated and had to start again. Fans of some clubs have at times had to conduct bucket collections and hold bake sales, even running online crowdfunding initiatives in order to keep their teams afloat, much to the mirth of rival supporters. Hibs fans have been spared that embarrassment. We've always had a team, and all that we are asked to do is pay for tickets and buy merchandise, which is never a hardship. No jumble sales, no sponsored walks, no begging for extra cash from already hard-up supporters.

Sir Tom Farmer was and remains Hibernian's most successful owner, ever. Infrastructure and stability off the park, relative success on it. Outwith the old firm, only Hibs, Aberdeen and Hearts have won more than two major trophies in the last 30 years. Hopefully, our new owner can maintain and even improve on our relative success and we all wish him well in that. But remember, without Douglas Cromb, Kenny McLean and Sir Tom Farmer, the last 30 years may have been very different, and almost certainly dark. Moreover, how things have panned out for Hibernian since the Hands Off Hibs episode completely vindicates the actions and involvement of the fans and of the aforementioned people. Hands Off Hibs and the 1991 restructuring gave us everything that we have and everything that we have enjoyed as Hibs fans in the last 30 years. Now, that's quite enough of the football finance chat, let's get back to the beautiful game …

We can cross the race divide
Bridge a gap that wasn't really there
When I hold her in my arms
I feel like Fred Astaire.

LAID – SEASON 93/94

'Forever and ever, we'll follow the boys, the
Edinburgh Hibees, the Tim Malloys
*For we'll be mastered, by no 'other' b*stard,*
we'll keep the green flag, flying high, so ...'

THE SUMMER of 1993 saw boyband Take That achieve their first number one single with 'Pray'. As season 1993/94 got underway the charts were topped by the late Freddie Mercury's single 'Living on My Own'. At the cinema, punters were going crazy for *So, I married an axe murderer* and *The Fugitive.*

In UK news, NHS waiting lists had reached breaking point with over 1m people waiting for operations, while a new fringe political party had just been formed to oppose the Maastricht Treaty; it was called the UK Independence Party. The governing Conservative Party spent much of the summer mired in sleaze scandals. Globally, a company named Microsoft had just launched a new computer program called Windows, Russia was in the process of withdrawing troops from Lithuania and a probe sent by NASA to investigate Mars vanished just before entering the planet's orbit.

The year 1993 had seen Scotland's bid to qualify for a sixth consecutive World Cup falter and fade as the year progressed. The nail in the coffin had been a 0-5 drubbing from Portugal in Lisbon. In that match Scotland and Rangers striker Ally McCoist had suffered a broken leg and was not expected to play football again until 1994. Scotland manager Andy Roxburgh stood down after failing to get the national side to USA 1994, and was replaced by Craig Brown, who at the time was best known for guiding Scotland's under-16s to the final of their own 1989 World Cup tournament, held in Scotland. England had also failed miserably to qualify for USA 94.

Celtic manager Liam Brady was sacked early in season 93/94 and was replaced by Lou Macari. Rangers' seemingly endless pursuit of Dundee United striker Duncan Ferguson came to an end in the summer of 1993, when they finally signed him in a £4m deal. The close season had also seen Jim McLean step down as Dundee United manager after 22 years at the helm, replaced by Yugoslavian coach Ivan Golac. Over at Tynecastle, Sandy Clark had replaced Joe Jordan in the Hearts hot seat, ex-Scotland hero Jordan having been fired after the Jambos' 6-0 humiliation at the hands of Falkirk back in May. Season 93/94 saw a rule change in the Scottish League and League Cup, with clubs being allowed three substitutes instead of two, though the SFA's Scottish Cup didn't follow suit until several years later.

At Easter Road there were changes, too. Cult hero and cup-winning goalkeeper John Burridge left the club, leaving Hibs with just Chris Reid and young Jason Gardiner as cover. A solution to the goalkeeping situation was required, as in season 92/93 Hibernian had only kept a clean sheet in 12 out of 53 competitive matches. Alex Miller's answer was initially to raise a few eyebrows but would ultimately prove to be one of the best decisions that he made while at Easter Road.

Jim Leighton had been Scotland's best goalkeeper of the 1980s. He was a great success with Aberdeen and at Manchester United under Alex Ferguson and had won many domestic honours as well as a Cup Winners' Cup medal with the Dons. He was in the squad for the Spain '82 World Cup and was in goal for Scotland in all six matches at Mexico 86 and Italia 90. However, in 1990 Leighton made some errors in Man Utd's FA Cup Final against Crystal Palace, which ended in a 3-3 draw. Leighton was dropped for the replay and fell out of favour at Old Trafford. He also lost his place as Scotland goalie to Andy Goram. After two years of reserve football and being out on loan, Dundee signed him in 1992, but Leighton was dropped from the Dundee side in August that year after the Dees were thrashed 3-6 at home by Partick Thistle, and was replaced by Paul Mathers. More reserve football followed and then another loan spell, before Leighton signed for Hibernian on a free transfer in the summer of 1993. His arrival meant that all three of Scotland's most recent number-one goalkeepers, Rough, Goram and Leighton, had played for Hibs.

Hibs fans knew of Leighton's fall from grace but were, as with so many other players, keen to give a man with proven ability a chance. Some of the press questioned Alex Miller's judgment in signing the 35-year-old player, but Miller was rightly defiant. He knew that the signing was a masterstroke.

With Pat McGinlay having joined Celtic and three other regular players having departed, more players were needed to bolster the Hibees' squad for the coming campaign. Alex Miller knew that replacing a free-scoring box-to-box midfielder like McGinlay on a like-for-like basis with Hibs' budget would be difficult, so he tried something different. In came Falkirk winger Kevin McAllister and Dundee

United midfielder Michael O'Neill. McAllister, nicknamed Crunchie, was a pint-sized wee skilful winger very much of the old-school Scottish variety, akin in style to Jimmy Johnstone, John Colquhoun and even Mickey Weir. He had played over 100 matches for Chelsea and been part of their two SIMOD Cup wins – a knockout tournament played in England when English clubs were banned from Europe after the Heysel Stadium disaster of 1985. Kevin had even been in the Chelsea side that had played Hibs at Easter Road in a friendly in 1991, that had ended 2-2, Stevie Raynes and Keith Wright scoring for Hibs, Chelsea's goals coming from Kerry Dixon and a Dennis Wise penalty. With him having shone at Falkirk under Jim Jefferies after his return to Scotland, Alex Miller was impressed enough to pay Falkirk £235k for McAllister's services. Some fans learned that Crunchie was signed before others did. A Hibs XI was playing down in Peebles for pre-season one July evening; it was a midweek game so not many Hibbies were there, so Alex Miller invited the small group of fans to join him and the players for refreshments after that match. The manager was said to be excited, far more animated than anyone had ever seen him. Like a giddy schoolboy, he gleefully told the fans 'I've just signed Kevin McAllister!'

Irishman Michael O'Neill was a talented attacking midfielder who had enjoyed relatively successful spells at Newcastle United and Dundee United. He had impressed at Tannadice but had fallen out with then boss Jim McLean over signing a new deal and been dropped from the side. Even with his contract expired, under the old transfer system, which favoured clubs over players, Michael couldn't really just leave and sign for Hibs, as a player might now, as Dundee Utd held his registration. However, United wanted to cash in so O'Neill signed for Hibernian early in the 93/94 season, with his transfer fee to be decided by a tribunal. As with Darren Jackson a year earlier, the tribunal was more favourable to Hibs and decided that the fee should be around £250,000. United had wanted a lot more money for the gifted left-sided player.

The acquisitions of McAllister and O'Neill gave Hibs great attacking options to add to the threat posed by Wright, Jackson, Evans and Weir. Mickey Weir sadly suffered from recurring back injuries so it was a boon to Hibernian to sign two more players who were skilful going forward. The new season would also see utility man David Farrell step up to the plate and become a proper first-team regular. Faz took up a new role in the side, playing the defensive anchor role protecting the back four – and he played it rather well.

As usual, Hibernian prepared for the coming campaign with some friendly matches. Whitehill Welfare held the Cabbage to a 2-2 draw. Gala Fairydean were beaten 5-1 at Netherdale and Ayr United were defeated 2-0 at Somerset Park. Then came two glamour friendlies against English sides. Luton Town visited Easter Road on 30 July, the Hibees and the Hatters drawing 0-0. Sunday, 1 August saw Howard Wilkinson's Leeds United side visit Easter Road, on a glorious sunny afternoon. Wilkinson remains to this day the last English manager to win England's top-flight league.

Leeds had been English champions in 1992 but in season 92/93 had mounted the most inept title defence in decades, finishing 17th. A crowd of 9,204 fans was at Easter Road to see the challenge match. A large support had travelled up from Yorkshire to back Leeds and there were some disturbances in Edinburgh before and after the match. Michael O'Neill hadn't quite arrived at Hibs as of then but Kevin McAllister and Jim Leighton both played. The Yorkshire side had just signed striker Brian

Deane from Sheffield United for £3m and their line-up also featured David Rocastle, Gordon Strachan, David Batty, Rod Wallace, Gary Speed, Gary McAllister and Noel Whelan. Hibs' best chances in the match both fell to Darren Jackson, but John Lukic in the Leeds goal foiled him twice, brilliantly diverting a powerful drive by the striker and also saving a late Jackson penalty. The Leeds side was very strong and it was a really hard afternoon's graft for the green jerseys. Leeds won the match 2-0 thanks to goals by Noel Whelan and Brian Deane. The match featured the usual 'banter' between fans you get at Easter Road when an English side comes to visit, all good-natured, honestly. Leeds went on to re-establish themselves in the top half of England's Premier League in the coming season, finishing fourth. Though a defeat for Hibs, the game was ideal preparation for Alex Miller's men for what was to be a very topsy-turvy season.

On the eve of the new campaign, Alex Miller was quoted saying, 'We owe it to the public to supply top-rate league competition to Rangers; crowds will drop if the same team keeps winning the title. We intend to deliver good all-round entertainment to our fans in the new campaign.'

* * *

Wearing the same Bukta kit and with the same sponsor as the previous season, Hibs opened the 93/94 campaign with a home league match against Partick Thistle. For some reason, at every home match in both season 92/93 and 93/94, the PA at Easter Road always started with the same two songs, 'It's My Life' by Dr Alban, then 'Is it Like Today' by World Party. The records available may have been limited in choice due to PRS or because of the club's tie-in with Bandparts Music at the top of Leith Walk. Anyway, these two very different catchy pop tracks thus provided the opening sounds on home match days as the ground began to fill up, including before this Jags game. The match programme that day contained something rare – a scathing club statement about the casuals, because of all the bother connected to the Leeds United match. The Partick encounter was instantly forgettable, a typically drab Scottish League draw, and was by no means an indication of what was to come for the men from Leith in the new campaign.

Three days later, Alloa Athletic visited Easter Road in the League Cup second round. Billy Lamont's Wasps competed well but were stung by two Hibs goals from Keith Wright and from youngster Graeme Donald – back on the scoresheet for the first time since his brief but successful foray into the first team at the tail end of season 91/92. Most Hibs fans who were there will remember the Alloa fans on the Dunbar End that night – all 12 of them – bouncing around singing 'Ooh ah Alloa' to the same tune as Darren Jackson's own chant throughout the match, even when they were losing.

Saturday, 14 August saw the Hibees face their first big test of the season, heading west to take on Celtic at Parkhead. Almost 28,000 fans were in attendance, nearly three times the crowd of the sides' last meeting there. Charlie Nicholas gave the lesser greens the lead with a typically cool finish after ten minutes. Hibs, in purple and black, almost equalised just before the interval when Darren Jackson headed a pinpoint McAllister cross goalward, only for Pat Bonner to make an excellent save. Twice in the second half Jim Leighton produced amazing saves to deny Nicholas further goals. The Cabbage hurled everyone forward in the last 15 minutes and got a deserved equaliser with seven minutes remaining, when a superb volley from young Steven

Tweed bulged the net right in front of the large Hibs support behind the goal: 1-1. Celtic forced a series of corners in the dying minutes but Jim Leighton produced two world-class saves to keep the Hoops at bay. Alex Miller was actually scathing in a post-match interview, angry at his team's weak performance in the first half, but he must have been delighted with his new goalkeeper. Jim Leighton may have been low on confidence before joining Hibernian, but was surely brimming with self-belief now.

One week later saw the season's first Edinburgh derby played at Tynecastle. This match was the first modern Edinburgh derby in which a black player took to the field – though Hearts did actually have a black player from Leith named John Walker away back around 1898. The black player in 1993 was called Justin Fashanu. He had made his name in England many years before and had been Britain's first £1m black player. He was a tall, skilful striker and he also happened to be gay, and openly gay. Nowadays nobody would bat an eyelid at that but in the 80s and 90s when Fashanu was playing, many people did. Racism was still rife in much of society and in football; homophobia even more so. Prior to this match, if you'd been given a pound for every time you heard the following from some football fans in Edinburgh's pubs, clubs and on buses, you'd have had a few bob, sadly.

'He's gay, he's black, he's English, he plays for Hearts, no got much going for him, eh?'

Upon his joining Hearts from Swedish side Trelleborg, where he had played briefly after leaving Airdrieonians earlier in 1993, at least two contemporary newspapers 'affectionately' referred to Justin as 'The Queen of Hearts' – an example of the type of casual homophobia that was still commonplace then.

How did the Hibs fans on the Gorgie Road end react to Fashanu's appearance in a Hearts top?

Well, the player was targeted for abuse, like all opposition players are in derbies. There were a few idiots making fun of his skin colour, but far more fans aimed abuse at Fashanu over his sexuality at this game. In the first half, as Hearts attacked the Gorgie Road end where the Hibbies were, his every touch was greeted with wolf whistles. This type of nonsense plagued Fashanu's career, including during every match of his relatively short Hearts stint. Lots of Hibs fans that day didn't abuse him at all. Some of his own fans did. Big Fash was dignified and just ignored it. However, this match, watched by almost 18,000 fans, wouldn't be remembered for Justin Fashanu.

The game itself ran to a pattern which was becoming almost habit in the fixture. A Hibs team with plenty of good players suddenly forgot how to play football and offered virtually nothing in attack, against a Hearts team of equal ability but which was lethally better motivated. Darren Jackson had a terrible game, charging around committing fouls and getting caught offside, and was actually red-carded at the final whistle after a confrontation with Tosh McKinlay. The match was settled just after half-time when derby debutant Alan Johnston, 19, slipped his marker to fire high past a helpless Jim Leighton at the School End. Alex Miller's men had no reply and the encounter finished 1-0 to Hearts.

Hearts fans had a new song: '18 games in a row, it's magic, you know'. They had about another year to sing its variants.

On to the Tuesday and Dundee visited Edinburgh on League Cup business as part of back-to-back visits to Easter Road, as the two sides were to meet on league business on the Saturday. Hibs were without the suspended Darren Jackson for the cup tie. Jackson's first 18 months at Hibs proved he was a terrific player but also saw him display other qualities such as petulance and belligerence. He was often caught offside, talking back to referees and arguing with other players. Thankfully, Jacko grew up, and discovered weight training rather than trying to throw his weight around, and by 1994 was a far better footballer for it. The Hibees didn't need Jackson to defeat Dundee in this League Cup tie, anyway.

A sterling performance from new boys Michael O'Neill and Kevin McAllister and a goal apiece from Gordon Hunter and Keith Wright were enough to see off Jim Duffy's men 2-1. And it was 2-0 on the Saturday in the league meeting, this time Kevin McAllister and Dave Beaumont were on the scoresheet.

On 31 August, a lovely Tuesday evening, the League Cup quarter-finals took place. Hibs headed to Firhill to take on John Lambie's Partick Thistle. Some recent encounters between the sides had been turgid, boring affairs, but on this late summer night, it was absolutely a case of 'Firhill for thrills'.

Hibernian had never before faced Partick in a one-off League Cup knockout tie. The sides had met in the 1949 quarter-finals, but that had been a two-legged affair, Hibs winning 6-4 on aggregate. There had also been four instances of the two teams being in the same section in the tournament's group stages, all between 1951 and 1961. An impressive 37 goals had been produced by these eight matches, Hibs winning four, drawing once and losing three times – all three defeats had come at Firhill.

The roughly 8,000 fans in attendance were treated to a fast-paced cup tie from the off, but had to wait until the

35th minute for the first goal. A Thistle high ball into the box drew Jim Leighton from his line, but the goalie misjudged his jump and was beaten to the catch by the head of Partick striker Roddy Grant. The ball looped into the empty net and put the Jags 1-0 up. The large Hibs support on the terracing didn't seem too worried and were roaring encouragement to their heroes almost as soon as the goal was given, as Hibs fans often do when the team goes behind. Add that to the celebratory noise of the home fans and quite an atmosphere now engulfed that old Maryhill stadium.

Hibs went straight back onto the attack; great dribbling and shielding by livewire Kevin McAllister allowed the winger to gee up Gordon Hunter, whose long-range thunderbolt was brilliantly saved by Craig Nelson in the Partick goal. It was 1-0 at half-time, but the green jerseys upped a gear after the interval and got their reward. A simple pass from Billy Findlay on 65 minutes found McAllister on the edge of the box. He brilliantly turned one Jags defender then dummied another before firing low past Nelson into the bottom corner to make it 1-1. Minutes later, Gareth Evans – starting in place of Jackson, who was on the bench – weaved past Thistle's left flank and sent in a cross to the near post. Sandwiched between two Jags defenders and with Nelson to his front, Keith Wright managed to beat both defenders to the jump and nodded the ball at an acute angle past the despairing goalie, only for the ball to come back off the upright.

Keen to finish Thistle off, Alex Miller threw on Darren Jackson, who had been warming the bench since his derby red card. In the dying minutes of the 90, Jackson went on a blistering run with the ball, ghosting past two defenders before firing in a perfect cross to the far side of the box. Keith Wright connected brilliantly with the ball and sent a thunderous header towards the far top corner, across Nelson. However, the goalie matched Keef's header and pulled off a fantastic diving save to keep the score level and take the match into extra time. Nelson and Jim Leighton were both having excellent matches; Leighton had already atoned for his earlier error by making three wonderful saves himself.

Hibernian drew first blood in extra time. Michael O'Neill rampaged down the left and played a superb 20-yard chipped ball along the Partick defence, with pinpoint accuracy, to the feet of Kevin McAllister, who made no mistake, beating Nelson from 16 yards to add his and Hibs' second. Many Hibs fans thought that goal would settle it, it sure did not. Albert Craig equalised for Partick, his header going in after an almost slapstick game of head tennis in the Hibs box: 2-2.

Partick ended the 120 minutes with ten men after David Byrne (not the Talking Heads frontman) was red-carded for a violent reaction to a niggling foul by Jackson. And so it came to pass that the sides couldn't be separated by ordinary football and the tie was to be resolved by a penalty shoot-out.

Michael O'Neill, Keith Wright and Darren Jackson all scored for Hibs. Billy Findlay and Tommy McIntyre did not. Jim Leighton pulled off three superb saves to deny Paul Kinnaird, Roddy Grant and Ian Cameron, and was mobbed by his team-mates at the end for doing so. Hibs won the shoot-out 3-2 and were into the semi-finals of a major cup for the second time in five months. The pace and skill of McAllister and O'Neill had made all of the difference while Gordon Hunter was named man of the match. However, Hibbies' real hero of the night was Jim Leighton. The 35-year-old goalie truly deserved the loud acclaim of the Hibs faithful, and that night a new chant was born among the Hibbies on the Firhill terracing.

'Scotland's, Scotland's number one! Scotland's number one.' Well, not exactly a new chant. We'd sung it when Andy Goram was our goalie and was trying to oust Jim Leighton from the Scotland team. Now the chant filled the Glasgow air as we saluted our new super-goalie.

The chant was to prove to be prophetic for the rejuvenated goalkeeper. By November, Leighton would be back in the Scotland team, starting in a 2-0 victory over Malta, and he remained in the Scotland squad until October 1998!

The draw for the semi-finals contained Hibs, Dundee United, Rangers and Celtic. With Hampden Park still closed for refurbishment the ties would be played at neutral venues. Most Hibs fans wanted Dundee United, not just because it might be an easier tie to win but also because such a tie would almost certainly be played at Tynecastle, handy for a midweek cup tie for most Hibs fans. They got their wish as they were indeed drawn to play the Terrors, at Tynecastle, on Tuesday, 21 September. The following evening would see Rangers take on Celtic at the neutral venue of … Ibrox. Without Hampden, there was no suitable large venue for those two teams to play each other so the venue was decided by the SFL on the toss of a coin. For that match, in the interests of fairness, Celtic fans got half of Ibrox, despite their much lower average home attendances than Rangers at the time – logic which would not be used by the tournament's organisers when it came to the tournament's final.

Before the semi-finals, Alex Miller's men had three league matches to contend with. Gareth Evans scored in a 1-1 draw against Tommy Burns's newly promoted Kilmarnock down at Rugby Park. The following week Hibs beat Aberdeen 2-1 at Easter Road thanks to goals from Kevin McAllister and Keith Wright – ending a bleak winless spell against the Dons. Then came a trip to McDiarmid Park, that soulless 'legoland' arena. Michael O'Neill put Hibs one up after just two minutes with an 18-yard drive to finish off a superb move. Four minutes later, the pace of Gareth Evans and McAllister combined to double Hibernian's lead, Crunchie getting the goal after the pair had run through the Saintees' defence as if it wasn't there. Both goalkeepers made some fantastic saves. In the second half, McAllister, despite being fouled, stayed on his feet to beat two defenders then floated a wonderful cross onto the head of Keith Wright, who beat Rhodes all ends up. Hibs were on fire, St Johnstone had no answer to the skill, pace and trickery of Hibs' two wingers and Gareth Evans, plus the pace and power of Wright. Hibs pinned the Perth men back for most of the second half but didn't add to the lead. Paul Wright pulled one back for the home side in the last minute, with a superb long-range effort, though, and it finished 3-1 to Hibs.

This was an important victory for Alex Miller's men as, not only was it emphatic, it also showcased the new-look Hibs team. A solid goalkeeper, two skilful wingers, an industrious midfield and razor-sharp strikers, playing a wonderful passing game, the type of football all Hibbies love to see. The match was also a milestone for Hibernian, as 17-year-old Kevin Harper came on in the second half and thus became the first black player to feature for the first team (a black player from Bermuda called Ricky Hill had donned the green as a trialist around 1981 under Bertie Auld but never played a competitive match for Hibs, not the famous Ricky Hill of Luton, though). Harper was fast, direct, skilful and tenacious – all of the ingredients needed for a player to thrive in Scottish football. He had won the BP Cup with Hibs' excellent youth side in 1992 and would go on to be a fans' favourite for the next five years and to this day. We loved him.

Just like for the Jambos during Justin Fashanu's spell at Hearts, Kevin's introduction to the side forced some Hibs fans to have a discussion about racism, which was ultimately a good thing, as the minority of racist arseholes were largely silenced and soon changed their tune when they saw just how good a player Kevin was. Of course, it's sad and in all honesty a bit of a 'beamer' that it took Kevin's brilliance in the green to make that minority change their tune, or that people even had such a 'tune' at all, but such were the times. Most racist Hibs fans you encountered (there weren't *that* many) would usually say something idiotic and ignorant like, 'I hate blacks but I dinny mind Kevin Harper.' You could usually demolish their prejudice fairly quickly after that, or at least shut them up, by pointing out that such an attitude was both wrong and moronic. That doesn't mean that Hibbies or Hibs had a big racist problem back then: it was wider society and football in general where attitudes sometimes stank, football being a microcosm of society. Football supporters tend to have a higher proportion of utter zoomers among them, though, so in football it seemed more amplified. Though guys like Kevin Harper and Justin Fashanu did face racism in Scottish football, things had improved slightly since the late 80s when Paul Elliot of Celtic and Mark Walters of Rangers had been showered with abuse, monkey noises and bananas by their clubs' rival fans, and by some Hearts fans, too. Gus Caesar of Airdrie was also a target for such knuckledraggers when he played up here from 1992–94. Historically, most prejudice in Scotland and in its sport tends to have been based around regional tribalism and on religious intolerance rather than on skin colour, but there was always a bit of racism, too. It's weird, and perhaps *very* Scottish, that most racism in Scottish football retreated to the fringes after the mid 90s but that tribalism and religious intolerance didn't. Anyway ...

The 3-1 victory over St Johnstone made Hibernian top of the Scottish Premier Division. Five points from three games was ideal preparation for that looming cup semi-final against Dundee United.

That Tuesday night, almost 20,000 fans were at Tynecastle. Once again, Hibs fans occupied the shed and other areas of the ground usually reserved for home fans and once again the Hearts shed reverberated to the unfamiliar sound of Hibs anthems. The Arabs occupied the Gorgie Road end and around one third of the old main stand. Hibernian had faltered at this very ground in the Scottish Cup semis just five months earlier, now they set their sights on going one better in the League Cup.

These sides had met in the League Cup four times before. Dundee United had won the most recent encounter 2-0 at Easter Road in the quarter-final of the 1986/87 tournament. By 1993 only Gordon Hunter and Joe Tortolano remained from that side. The other three times the sides had met in the League Cup had been two group-stage home and away meetings in 1961 and 1963, all four matches of which were won by the Cabbage, and a 5-2 aggregate victory for the Hibees in 1972, which was, of course, on Hibernian's way to lifting the trophy against Celtic.

With 'Hail Hail' and 'Triumphal march' booming from the Hibby-occupied terracing behind the goals, Alex Miller's green jerseys and Ivan Golac's Terrors faced off on what was a typically windy yet pleasant autumn evening.

Hibernian attacked the School End of Tynecastle in the first half, which housed the Hibee faithful. Hibbies didn't have long to settle into their seats or standing places before they found themselves standing and, in many cases, leaping around in rapture.

After 11 minutes, a bungled Dundee Utd attack saw Hibs break quickly, a surging run from McAllister taking the ball right up to the edge of the box. McAllister then played a slick but simple lay-off to Jackson on the edge of the box, which Jackson chose to hit with his weaker left foot, low and straight into the bottom corner, beyond Alan Main. Using his left peg was clever; it completely wrong-footed United's defenders and goalie. Three sides of Tynecastle erupted, the sea of green and white rippling against the glare of the floodlights while the thunderous noise of the Hibs faithful was allegedly heard from as far afield as Broomhouse. When the goal cheers settled down, that song came booming out of the shed, the open terracing and from two thirds of the main stand:

'Ooh ah, Jacksona, say ooh ah Jacksona!'

Once again, the striker revelled in the acclaim. He deserved it. A few weeks earlier he had been the villain of the piece at Tynecastle, now he was the hero. Jacko, who had done some bench-warming prior to the tie, had publicly promised Alex Miller that he would score if chosen to start the tie. He kept his word.

Dundee Utd, unbeaten in all domestic competitions thus far, weren't about to lie down and let Hibs walk all over them. The match became an intense battle, with as much strength and commitment on display as there was skill. Soon after Hibs scored, United had a chance to level through youngster Andy Maclaren, but Jim Leighton bravely dived at the striker's feet to save the day. The green jerseys had a chance to double their lead before half-time, when Main picked up a back pass from Brian Welsh. The passback rule then was little more than a year old and some goalies were still getting used to it. As so often happened with the near farcical indirect free kick situations caused by back-pass violations, though, there was a lot of fuss but nothing happened. Michael O'Neill failed to guide his shot past the entire Dundee Utd team standing on the six-yard line, and the half ended, 1-0 to Hibs.

Throughout the second half, the noise inside Tynecastle was deafening, as the Hibs fans partied on Hearts' patch, revelling in desecrating the home areas of the ground with their Hibee anthems.

Keith Wright had a goal-bound effort brilliantly saved by Alan Main. Jim Leighton in turn saved superbly from another Maclaren effort and also blocked a long-range rocket from Freddy van der Hoorn. A few minutes later, Christian Dailly – a striker back then – bulleted a header goalward but Leighton was once again the hero, somehow managing to tip it over the bar. The closing stages of the match saw United besiege the Hibs goal with a series of long balls, but as time wore on these attacks began to look desperate. United could find no way past Jim Leighton and the impressive central defensive pairing of Hunter and young Tweed.

'Scotland's number one' rang out time and again from the Hibs support whenever Leighton gathered the ball. The colossal jubilant roar with which the Hibs fans greeted the final whistle made many a hair on many a neck stand on end. After saluting their heroes, the Hibbies made their way home into the dark autumn Edinburgh evening, Roseburn, MacLeod Street and Dalry echoing to a multitude of Hibee anthems. Hibs were top of the league and in a cup final. Hibernian FC and their supporters were flying. It was Hibernian's first win in a competitive match at Tynecastle in almost five years, and though it hadn't come against Hearts, there was one more sweet irony that evening which is often forgotten. After his goal, Darren Jackson had celebrated in front of the Hibs fans with both of his arms in the air. Steve Archibald had done the same five years earlier when he had scored what had been Hibernian's last winner in Gorgie.

Alex Miller praised the players' commitment and Jim Leighton, in particular, after this match, saying what most Hibs fans already knew and what most of Scotland would soon realise.

'Jim Leighton didn't lose his ability; all he ever lost was some of his confidence.'

Hibernian's second League Cup Final appearance in just two years would be against Rangers or Celtic. The other semi-final was played the next evening at Ibrox, with Rangers winning 1-0 despite being down to ten men. The all-conquering Govan side's victory meant that the final would be played on 24 October at Celtic Park, a neutral venue. Thus, as the newly all-seated Hampden would be ready by May to host the Scottish Cup Final, the 1993 Scottish League Cup Final would be the last major final contested in Scotland where fans were allowed to stand on terraces.

* * *

Back to league business and Hibs continued their good form. A cup-final dress rehearsal against Rangers at Ibrox brought a narrow 2-1 defeat, Gareth Evans scoring for the Hibees in a match that the light blues were lucky to win. The loss knocked Hibs off top spot in the table but only for two weeks (there wasn't much in the way of points between the top six teams). Dundee United returned to Edinburgh a week later, once again to be put to the sword by Hibs, and once more the swordsman was Jackson, who bagged a brace in a 2-0 win. Next, Raith Rovers were beaten 3-2 at Easter Road, McAllister, Jackson and O'Neill scoring. Wright and Jackson both scored in a 2-0 win at Fir Park. Celtic then visited Easter Road, under the temporary charge of Frank Connor as Liam Brady had just been sacked as their manager. Gareth Evans gave the Hibees the lead after 65 minutes but the Hoops got a late equaliser through Gerry Creaney and it ended 1-1.

After a slow start to the season, Hibernian had spent September and October playing sexy soccer; the new signings were more than proving their worth, while the longer-serving players were also performing magnificently. The fans had regained their swagger and were enjoying the season. Top of the league with one quarter of the season played and having lost just two out of 16 matches, Hibs fans had every reason to be confident ahead of their next match, the League Cup Final against treble holders Rangers.

Another October Sunday, another League Cup Final in Glasgow for Hibernian. In season 93/94 the tournament had no main sponsor: SKOL had stopped sponsoring it the previous season and the new deal with Coca-Cola wasn't to begin until 1994. Almost 50,000 fans were expected at Celtic Park to see the current table-toppers take on the champions and cup holders. Despite the fixture's billing, Alex Miller's men had a mountain to climb if they wanted to receive anything more than a runners-up medal.

Rangers in this era were virtually unstoppable in the domestic set-up. Backed by Bank of Scotland and under the leadership of millionaire businessman David Murray, they carried all before them in Scotland. They did occasionally lose matches but tended to turn up for every important one. They were less solid in Europe. For instance, their good 92/93 Champions Cup campaign was followed by an ignominious first-round exit in the same tournament to Levski Sofia in August 1993, and they were soon joined in the Scottish Euro bin by Hearts, who lost to Atletico Madrid, and by Celtic, Aberdeen and Dundee Utd, all of whom were eliminated early.

Rangers had won the League Cup 18 times in their history and were looking to make it 19 against Hibernian. Alex Miller's men, at the time, were the last side to have beaten Rangers in a domestic cup match, that being the 1991 SKOL League Cup semi-final at Hampden, on Hibs' journey to lifting the coveted trophy. Hibs had also triumphed against the Gers when the two sides had met in the same competition at the same stage in 1985, John Blackley's side winning a two-legged affair 2-1 on aggregate, only to lose the final to Aberdeen. Eddie Turnbull's Hibs had beaten the light blues 1-0 in the 1972 semi-final en route to lifting the trophy. Going further back, Rangers had beaten Hibernian in the 1947 semi-final of the tournament, but this was the first and to date only time that Hibs and Rangers had contested a League Cup Final.

Despite it being a neutral venue, the SFL saw fit to give Rangers a de facto home advantage. That is to say, Hibs got around 20,000 tickets and were given the East End behind the goals and about a third of Celtic Park's main stand. A Hibs terracing ticket that day cost £8. Rangers fans occupied the west terrace behind the other goal, the rest of the main stand *and* the whole of Celtic's famous jungle – which Celtic's soon-to-be-ousted owners had seated in the close season. There would have been, ahem, difficulties in segregating the stadium in any other safe way, to be fair, but nevertheless, 20,000 Hibs fans to almost 30,000 Rangers fans really wasn't a fair split for a cup final. Scottish football authorities didn't bother to make cup finals a fair 50/50 split until the 2001 Scottish Cup Final between Hibs and Celtic.

The Hibee faithful choked the M8 on Sunday, 24 October 1993 as fans from Leith, Longstone, Danderhall, Muirhouse, Granton, Livingston, Fife, Coatbridge and 1,000 other places descended on Scotland's second city. The fans were in confident mood. It was a relatively nice day for late October. Meat Loaf had just begun a seven-week stint at number one with his single 'I Would do Anything for Love', while Quentin Tarantino's *True Romance* was popular in cinemas that week. However, that Sunday, it was the romance of the cup that was on the mind of much of Scotland's populace.

With all the Hibs fans rammed into one end of the ground, it was easier for the underdogs' fans to sing one loud song together. During the match build-up the usual party songs emanated from the Rangers end, 'The Sash', 'Derry's Walls', etc, but there was another song booming around Celtic Park that day and, bizarrely, it was being sung by both sets of fans, though not together. The song in question was 'Triumphal March' from Verdi's 1871 opera, *Aida*. The song didn't have any words; fans just sang the tune with 'do do …' and jumped around on the terraces a lot whilst singing it. It was a catchy tune but football fans aren't exactly associated with the opera, so where did this song, which first appeared on British terraces in season 92/93, come from? The answer is, *Football Italia*. From 1992, Channel 4 was showing live Italian football every Sunday and the chant was popular in Italy, so fans in the UK started singing the ditty, too. Fan sharing of songs, dear reader, antedates the invention of YouTube. There are other theories about where this chant appeared from but *Football Italia* is the most likely source. It's one of the few tunes that every team in Britain sang at the time.

Pre-match entertainment at Celtic Park came in the form of cheerleaders, and a Scottish steel drum band called Mackumba. The talented band of steel-drummers did a lap of the pitch, drumming away furiously, playing Caribbean and African tunes with a Scots twist; however, both sets of fans sang over them and when the band walked in front of the Hibs fans it was showered with jeers, abuse and pies. Some Hibs fans didn't think that having any sort of marching drum band on the park when we were playing Rangers was very neutral or entertaining at all, others didn't like the racket, others jeered them simply because they were drunk.

The PA then blasted music right up until before kick-off, the final track being 2 Unlimited's number one 'No Limit'. Then, with the stadium full and looking like a huge Roman amphitheatre, part blue, part green, the gladiators took to the field.

Former Hibs hero Andy Goram had excelled at Rangers but had also developed serious knee problems by 1993 and was injured, replaced in goal by former Motherwell man Ally Maxwell; that gave Hibs fans some hope. Likewise did the absence from the Gers starting XI of prolific striker Ally McCoist. 'Super Ally' had only just recovered from the broken leg he had suffered in Lisbon earlier that year, so he was on the bench, though he had played his first comeback game a week earlier against St Johnstone at McDiarmid Park. To this day there's a popular misconception that McCoist's comeback game was this final – it wasn't. Those absences aside, Rangers lined up with Maxwell in goal, Stevens, Robertson, McPherson and Gough at the back, Huistra, McCall, Ian Ferguson and Trevor Steven in midfield, with Mark Hateley and Ian Durrant up front. They had Scott, Mikhailichenko and McCoist on the bench and were managed by Walter Smith.

Hibernian lined up with Leighton in goal, Miller and Mitchell as full-backs, Hunter and Tweed in central defence, McAllister and O'Neill on the flanks, Farrell and Hamilton in the middle and Wright and Jackson up front. On the bench were Chris Reid, Gareth Evans and Dave Beaumont. Only five players in that XI had played in the 1991 cup-final win. Jim McCluskey was the referee. Hibs fans welcomed their heroes onto the pitch by singing 'Hail Hail', 'You'll Never Walk Alone' and 'Glory Glory to the Hibees', all of which were booed loudly by the Rangers fans.

Rangers attacked the Hibs end in the first half and were first to have a good chance, Trevor Steven weaving through the middle then unleashing a shot which Leighton did well to save. Then Hateley managed to head a pinpoint Peter Huistra cross wide when it looked easier to score, though the big striker had to try to mount Gordon Hunter in order to connect with the ball. Another Rangers attack saw Ian Ferguson blast the ball over the bar with the goal at his mercy. Hibs were largely on the back foot in the first half but, crucially, were not overrun.

Kevin McAllister played a laser-esque through ball to Keith Wright which sent the striker hurtling through on Ally Maxwell. Keith hit the turf just inside the box when challenged by Maxwell but the referee was having none of it. Instead of a penalty, Keith got a yellow card. From the Hibs end it had looked a stonewall penalty, but that wasn't to be. Much of the match was a midfield battle. Brian Hamilton and David Farrell did exceptionally well for much of the contest, holding their own against Rangers' tough and skilful middle men.

The teams were level at the interval, an interval which saw both of the terraced ends of the ground covered in huge flags, a marvellous spectacle for all. Not so marvellous was the reappearance of Mackumba.

The second half got underway with both sides attacking the ends which housed their own fans. Ian Durrant, playing as an auxiliary striker, started a clever move which saw him play a one-two with Mark Hateley, then finish the move himself, Durrant lobbing the helpless onrushing Leighton from 14 yards: 1-0 to Rangers after 55 minutes.

After the goal, the Rangers fans indulged in singing a song about not being able to hear the Hibs fans singing, you know the one. Ironically, this seemed to galvanise Alex Miller's men.

Michael O'Neill got Hibs' first attempt on target soon afterwards, hitting a low long-ranger straight at Maxwell. The Hibs fans behind the goal were by now loudly roaring on the team, as the Hibees finally began to string their passing game of the previous weeks together.

That passing game began to pay off and the Hibs faithful were rewarded for their patience. Pinned back, Gary Stevens, under pressure from Jackson, played a looped pass across his own penalty area to nobody. Keith Wright and Ally Maxwell went for the ball, this time Keith Wright steered the ball past Maxwell but his momentum carried him wide almost to the touchline, so, with two Rangers defenders on the line, Keith did the sensible thing and hammered the ball directly towards them. There was no Hibs player in the middle but Keith's shot smacked Dave McPherson on the side of the head and bounced into the net. Hibs were level, 1-1. The announcer at the time credited Keith with the goal but it has since been revised to be a McPherson own goal. Keith still claims it as his goal to this day, and it really was.

When the ball hit the net there was pandemonium in the Hibs end. Fans on the terraces jumped around, hugged each other, and gesticulated towards the opposition fans. A sea of green and white leapt into the air as one, then surged forward, then back, safely, because terracing was safe. Alex Miller, the Hibs players and the fans scented blood now. The Rangers support stood aghast, in near silence, as 20,000 Hibs fans belted out 'Glory Glory', at deafening volume, then came an equally loud rendition of 'Hail Hail'. It was all to play for in the last 20 minutes and Hibs had the best of the remainder of the match.

Hibs pushed on. There were chances to score but they fell to skipper Gordon Hunter, David Farrell and to Brian Hamilton, and they weren't clear-cut chances. McAllister, too, came close late on, a clever angled effort of his being headed off the line by Gary Stevens.

Sometimes as a football fan, your team gets a fairytale ending. Other times your team has a nightmare. But there are other occasions as a football fan, too, and some such occasions involve your team playing very well but ultimately ending up as the bit-player in someone else's fairytale. This was one such occasion.

Enter stage left with 69 minutes gone, Ally McCoist, recently back from a six-month layoff following that horrific injury. With nine minutes remaining, a long throw by David Robertson into the Hibs box was knocked on by Hateley to McCoist, who controlled the ball on his chest then scored a wonderful overhead kick from around 12 yards, despite the nearby attentions of four Hibs defenders. It was a truly excellent goal, and it utterly sickened us in the Hibs end. If you were there, you probably had that dreadful sinking feeling as McCoist scored and three sides of the stadium, clad in blue, rose in jubilation, with a seemingly endless roar. Rangers fans would feel exactly the same way in 2016, when David Gray scored the winner against them for us at Hampden.

Hibs did pin the Gers back in the closing minutes but there was nothing doing in the way of clear chances. Rangers won the match 2-1 and lifted the cup. It was a cruel way for Hibs to lose, and yet, something beautiful happened at the end. With the Rangers players celebrating with their fans at the other end, along with comedian Andy Cameron and TV's Mr Blobby (why was he there?), the Hibs fans, many of who had stayed behind, held aloft their scarves and sang 'You'll Never Walk Alone' to salute the team's effort and to show defiance. A mass of green and white scarves, a beautiful song, right after a defeat – that's Hibs class. Then came the usual 'We'll Support You Evermore' as the Hibs fans started to leave the ground and head home. There were 71 arrests after the match, mostly for public-order offences like pissing in the street.

It had been an effort to be proud of for Alex Miller's men. Walter Smith praised Hibs after the match, while Alex Miller said that he was proud of his players. He had every reason to be. His side had competed well for most of the match and had dominated possession for much of the second half.

The cup dream over, it was now back to league business for Hibs, with Hearts due to visit Easter Road in just six days' time.

The season's second Edinburgh derby took place on 30 October. Around 19,000 fans were in attendance, including a large Hearts support, buoyed by Hibs' cup-final heartbreak. In those days the PA at Easter Road didn't play continuous music, which meant that opposing fans could have a right good shout at each other in the 30 minutes before kick-off. On this occasion, the Hearts fans had but one song, and they sang it loudly, all afternoon. It went like this:

'Super Ally, Super Ally, ole ole ole!'

Hibs fans, hoping to see their brave heroes from the cup final come onto the pitch and shut the Jambos up, were to be disappointed, as a very jaded and predictable Hibs team took to the field instead. The same starting XI who had so valiantly battled Rangers gave up and lay down to a very mediocre Hearts side. The atmosphere on the East Terrace wasn't good at all and worsened after Hearts took the lead through John Colquhoun in the first half. There were virtually no loud Hibs songs thereafter. The Cabbage only had one shot on target, a weak Graham Mitchell effort. Colquhoun scored again in the second half and it finished 2-0 to Hearts.

The press seemed to enjoy telling their readers that Hibs now hadn't beaten Hearts in 19 attempts. The same press rarely mentioned that Hearts hadn't won a trophy in more than 30 years. After this defeat a story appeared in one newspaper claiming that a Caribbean witch doctor had offered Hibs his services in helping to shake off their Hearts hoodoo. Voodoo for a hoodoo? Whether true or not, that story sums up how some of us as Hibs fans felt about our run in the fixture. Some fans were annoyed at the manager as, sometimes when asked about the hoodoo, Alex Miller was quick to say that a derby was just like any other match. Results clearly belied that viewpoint. Since the 0-1 Tynecastle derby defeat, Hibs had played 13 matches and only lost two – both of those to Rangers – yet once again at Easter Road a hungrier Hearts team had won easily. Hibs had also been knocked off the top spot in the league during the two weeks since their 1-1 draw with Celtic prior to the cup final.

Hibernian's players lost their way at times in the following weeks;4 the cup-final exertions and disappointment had indeed taken their toll.

A tediously dull 0-0 draw with Partick Thistle at Firhill on the Tuesday after the derby followed, though Hibernian were still second in the league after that match. Next up, the Cabbage visited Dens Park to take on bottom side Dundee. Dundee's four new foreign imports – including Dariusz Adamczyk and Dragutin Ristic – combined to overwhelm the men from Leith, the Dees winning 3-2. Hibs goals came courtesy of a quite spectacular own goal by Dundee's player-manager Jim Duffy and a late Keith Wright effort.

On Tuesday, 9 November Kilmarnock visited Easter Road. The Ayrshire side had the best of the first half, with their strike force of Bobby Williamson and Tom Brown giving the Hibee defence a torrid time. Killie led at half-time through a Tom Brown header but Steven Tweed equalised with a header of his own just after the interval. Killie deserved something from the match but got nothing, as a late Gordon Hunter goal meant Hibs won 2-1. Kilmarnock's midfielder Andy Millen was man of the match. That victory ended a five-match winless run for the green jerseys.

On the Saturday the Hibees were up at Tannadice and were 2-0 down at half-time, largely thanks to Dundee Utd striker Craig Brewster, who had scored one and made one. A half-time roasting from Alex Miller turned things around and Hibs fought back to earn a point, thanks to goals from Jackson and Hamilton. Graham Mitchell was sent off late in the game.

Rangers came to Leith on league business on 20 November and won 1-0, Mikhailichenko scoring the game's only goal. A week later Hibs went up to Pittodrie and were mauled 4-0 by league leaders Aberdeen, Hibs legend Paul Kane being among the Reds' scorers. On the Tuesday, St Johnstone came to Easter Road and drew 0-0 in cold, rainy conditions, in a match that many Hibs fans remember as being one of the most boring encounters ever. Goals from Billy Findlay and Keith Wright were enough to ensure two points for Hibernian a week later, with a 2-1 win against Jimmy Nicholl's Raith Rovers at Stark's Park.

On 11 December Easter Road witnessed a thrilling Saturday afternoon match, with five goals in the second half, as Hibs took on Motherwell. Keith Wright gave the home side the lead with a great header but the Steelmen equalised almost immediately through Ireland striker Tommy Coyne. Coyne then put Well in front with an impressive lob over Leighton, only for Billy Findlay to haul the home side level just 50 seconds later. Motherwell had Miodrag Krivokapic sent off late on for a professional foul on Keith Wright and the Lanarkshire side promptly folded, Hibs winning 3-2 with Graham Mitchell heading home a Joe Tortolano corner for the winner.

Saturday, 18 December came and Hibs played their last match before Christmas, putting in a weak display against Celtic at Parkhead, but only losing 0-1 to a late Paul McStay goal.

Hibernian FC's final match of 1993 was at Easter Road on Monday, 27 December. Partick Thistle were the opponents on a bitterly cold festive afternoon, with over 10,000 in attendance. The first half wasn't much of an affair, though Hibs did lead 1-0 at the interval thanks to a scrambled effort credited to Brian Hamilton. The second half was much better, both as a game of football for the neutral, and for Hibernian fans. Thistle actually equalised,

Grant Tierney scored a marvellous overhead kick at the Dunbar End which went in off the crossbar (a strike which is still remembered fondly by Jags fans), and led to jubilant celebrations by the 500 or so Jags fans behind the goal, but their joy was to be short-lived. David Farrell headed a Tortolano cross past Andy Murdoch and into the net just one minute after the Jags' equaliser, to put Hibs 2-1 up.

It was Faz's first goal for Hibernian in five years at the club, and boy did he celebrate. He had also had two long-range piledrivers superbly saved by Murdoch and could have had a hat-trick. In that second half, the confident, swaggering, passing and pacey Hibs side which had scarcely been seen since the cup final returned with a vengeance. A Darren Jackson penalty and a wonderful solo goal by McAllister put the home side 4-1 up and on easy street as Thistle collapsed beneath the weight of the green and white onslaught. Nine minutes from full time Keith Wright got the match's final goal and Hibs had won 5-1. It could easily have been 10-1. For those of a green persuasion, it had been a Christmas cracker! Five different players had scored, the team's confidence had returned and, it seemed, just in time, too. Hibernian's next opponents were to be Hearts at Tynecastle on New Year's Day. On that freezing December day against Thistle at Easter Road, 5-1 up, the Hibs fans chanted loudly 'Bring on the Jam Tarts' over and over again. The fans had reason for such renewed confidence, as not only were there signs that Hibs were back to their best, Hearts had problems, too. Two of their best players were injured; another was suspended for the derby. Hearts were languishing in the table's bottom half where they had spent most of the season. Hearts were in off-field turmoil, too, with fans increasingly pissed-off at Wallace Mercer and the club's lack of real success; indeed, were it not for the unbeaten run against Hibs, the Hearts support might have been in open revolt against the club's owner much sooner. In fact, Hearts at year's end were ten matches without a win, their last victory having come against, that's right, you guessed it, Hibs. Hibs fans felt that the New Year derby would see them end their 19-match winless run in the fixture.

The 1994 New Year derby was postponed due to bad weather, not once, but twice. Cynics say that Wallace Mercer wanted the games called off so as to avoid paying treble-time holiday rates to police and to allow his injured and suspended players a chance to return to face Hibs. Regardless of such conspiracy theories, the weather was very bad, so the derby was delayed by 12 crucial days.

On 8 January, Dundee returned to Easter Road for the third time that season, and again, Hibernian beat them 2-0, this time with goals from Joe Tortolano and McAllister.

Wednesday, 12 January saw almost 25,000 fans gather at Tynecastle for the rearranged Edinburgh derby. Hearts were back at full strength, Hibs also had no notable absentees, though Darren Jackson started on the bench. No Edinburgh derby played in Scotland's capital has had a larger attendance since. Fans crammed onto the terraces in the eerie, freezing January evening. Lots of woolly hats were worn. The usual 'banter' was exchanged between men in the Hibs end and young women who were watching the match from the windows of flats in Gorgie Road which looked right out onto the away end. The party songs and Hearts anthems emanating from the home end were met with chants of 'No cups in Gorgie' from the green and white legion. 'I Beg Your Pardon' by Kon Kan – played regularly at Tynecastle for some reason – added to the atmosphere, then on came the Hearts song, first the 80s disco version, then the old Hector Nicol one. The Hibs fans sang along to the Hearts song with their own lyrics, as usual. The noise and atmosphere inside Tynecastle was electric as the match kicked off, with Hibs attacking the School End. It was the last Edinburgh derby at Tynecastle where fans stood on terracing.

Unlike the previous few derbies, the match was actually a decent game of football, tight, but largely devoid of venom. Hearts came close in the first half when Gary Locke forced a superb save from Jim Leighton. Hibs' best chance in the first half came from Keith Wright, who curled a dangerous shot past Smith but also just past the post. Hearts winger Wayne Foster almost scored after being put through one-on-one with Leighton but the goalie cleared the danger just as Dave Beaumont clattered into the back of Foster. Beaumont was booked for the foul on Foster, but Hibs survived. At half-time it was 0-0.

Hibs came out for the second half and threw everything at Hearts, sensing a real chance to end the winless run. Tortolano forced a good save from Henry Smith. Then, on 54 minutes, Graham Mitchell stormed down the left and crossed to Keith Wright. With the Hearts back line looking on like statues, Keith rose to head the ball into the net, past the helpless Smith. Hibs were 1-0 up. The Gorgie Road end erupted, hats went flying, many fans ended up 20 paces away from where they had been standing before the goal, such was the surge. Tynecastle reverberated to 'Hail Hail' and chants of 'Keef, Keef, Keef'. The Jambos were stunned.

Hearts hit back. Leighton saved a good Robertson overhead kick, then Willie Miller cleared a Scott Leitch corner off the line. Hibs looked dangerous on the break and their players seemed calm and confident. Two substitutions changed the game. Locke limped off injured and was replaced by John Millar. Hearts forced a corner. Alex Miller replaced McAllister with Jackson just beforehand. Up until this point, since the Hibs goal, the home support had been largely silent, standing aghast in icy dread of losing their little unbeaten run. Then, 12 minutes from time, a Leitch corner was headed into the net by John Millar. A colossal roar of relief came from the Hearts end, sounding slightly different to their usual racket. Hearts fans knew that their team had gotten out of jail. When Jackson had come on for Hibs he had given instructions from the boss to certain players just before the corner and the Hibs defence had reconfigured to plug a gap which wasn't really there. In that process they had opened up a real gap and that's how Hearts, somewhat scabbily, made it to 20 matches unbeaten against Hibernian.

Hearts had still only won one match in their last 18. The point meant that Hibs remained in fourth place in the table, but many Hibs fans saw the derby not only as a point dropped but also a wasted opportunity to beat Hearts. Would Hibs have won the match had it been played on 1 January? We'll never know. Nevertheless, Hibs put in their best derby performance since the first derby of season 92/93, and most fans were sure that Hearts' run would end soon.

The following Saturday gave Hibs fans a winter trip to Ayrshire to take on Kilmarnock. The green jerseys carried on where they had left off against Partick Thistle and easily beat Tommy Burns's men 3-0; goals came from Dave Beaumont, Gareth Evans and a screamer by David Farrell, who again celebrated in style. Much is made of the likes of O'Neill and McAllister's contribution to the season in question, yet Farrell, relishing his midfield role, was by far the most improved player in the squad during that campaign.

Perth was Hibernian's next destination, to take on St Johnstone. The Saintees took the lead through

Paul Wright, but the striker was stretchered off with a recurrence of the dreadful knee injury he had suffered at the hands of Neil Berry in an Edinburgh derby three years earlier. Michael O'Neill levelled the match from the penalty spot after 66 minutes. St Johnstone regained the lead against the run of play through young Billy Dodds, but Jacko came off the bench to level the match with six minutes remaining. Jackson had been benched by Miller quite a few times since the season's first Edinburgh derby back in August. After this match, one reporter asked Alex Miller if Jackson's goal would mean that the striker would return to the starting XI for the next match. Alex Miller said no. But, he did …

The last Saturday of January saw the Scottish Cup begin for Hibernian, with a home tie against Clyde. The Bully Wee, managed by Alex Smith, came to Easter Road with a crude but effective game plan, and it almost worked. Graeme McCheyne stunned Easter Road by heading the visitors into the lead, and the dynamic of the match caused great nervousness among the home support. Clyde put up a real fight. Michael O'Neill eventually hauled Hibs level late on with a fine strike from 15 yards, and most Hibs fans began to think of the replay, which was to be at Clyde's new home at Broadwood in Cumbernauld. However, thankfully, Kevin McAllister's persistence and fine late, late goal cancelled that particular away day and Hibs, rather fortunately, won the match 2-1 and progressed to the fourth round.

The draw for the fourth round came immediately after the match and many Hibs fans heard it on the radio in their cars or in the pub just after leaving the Clyde match. Fans of both Edinburgh clubs who were around at the time will remember that voice well.

'Hibernian will play Heart of Midlothian.'

Hibs and Hearts had been drawn together in the cup for the first time since the 70s. The next 22 days saw Edinburgh's football fans whipped up into a frenzy by the media. Who can forget the constant radio advertisements for the tie? 'Two Tribes' by Frankie Goes To Hollywood, with the audio of the cup draw played over it. The tie was to be played on Sunday, 20 February at Easter Road and would be shown live on BBC. Hibernian had a great chance to end that hoodoo in style, the last derby had given the fans every confidence. Hearts fans were apprehensive about the tie but also confident.

Hibs had two league matches to play before the big cup derby. Aberdeen visited Easter Road on 5 February. Lee Richardson gave the Dons the lead but Hibs fought back, winning the match 3-1 thanks to a double from Wright and a great goal by Danny Lennon, the latter putting in by far his best performance in the green jersey. A week later the men from Leith went down to a 0-2 defeat to Rangers at Ibrox, Trevor Steven and ex-Hibee Gordon Durie netting for the light blues in a match in which Gordon Hunter was sent off for, well, doing a decent job of marking Mark Hateley. The Ibrox loss wasn't ideal cup-derby preparation but wasn't harmful, either. That said, Hibernian had now gone 12 matches against Rangers without a victory. Now Hibs had to try to beat struggling Hearts, whom they hadn't beaten in 20 attempts. Hibs had met Hearts in 27 Scottish Cup matches before the 1994 meeting, winning nine matches and drawing eight.

Around 21,000 fans were at Easter Road for the cup tie against Hearts. The irritating Hearts support on the Dunbar End had a new ditty, sung to the tune of The Pet Shop Boys' chart cover of 'Go West'. They were also still singing 'Super Ally'. The Hibbies, though, were in fine voice, too, and Easter Road was almost shaking with noise when the match kicked off. Home fans sang a loud 'Glory Glory' before kick-off. Hibs were at full strength, asides the absence of the suspended Gordon Hunter and Graham Mitchell.

Mo Johnston, the controversial ex-Celtic and Rangers striker, was in the Hearts starting line-up. Hibs fans hated the player and sang 'Mo, Mo, f..k yer Mo' at him, loudly, during the warm-up. Terracing tickets for the match cost £7. For a whole generation of Hibs and Hearts fans, this was their first cup derby. Battle was soon underway on the pitch.

In the third minute, Tosh McKinlay played a simple ball to John Robertson at the near post. Two Hibs defenders didn't see the danger and were ball-watching when Robertson stabbed the ball past Leighton at the Cowshed End to put Hearts 1-0 up. Hibs fans were stunned, but kept singing: this was the cup; it was different.

Sure enough, Hibernian took command of the match as the first half wore on, dominating possession and looking stronger, more like the 'good' Hibs team the fans had seen for much of the season. Hearts were no mugs, though, and the match became a battle. On 42 minutes, a delightful cross from Michael O'Neill found Keith Wright unmarked in the box, and the Hibs hero rose to nod the ball downwards past Smith and into the net: 1-1.

Three sides of the stadium roared with joy as Keith ran to celebrate in front of the east terracing, which housed Hibs' noisiest fans. Hibbies then sang Verdi's 'Triumphal March' again, at ear-splitting volume. A minute later, Kevin McAllister ran through the Hearts defence and cleverly dinked the ball past Henry Smith. The ball came back off the inside of the post and would surely have been put over the line by the onrushing Brian Hamilton, but for a timely intervention by Hearts defender Craig Levein. Sandy Clark later admitted that had that chance gone in his team would have lost the match. Levein gets a lot of stick from Hibs fans today. That's unsurprising as he played for our city rivals and managed them twice and even has a good record against Hibs. However, it should be noted that he was one of the best defenders at the Edinburgh clubs of the 80s and 90s. It was 1-1 at half-time.

The second half was more of a typical derby, but Hibs were matching Hearts physically and had the best of the 45 minutes, save for one fatal lapse in concentration.

Both sets of fans were by now thinking of a replay at Tynecastle. Then, with four minutes remaining, Gary Mackay thumped a long ball up the pitch which missed out the whole midfield, and fell to Hearts substitute Wayne Foster. The attacker hurtled through on goal, Jim Leighton came out to narrow the angle and Dave Beaumont was right behind Foster, but, unlike in the previous derby, Beaumont chose to let Foster run rather than having him chew the grass. Foster finished well to beat Leighton and the away end erupted. Hearts won the tie 2-1 but were unceremoniously dumped from the cup in the very next round, losing 2-0 at Ibrox. Had Beaumont chopped Foster and ended up suspended for the replay, the truth is that nobody knows what the outcome may have been. The defeat wasn't anyone's fault, that's just football.

As Hibs fans, we all have our annoying memories of matches gone awry. Two generations of Hibbies were haunted by this goal for six months, some for even longer. What Hibby who saw the game can forget the sinking feeling as Foster, hitherto a figure of ridicule to both sets of fans, went through on goal, as if in slow motion, wasn't challenged and scored, sending the numpties on the Dunbar End delirious?

As a fan, your sad experiences at matches shape you just as much as your delightful ones. I was 15 when I was at this game, and I don't believe I spoke a word to my mate and his dad for the duration of our journey home. Many other Hibbies were in similar shock. We all were. A lot of us stayed in shock until August.

And so, it was back to the grind of the domestic league. Hibs were still fourth in the table, just five points behind leaders Rangers. Six days after the derby defeat, Hibs lost 1-0 to Dundee United at Easter Road, Trinidad and Tobago striker Jerren Nixon bagging the game's only goal. Alex Miller recalled Tommy McIntyre and Billy Findlay for the next match, at home to Raith Rovers. Tommy's steel revitalised the defence while Findlay added some much-needed guile in central midfield. The Hibees won 3-0, Findlay scored a great goal and Keith Wright bagged yet another double.

Next came two 0-0 draws, away to Motherwell and at home to Celtic, then a 0-1 defeat away to Partick Thistle. Then, 29 March brought some cheer, as the men in green pulled off a surprise win, 3-2 up at Pittodrie, thanks to another double from Wright and a goal by Steven Tweed. Another boring 0-0 draw at home to St Johnstone followed, and then on 16 April a woeful performance by the green jerseys saw them thumped 3-0 by Dundee Utd at Tannadice. A week later, Motherwell beat the Cabbage 2-0 at Easter Road in a dreadful match, made all the more farcical as Hibs, by now plagued by injuries and suspensions, were forced to give 36-year-old coach Eamonn Bannon a game in central defence!

On the next Tuesday Hibs were held to a 1-1 draw by Raith Rovers at Stark's Park, Keith Wright once again getting on the scoresheet, this time with a superb 20-yarder.

Colin Cameron equalised for Raith but the result meant that the Kirkcaldy side were relegated.

The season's final Edinburgh derby was perhaps the most awful match of Hibernian's winless run in the fixture. The 0-0 draw, played in front of fewer than 15,000 at Easter Road, almost bored both sets of fans to death. There were no real chances to score; it was a tepid affair, devoid of passion from either side or either set of fans. The point Hearts gained meant that they wouldn't be relegated that season – three clubs were being relegated as the top flight was moving to a ten-team set-up. That was the last derby at Easter Road where we got to stand on terracing.

Tuesday, 3 May brought title-seeking Rangers to Easter Road. They were without their two senior goalies so young Colin Scott was in goal. Almost 15,000 fans turned up. Tommy McIntyre marked Hateley to a standstill; Kevin McAllister and Michael O'Neill were excellent. Jim Leighton made three excellent saves. On what was a lovely May evening, the match was settled by a Keith Wright goal at the Dunbar End, right in front of the Rangers fans. Hibs won 1-0. This was an important match as it was the last time at Easter Road when fans got to stand on open terraces. New regulations meant that all-seater stadiums were required for season 94/95, so the last terraced match at Easter Road quite literally ended with Hibs fans doing the Hibees Bounce on the terracing whilst singing 'Can you hear the Rangers sing?' Thus ended Hibernian's 12-match winless run against the Gers.

The remaining two matches of the league season saw Hibs hammered 0-4 by Jim Duffy's doomed Dundee up at Dens Park, then in the season finale at Easter Road, with the terracing closed, the Hibees fought out a 0-0 stalemate with Kilmarnock, watched by a large away support as Killie needed a point to stay up.

Season 1993/94 had been a good one for Hibs. Though the club finished fifth in the league they had spent much of the season in the top three. The goal difference was back in the black, 53 had been scored in the league to 48 conceded; 16 matches had been won, 15 drawn and 13 lost. A magnificent League Cup campaign had been enjoyed while the Scottish Cup had been a bit of a damp squib. The new signings had done exceptionally well – Kevin McAllister had scored nine, Michael O'Neill had bagged four. Keith Wright had bagged 19, the fans' favourite bettering his 91/92 tally of 17. Darren Jackson had only scored eight but had contributed in other ways. Steven Tweed had gone from fringe player to first-team regular while David Farrell had also been impressive, mostly. Mickey Weir didn't feature at all that season. Jim Leighton was ever-present and kept 16 shut-outs, four more than the Burridge/Reid 'jobshare' had managed the previous season.

The only real downside to the campaign, other than the end-of-season dip in form, had been the derby matches. Three defeats and two draws had extended Hibs' winless run in the fixture to 22 matches and, partly thanks to media obsession with that run, this had distracted from what was an otherwise good campaign from a club who just three years earlier had been on the brink of extinction. The campaign's standout performances had been in the semi and final of the League Cup, the early season 3-1 win at St Johnstone, the 5-1 mauling of Partick Thistle and in the New Year derby. The worst showing by the team had been in the 'Colquhoun' derby at Easter Road just after the cup final. It's hard to pick a single 'best player' for season 93/94 – O'Neill and McAllister were both superb, Jim Leighton was outstanding and Davie Farrell was the most improved. For much of the season we had played very well and when on song we were really battering teams.

There were some departures at the season's end. Danny Lennon left to join Raith Rovers, having scored two goals for Hibs in a sporadic first-team career spanning six years and 40 appearances. By far the biggest name to depart was defender Tommy McIntyre. Big Tam had made 152 appearances in the green jersey since joining Hibs from Aberdeen late in 1986. He'd scored 12 goals including four penalties, the most famous being the one against Dunfermline in the 91 cup-final win. He was and remains a Hibernian cup-winning legend. Tommy left to join Airdrieonians and is now a top youth coach at Celtic.

Those departees would need replacing, but money was tight with the new campaign ahead and with stadium refurbishment on the agenda. Big changes would come to Hibs and to Scottish football in 94/95, big changes indeed; on and off the park. The Hibs went marching on …

Elsewhere in Scottish football, Rangers had easily won the title for the sixth consecutive time. Dundee United won the Scottish Cup for the first time in their history, beating Rangers 1-0 at the newly all-seated Hampden Park, future Hibee Craig Brewster scoring a historic winner. St Johnstone, Dundee and Raith Rovers were all relegated, while Jim Jefferies's Falkirk side were promoted from Division One as champions. Rangers qualified for the Champions League, while Dundee Utd went into the Cup Winners' Cup. Scottish clubs' poor performances in Europe that season saw Scotland's UEFA Cup places for the 94/95 campaign cut from three to two, so Hibs didn't get in as

League Cup runners-up. Scotland's UEFA Cup places went to Motherwell and Aberdeen.

The therapist said not to see you no more
She said you're like a disease without any cure
She said I'm so obsessed that I'm becoming a bore, oh no …

COME HOME – SEASON 94/95

'Bring on the Hearts the Celts and Rangers
bring on the Spaniards by the score
Barcelona, Real Madrid
*Who the F*** you trying to kid?*
For we're out to show the world what we can do!'

AUGUST OF 1994 crowned what had been a hot, eventful summer. Brazil had just won the World Cup in the USA, beating Italy in the final after penalties. The horrific genocide in Rwanda had just come to an end, with a butcher's bill of over a million dead. Tony Blair had just been elected to lead the Labour Party, the Irish Republican Army had recently ceased all military operations, and in America, some fella named Jeff Bezos founded a new start-up company – it was called Amazon. The European Economic Community had recently changed its name to the European Union.

It had been a big summer in cinema and music, too. Film lovers had flocked to see *The Mask*, *The Lion King*, *True Lies* and *Forrest Gump*. The UK charts that summer were topped for 15 weeks by Wet Wet Wet's cover of 'Love is All Around', originally sung by The Troggs. The cover version was from the soundtrack of another hit movie of that year, *Four Weddings and a Funeral*, and was still number one when the football season began, remaining there until knocked off the top spot by Whigfield's 'Saturday Night'. August 1994 also saw the release of the debut album by a band that was spearheading a revival in British guitar pop; I speak, of course, of *Definitely Maybe* by Oasis.

While a Brit-pop revolution swept Britain, another revolution was sweeping Scottish football; in fact, it was a revolution which still affects our game today – for the positive.

Scotland's pool of 38 senior clubs was increased to 40 by the addition of two Highland League sides, Ross County and Inverness Caledonian Thistle – the latter formed by merging Caledonian FC and Inverness Thistle. No doubt whoever came up with the name for this new entity was up all fucking night agonising over which name to choose, eh? This move ended years of calls from many quarters to include highland clubs in the senior set-up, as they already played in the Scottish Cup. While two new senior clubs were born, another one was about to die; 1994/95 was the last season in which Edinburgh's Meadowbank Thistle were to grace Scottish football, as the then Division Two side were moving to West Lothian and changing their name to Livingston FC.

The World Cup in the USA had seen the number of points awarded for a win in the group stages increased from two to three, in one of FIFA's constant efforts at the time to eradicate negative football tactics. As a result, most of the world's domestic leagues, including Scotland's, switched to 'three points for a win' from 94/95 onwards, though some countries including England had been using that system since the 80s.

Scotland's 40 senior clubs were reorganised into four leagues of ten. The league had a new sponsor in the shape of Bell's Whisky, while the League Cup began a four-year sponsorship deal with Coca-Cola. Tennent's Lager continued to sponsor the Scottish Cup.

Another big change that came with season 94/95 was the implementation of the Taylor Report. As a result of the 1989 Hillsborough disaster, big clubs in the UK were forced by law to have all-seater stadia by the summer of 1994. Some clubs like Aberdeen and St Johnstone already had seated grounds; others like Rangers only had small terraced areas remaining which needed to be seated. For Hibs, Hearts, Celtic and most other Scottish clubs, though, this would prove to be a huge challenge. Celtic had already seated their famous jungle but Parkhead needed so much work to comply with the new safety regulations that doing so became impracticable. The new Celtic owner Fergus McCann initially thought of challenging the Taylor Report in court but eventually made a £500,000 deal with the SFA to lease Hampden Park for one season. Hampden had indeed been made all-seater, but in essence, it had been a patchwork job. The two uncovered terraces were given roofs, while all three terraced sides simply had seats added to the terraces, while the old rickety main stand was left largely intact.

Hearts, too, needed major stadium work done and towards the end of season 1993/94 had demolished their School End and the side of the ground opposite the main stand. What was left of the Gorgie Road end had seats put onto it for the new campaign, while a new Wheatfield Stand was built opposite the main stand, funded in part by some Hearts fans who donated £500 each. Hearts played season 94/95 with no stand at the School End.

Hibernian FC had spent much of 1992–94 in dialogue with fans, builders and politicians over a possible move to a brand-new stadium on the city's southeast outskirts at Straiton. There's a separate chapter in this book covering that episode. The first idea of a 25,000-seat modern arena on the city outskirts with great travel links etc did seem a good one and many fans were for it, or were at least open-minded about it, but when the plan was later revised to an initial 12,000 or so seat ground without much of the extra revenue raising facilities like the reserve stadium, tennis ranch and hotel, etc., the fans turned against the idea. No Hibs fan really wanted us to move to a green version of McDiarmid Park. As 1994 wore on, the move looked less likely, so temporary changes were made to Easter Road. With hindsight, remaining at Easter Road was the right thing to do, especially as a famous change to the player transfer system in 1995 was to turn football finance on its head.

To comply with the Taylor Report, seats were installed on the East Terrace, which was re-christened the East Stand. The bucket seats were only ever supposed to have been a temporary measure but ended up remaining in place until the structure was completely replaced in 2010. The East Terrace was the home of the more vocal element of the Hibs support and many fans were worried about the prospect of reduced atmosphere in the coming campaign. The Dunbar End also had bucket seats fitted to it, but remained uncovered, frankly looking a bit ridiculous, but most Hibs fans didn't care about that as it was only away fans who would be getting soaked – mostly. Hibs, like Hearts, were given an extension with respect to the new rules about uncovered areas. This meant that during matches at Easter Road where there was bad weather, away fans (and some home fans in the Cowshed and enclosures) were issued with luminous yellow-hooded ponchos to keep them dry and a foam cushion to put onto their seat. This was a temporary arrangement. Thus at the start of season 94/95 Easter Road's capacity was slashed by over a third, to just 13,800, and would be reduced even further towards the end of the campaign. By October 1994 the Straiton proposal was dead so the Dunbar End and the Cowshed were actually demolished late in the season and replaced with modern two-tier stands.

Though *some* public funding was available to clubs via the Football Trust, to partially assist with stadium redevelopment costs, for most clubs, complying with the Taylor Report meant financial hardship. In Scotland this meant that almost every top club, except Rangers, needed its money for builders rather than for players that summer. The sad thing was that the Taylor Report was based upon initial police reports about the Hillsborough disaster which had blamed the death of 96 Liverpool fans on fan misbehaviour and on stadium design, when in reality the tragedy was caused by inept policing. Every big club in Britain had to go all-seater and subsequently spent millions of pounds because of this deeply flawed legislation, for no good reason – though going all-seater did turn out to be a positive for football over time with regards to encouraging more families to come along, improving the fan experience and improving some aspects of safety. Yet with the loss of terraces, British and Scottish football lost something in atmosphere, something that the game has tried and invariably failed to recover ever since.

Alex Miller made no major signings in the summer of 1994. Most fans understood why and accepted that state of affairs, though there would be recruits added as the season progressed, as there was no transfer window back then. Jocky Scott, the ex-Dundee, Aberdeen and Dunfermline boss, joined the coaching staff.

Hibs not only had a new-look stadium, they also had two new sponsors. Calor Gas replaced Macbean as the main sponsor, while Mitre began a four-year kit sponsorship deal, taking the place of Bukta. Together these deals reportedly netted the club around £750,000. The new home kit featured a green jersey with green and white striped sleeves, white shorts and green socks, while the away kit's jersey had green and purple thick vertical stripes – the latter remains a fans' favourite even to this day.

It had been a busy summer for Scotland's other clubs as well. Tommy Burns replaced Lou Macari as manager of Celtic. Sandy Clark had lost the Hearts hot seat to ex-Motherwell boss Tommy McLean, who had revamped the Jambos' squad. Hibs' city rivals' season preparations weren't helped by some off-field drama. Wallace Mercer sold his majority shareholding to catering businessman Chris Robinson and solicitor Leslie Deans, while an infamous punch-up between Hearts defenders Craig Levein and Graeme Hogg during a friendly at Stark's Park brought more turmoil to Tynecastle, and much mirth to the rest of Scottish football. Raith, inspired by Danny Lennon, had won the match 2-0. Hogg ended up leaving Scotland. Over at Rangers, Danish international and Euro 92 winner Brian Laudrup joined the club from Fiorentina, while the Ibrox side also signed French international Basile Boli and Hearts defender Alan McLaren. The latter's exit from Tynecastle and the Stark's Park episode fallout left the Jambos short of defenders – that would prove useful to Hibs.

* * *

Hibernian's campaign began with a friendly against English Premier side Sheffield Wednesday on Sunday, 7 August, Easter Road's first all-seated match. Just fewer than 7,000 fans were in attendance, with a small contingent of Owls fans perched on the new bucket seats on the Dunbar End. Trevor Francis's side was a strong one, and included Mark Bright, Des Walker and even Romanian USA 94 star Dan Petrescu, who was on the bench as a trialist, about to sign for the Yorkshire side. Hibs wore the new green and purple away kit for the first time. Many Hibs fans looked aghast at the new East Stand where they used to stand to watch matches, and it took supporters a few games to get used to the seating arrangements, amid many a cry of 'sit doon' when fans stood on seats so that they could see action at the pitch's extremities.

Keith Wright had picked up a serious injury in pre-season and was unavailable for this match and indeed would be out until Christmas. As for the match itself, it was a real pre-season treat. Great work by McAllister set up Jackson after just eight minutes, Jacko firing past Kevin Pressman from the edge of the box to put the green jerseys, or rather, purple and green jerseys, in front. Ten minutes later Jackson was again on target, getting on the end of a long ball from Steven Tweed to rifle past Pressman from a tight angle. 'Oooh, ah Jacksona!' rang around the newly seated home of the Hibees. The Owls hit back just before the interval through Ian Taylor to make it 2-1 to Hibs at half-time. Mark Bright equalised for Wednesday just on the hour mark with a brave diving header. For a time, the match looked like it could go either way, until 12 minutes from full time, when Tweed lobbed the ball forward, bypassing everybody on the pitch except Gareth Evans, who had remained onside and rushed forward, in a headlong contest for the ball with Owls' goalie Pressman. The ball bounced and Evans, somehow, beat Pressman to it and looped a brave header up and over his arms and into the empty net, to great acclaim from the watching Hibbies. Hibs won the friendly 3-2, Alex Miller praising his side's performance and stating that the match had been 'an ideal workout'.

The league campaign began on 13 August with a Saturday 3pm meeting with Dundee Utd at Easter Road. Pre match, Alex Miller told the media, 'Everyone at Hibernian is raring to go, the players are keyed up and there is confidence throughout the squad.' He wasn't wrong. Billy Findlay put the home side in front with a stunning volley from the edge of the box, after great work on the other flank by McAllister. Crunchie had the Terrors' defence at sixes and sevens from the off, so much so that Alex Cleland was red-carded in the first half for persistently fouling him. Darren Jackson put Hibs 2-0 up with a sublime 20-yard angled lob, then added a third from the penalty spot and it was game over before half-time, Jackson once more putting his old club to the sword. In the second half, Kevin Harper bagged his first goal for the club, then set up O'Neill who scored Hibernian's fifth with a great chipped effort. The green jerseys had treated Ivan Golac's side like a rabid dog might a rag doll, demolishing the Terrors. It was about as perfect a start to the season as Hibs could hope for, and once again, Hibs were top of the league.

Midweek brought a trip to Palmerston in the Coca-Cola League Cup to take on Queen of the South, the Hibees easily beating Billy McLaren's men 3-0 with goals from Evans, Tweed and O'Neill. A 0-0 draw with Kilmarnock followed at Easter Road, in the league.

Saturday, 27 August brought the season's first Edinburgh derby, at the new-look Tynecastle. Hearts were having a party, opening their new £2m Wheatfield Stand on a glorious sunny afternoon. All Hearts needed was the presence of that team who couldn't beat them, to complete what would be a great, memorable Tynecastle occasion. Hearts were without Graeme Hogg, for obvious reasons, but their fans were still confident of extending their unbeaten run in the fixture. The police didn't charge Levein or Hogg over their scuffle, though both were initially given lengthy bans and put up for sale by Hearts. Levein was also stripped of the Hearts captaincy, but pressure from Hearts' corporate sponsors ultimately saw him retained at Tynecastle. Levein did play in this derby, though, as the Stark's Park affair dragged on for several months.

The day before the derby match, Alex Miller told the press that his only concern was 'going out tomorrow and winning'.

Hibs fans standing among the bucket seats on the old Gorgie Road end got an early fright when Jim Leighton had to dive and tip a Gary Mackay rasper over the bar. At the other end, Gareth Evans tested Hearts goalie Nicky Walker with a good shot from outside the box, which the ex-Rangers man did well to tip onto the post. Just before the interval, Jim Leighton showed his class once more, with a brilliant double save to keep out first Robertson and then Leitch. The Hibs goalie moments later had to save a Colquhoun shot. It was 0-0 at half-time and Hearts had been marginally the better side.

Hibs had still played well thus far but some fans were all too aware that just one Hearts goal could trigger a familiar reaction in the green jerseys which would lead to yet another loss. The second half saw the match swing back and forth, until the hour mark. At the Gorgie Road end where the Hibs fans were, Michael O'Neill whipped in a corner which was knocked on by Dave Beaumont in the middle to the back post, where Gordon Hunter, from a difficult angle, smashed the ball past Nicky Walker and into the net: 1-0 to Hibs! A mass of green and white behind the goal went bananas in celebration, and in the stadium, you could feel that something had changed. Sullen Hearts fans looked on – Hibs hadn't read the script!

Just 18 minutes from the end, and with Hearts chasing the game and their fans becoming ever more agitated, Gary Mackay was red-carded for a second bookable offence. Many Hearts fans knew that the game was up, while many Hibbies, though delighted at being in front, also had the creeping feeling of dread, based on derbies from the last five years, that Hearts would grab an equaliser and be singing '23 games in a row' at the final whistle. That didn't happen.

Indeed, the green jerseys almost went 2-0 up in the dying seconds, when a Michael O'Neill shot beat Walker but came back off the bar. Some Hearts fans left the stadium rather than watch Edinburgh's green and white army celebrate at the final whistle, others hung on until the bitter end, waiting for that equaliser that never came.

Hibs won 1-0. At the final whistle, joy, relief and jubilation engulfed the Hibs support; celebrations were passionate, emotional, defiant and even tearful. Alex Miller's men had finally consigned their rivals' unbeaten run to the rubbish bin. Hibs had beaten Hearts, brought joy to the fans, given the press something new to write about and had utterly ruined for the Jambos what was supposed to have been a gala day out at Tynecastle. Instead of enjoying a grand opening day, Hearts fans had to leave their stadium with Hibernian victory songs and cries of 'f..k yer new stand' ringing in their ears. Alex Miller hugged the players at the end. Not only did Hibs fans regain the city bragging rights, but the win put Hibs back on top of the league and sent Hearts into second bottom and a relegation dogfight that would encapsulate their whole season. Even better for

Hibs, Hearts had played quite well, so there was nothing to take the shine off this fine victory. It was fitting that skipper Gordon Hunter scored the goal; he along with Gareth Evans and substitute Joe Tortolano were the only Hibs men in the squad that day that had played in 1989 when the Hibees had last beaten Hearts. That night, the green half of Edinburgh partied.

On to the Tuesday, and the Cabbage were back in League Cup action, easily beating Bert Paton's Dunfermline 2-0 at Easter Road, thanks to a Michael O'Neill double. Hibs were in the League Cup quarter-finals once more. Dunfermline's goalie that night was young Jim Will. He'd been the Scotland goalie for the under-16s in their 1989 World Cup Final. Released by Arsenal, where he'd been for years, he tried his luck at Dunfermline and this cup tie versus Hibs in Edinburgh was one of his few senior football matches.

Aberdeen were next to visit Easter Road on league business and the men in green were soon 2-0 up, going into a commanding position thanks to O'Neill and Jackson, only to be pegged back to 2-2, Billy Dodds and Brian Grant earning the Dons a point. The following Saturday brought another draw, this time it was 1-1 against Motherwell at Fir Park in which Michael O'Neill scored our goal.

Wednesday, 21 September brought Hibernian back home to Leith to take on Airdrie in the quarter-finals of the Coca-Cola League Cup. Hibs were a whisker away from yet another cup semi-final and almost 10,000 fans were at the match. Alas, the Diamonds, who already had one other Premier League scalp in the form of Motherwell in the previous round, were 2-0 up inside the first half hour, goals coming from Andy Smith and Alan Lawrence. Airdrie played very well, their back line of Sandison and one

Tommy McIntyre held firm until the 75th minute, when Gareth Evans pulled one back for Hibs. John Martin in the Airdrie goal – taunted all evening with chants of 'scab' from the Hibs fans for some reason – got in the way of everything Hibs threw at his goal. Even a late McIntyre red card didn't turn the tide. It was another shock 1-2 exit for Hibs at the hands of that pesky Lanarkshire side.

Hibs were at Hampden the following Saturday, to play Celtic in the league. Alex Miller's men played very well, but lost 2-0, O'Donnell and John Collins scoring. Hibs blew away Partick Thistle at Easter Road a week later, winning 3-0 thanks to a Darren Jackson double and a rare first-team goal by Mark McGraw. It could easily have been six or seven to Hibs. At this match, the East Stand boomed out 'Jackson for Scotland', a unanimous vocal plea for the player to receive international recognition. Jackson did deserve a call-up and as Alex Miller was by then also Scotland assistant boss, Jacko was on Craig Brown's radar, at least.

Big-spending champions Rangers came to Easter Road on 8 October. Basile Boli headed the Govan side into the lead, which they held at the interval. Hibs responded with a terrific second-half performance, Michael O'Neill putting in crosses which first Hunter and then Harper scored from to give the Hibees a deserved 2-1 win. Boli was red-carded late in the match. Typically, Hibs followed up this fine victory by drawing their next two away games 0-0, with Falkirk and Dundee Utd.

On 29 October Hearts came to Easter Road for the campaign's second derby. The weather that Saturday was atrocious and, amid heavy rain, Hibs proved that lightning could indeed strike twice, putting their city rivals to the sword once again, in much easier fashion than in the previous derby. Hibernian's goals came from Jackson and

O'Neill. Hibs could have had more. Hearts did rally and pulled one back with a late Robertson penalty but it finished 2-1 to the men from Leith, their first back-to-back wins in the fixture since season 88/89. Jim Leighton captained Hibs for this fine derby win. Many fans remember this match not just for the football, but for those silly yellow ponchos some fans in uncovered areas of the ground had to wear because of the rain.

Two more away matches followed, bringing two more 0-0 draws against first Kilmarnock and then against Aberdeen, but these draws didn't bother the fans, for one simple reason. Hibs had signed a player. Paddy was home.

Pat McGinlay rejoined Hibernian in early November of 1994, for a fee of around £420,000. The move came as a pleasant surprise to many Hibbies as most were under the impression that the club had no money to spend on players because of the cost of construction work at Easter Road. Unlike when many former stars returned to Easter Road then and since, Pat wasn't coming back to use Hibs as a sort of retirement home, nor had he failed elsewhere. McGinlay had been Celtic's top scorer in season 93/94 and had been popular with Hoops fans. He had been used in a more forward role, as he had no chance of ousting McStay and Collins from Celtic's midfield engine room. There was a rumour that Pat's wife, Margaret, had been a nuisance to some of the other players' wives and girlfriends at Parkhead, simply by virtue of her impassioned, zealous vocal backing of Pat at matches, but even if true it's highly unlikely that this was the reason for the transfer. Celtic had three different managers during Pat's 16 months there – four if you include Frank Connor, who back then would step in whenever a boss left, much like Graeme Murty does at Rangers today. The Glasgow side had also been through enormous off-field turmoil, rescued from its out-of-touch owners and from bank debt by Canadian businessman Fergus McCann. In the autumn of 1994 the Glasgow side needed a left-back, and wanted Tosh McKinlay from Hearts, so Celtic sold McGinlay to Hibs to raise the funds to buy a player from Hearts. The move suited all parties – but Hibs got the best of it.

Douglas Cromb paid around £100,000 less to buy Pat back than Celtic had originally paid Hibs for him in 1993. In return, Hibs got a ready-made star, already familiar to and loved by the Easter Road legions and who had already done enough at Hibs to earn the tag of legend – he'd won a cup with Hibernian and played for the club in Europe. In season 93/94, most of Hibs' good attacking play had come down either flank, via McAllister or O'Neill. Fans that season had often wondered what the team would be like with McGinlay still in it. Now, late in 1994, the Hibs board had given them the opportunity to find out. The prodigal son slotted right back into life at Easter Road as if he had never been away.

Pat's second home debut came on 19 November against Motherwell at Easter Road. Though Pat didn't score, his return boosted the home crowd to almost 10,000 – just over 7,000 had attended the most recent comparable home fixture, against Partick in early October. The Steelmen went 1-0 up after eight minutes, when a defensive mix-up allowed Tommy Coyne to score. The green jerseys took the game by the scruff of the neck and upped a gear. After 31 minutes, McAllister pulled Hibernian level with one of his trademark 'dribble n shoot' efforts. McGinlay was denied a homecoming goal by a Rab Shannon goal-line clearance.

Just before the interval, one of the finest Hibernian goals of the 90s was scored. On the break, Kevin McAllister sent namesake Harper flying down the right flank, who crossed to Michael O'Neill on the edge of the box. The Irishman took the ball first time and fired a wonderful volley past Motherwell's ex-Hibs goalie Stevie Woods. In the 55th minute the visitors equalised, Billy Davies finishing off a good move by the impressive Well, and then Jim Leighton pulled off a wonder-save to deny Steve Kirk in the last minute. It ended 2-2. Both sides, Motherwell in second and Hibs in third, missed out on a chance to make up ground on pace-setters Rangers.

By November's end the destiny of one Scottish trophy and that of Scotland's clubs in Europe had been decided. Rangers failed to make the Champions League group stages once again, losing 0-3 on aggregate to AEK Athens. Dundee United had been eliminated from the Cup Winners' Cup by Slovakian side Tatran Presov, 4-5 on aggregate. In the UEFA Cup, Motherwell lost to Borussia Dortmund, while Aberdeen suffered a humiliating away-goal exit to Latvian minnows Skonto Riga.

The Coca-Cola Cup Final on 27 November was contested at neutral Ibrox by Celtic and First Division side Raith Rovers. Future Hibees Stevie Crawford and Shaun Dennis were in Raith's line-up, as the Fife side pulled off a huge shock, beating Celtic on penalties to lift the trophy, after the match had ended 2-2 after extra time. Celtic skipper Paul McStay had missed the deciding spot kick.

Three days after that final, Hibs welcomed the defeated finalists to Easter Road. John Collins put Celtic 1-0 up after just 90 seconds with a well-hit free kick. It was a curious match, full of cynical challenges, bad tempers and yet, also, some great goalscoring chances, both goalkeepers doing well. It looked like the visitors would grab the three points, until the 83rd minute. Mark McNally hauled down Jackson in the box at the Cowshed End and the striker took the resulting spot kick himself, blasting the ball into the net to give Hibs a 1-1 draw. The Hibs support sang 'Oooh ah, Jacksona' then launched into a chant poking fun at the away fans: 'Are you watching, are you watching, are you watching, Paul McStay?' The draw kept Alex Miller's men in third place and also prolonged Hibernian's unbeaten home league record that season.

The Saturday brought a bizarre encounter at Firhill, Partick's new signings, ex-Hearts duo Nicky Walker and Wayne Foster, making their Jags debuts. Hibs were winning 2-1 with just nine minutes remaining, thanks to goals from McGinlay and O'Neill, after Foster had given Partick the lead. The Jags, though, bagged an equaliser when Jim Leighton's error allowed Isaac English to tap the ball home on 81 minutes. The assist for that goal had actually been a clearance from Nicky Walker! After that, two Hibees saw red, Tweed and then Tortolano both getting their marching orders for fouls on Foster. Hibs saw out the remainder of the match with nine men and drew 2-2, despite having dominated most of the game.

The next weekend, Jim Jefferies's Falkirk side – flying high in the top five – came to Leith. Two ex-Hibees now in Falkirk blue combined to give the Bairns the lead after 20 minutes, veteran Eddie May setting up Colin MacDonald to score: the latter had, of course, played and scored in Hibernian's fine BP Youth Cup Final win over Ayr Utd back in 1992. Darren Jackson levelled things from the penalty spot on 81 minutes but Falkirk looked to have nabbed a victory after 85 minutes when another ex-Hibee, Brian Rice, put them back in front once more, also from the spot. It took a Michael O'Neill wonder-goal in the dying seconds to rescue a point for Alex Miller's men, in what was a fiercely contested encounter. Falkirk's Joe McLaughlin – who had played very well – was red-carded after 60 minutes, when an ongoing tussle with Gareth Evans led to a second booking.

In the summer of 1994, a newspaper took some comments by Hibs chairman Dougie Cromb out of context and wrote a piece claiming that he'd said that Hibernian FC would win the league within three years. Mid-December of 1994 saw Hibs sitting in third place, just four points behind leaders Rangers, unbeaten in 11 matches and having only lost one league match out of 17! If even half of the 11 draws that made up that incredible run had been victories, whoever misquoted Mr Cromb may have ended up being extremely prophetic.

That unbeaten run came to an end on Boxing Day at Ibrox, when first-half goals from Hateley and Gough and a great performance by Laudrup gave Rangers a 2-0 victory and a seven-point advantage in the league over the Cabbage. That match saw a lacklustre display by the men in green but did have one positive aspect – Keith Wright played his first match for Hibs in seven months.

Dundee Utd visited Easter Road on Hogmanay and were once again destroyed in Edinburgh; this time it was 4-0, with Keith Wright bagging a hat-trick to mark his home return – his fourth hat-trick in the green jersey. Hibernian's other goal came from Michael O'Neill, compounding the misery of his former club who were now slipping towards the bottom end of the table.

The win over Dundee Utd also brought to an end Brian Hamilton's time at Hibernian. Brian's Hibs contract had expired in November and he hadn't been offered what, in his or his agent's eyes, was a suitable deal. Hammy had played 232 times and scored 11 goals from midfield during his time at Easter Road and had played in Europe and won the League Cup with Hibs, to add to the Scottish Cup winners' medal he had gained at St Mirren in 1987, a kind of flip-reverse of what John McGinn would later achieve at the two clubs. He was allowed to sign for another club, but Edinburgh football fans were astonished when, on 5 January, he crossed the city divide to sign for Hearts. The fee was to be decided by a tribunal. The player had been a target for some of the boo boys at Easter Road in his last 18 months at the club, but his overall contribution in the green jersey was recognised by most fans. All of the Hibs players who played alongside Hammy say that they loved having him in the team, as he won the ball and did a lot of the hard work in the middle. Hearts were eventually ordered to pay Hibs around £270,000 for his services. Now Hibs were a man down in midfield.

On 7 January, Alex Totten's Kilmarnock came to Easter Road. With a number of English scouts in attendance eyeing up Michael O'Neill, the man from Ulster didn't disappoint and bagged Hibs' second in a hard-fought 2-1 win for the home side. Pat McGinlay had opened the scoring but Killie had levelled through Colin McKee, before O'Neill headed in a Wright cross after 69 minutes. That was O'Neill's 12th goal of the season and it also put Hibs into second place in the league, though they were now 12 points behind leaders Rangers. The following Saturday saw the Hibees make the short trip to Fir Park to take on Alex McLeish's Motherwell, the sides sharing the spoils in a 0-0 draw.

Wednesday, 18 January brought the season's third Edinburgh derby, with just over 12,500 fans in attendance at Tynecastle. Stadium redevelopment meant that both sides agreed to the same home-away staggering as in season 93/94. Scheduled for New Year, the match had, for the second season in a row, been postponed. With Brian Hamilton starting for Hearts, the midweek evening match saw Hibs put in a downbeat performance while Tommy McLean's men put in a decent one, beating the Cabbage 2-0, with goals from McPherson and Millar.

Alex Miller's men bounced back from derby disappointment on the following Saturday, as 8,805 fans at Easter Road were treated to a one-sided six-goal thriller. Jackson and McGinlay had Hibs 2-0 up on Willie Miller's Aberdeen inside 11 minutes. A Jackson penalty and a strike from Keith Wright – fumbled into the net by Theo Snelders – were enough to guide the green jerseys to a well-deserved 4-2 victory, Aberdeen's two consolation efforts coming from young Billy Dodds.

Links Park up in Angus was Hibernian's next destination, in the Scottish Cup third round. John Holt's men put up stubborn resistance and the Hibees had David Farrell red-carded, but class shone through and round four was reached, courtesy of goals by Darren Jackson and Pat McGinlay in a 2-0 win.

On Saturday, 4 February, struggling Partick Thistle visited Easter Road and managed to inflict Hibernian's first home league defeat of the season. Pat McGinlay had given Hibs the lead with a wonderful volley, but the Jags rallied and managed to win 2-1, their goals coming from Roddy MacDonald and Tommy Turner.

A week later, a purple and green clad Hibernian headed to Hampden to take on Celtic, with around 25,000 fans in attendance. An exciting match saw John Collins give Celtic the lead, which was cancelled out by a superb Hibs team goal finished by, you guessed it, Pat McGinlay. Big Willie Falconer headed the 'home' side back into the lead but the men in purple earned a deserved point, gaining a 2-2 draw when Mark McGraw netted the equaliser after coming off the bench.

It was back to Scottish Cup business for Hibernian fans on 18 February, as Motherwell came to Edinburgh to contest round four. Kevin Harper stole the show, scoring one himself and setting one up for Pat McGinlay in a fine 2-0 victory, a match in which Well stopper Brian Martin was red-carded. Kevin Harper's goal in this match finished off a superb passing team move, so good a move, in fact, that the strike is mentioned in the film adaptation of Irvine Welsh's *The Acid House*. Elsewhere that day, the shock of the round was at Ochilview, where Stenhousemuir, from Division Two, eliminated Aberdeen. The Warriors' goals came from Tommy Steel and Adrian Sprott, the latter having previously been famous for scoring Hamilton's famous winner over Rangers at Ibrox in 1987's Scottish Cup. The Warriors were managed by Terry Christie, whose day job was being headmaster of Musselburgh Grammar School. The Stirlingshire side had murdered St Johnstone 4-0 in a previous round as well, and they were a potential banana skin to whoever might draw them in the quarter-finals. Of course, Hibs were given that honour, drawn to face Stenhousemuir away. The press whipped up quite a frenzy about the looming fixture, predicting another Premier League scalp would be taken. Alex Miller said virtually nothing about the draw – two league matches were still to be played before it.

Three days after Hibs knocked Motherwell out of the cup, just over 4,000 fans were at Easter Road to see goals from Steven Tweed, Wright and Jackson give the home side a relatively easy victory. The home side, though, was Scotland B, who were playing against Northern Ireland B in a challenge match. Steven Tweed and Darren Jackson did both score but the Wright I mentioned who scored the other goal was Aberdeen's Stephen Wright. Pat McGinlay also got some long overdue international recognition, as he started this match along with his two Hibee team-mates and all three did exceptionally well. Young Alex Rae of Millwall and Motherwell's Paul Lambert also got their first chance at international level that night. Darren Jackson's performance convinced Craig Brown that the player would be suitable for the full international team and, the next month, he got his first full Scotland cap against Russia in the Euro 96 qualifiers. Hibs fans did play a part in this B international at Easter Road. The press had let it be known that the three Hibs players would be starting the match, so there were a few hundred East Stand regulars at that Scotland game, your intrepid author among them, many sitting together and singing Hibs songs like 'Hail Hail' and 'Ooh to be a Hibby' and also chanting 'Tweedy' and 'Ooh ah Jacksona', much to the bewilderment of those non-Hibs fans who had come along just to see Scotland.

Alex Miller's men slipped up on 25 February at crumbling Brockville, losing 0-1 to Falkirk, Steve Kirk netting for the Bairns. Then, one week later, Rangers visited Easter Road. It was the last match where the old Dunbar and Cowshed Ends were used, before they were demolished. A crowd of 11,900 fans saw the two sides fight out a draw. Stuart McCall put the visitors 1-0 up around the hour mark, but Alex Miller's men rallied and got their reward 15 minutes from time, when Willie Miller's excellent cross was powerfully headed past Ally Maxwell by Keith Wright. It ended 1-1. The draw virtually guaranteed Rangers the title, as they were by then 17 points ahead of Hibs in third and 16 ahead of second-placed Motherwell.

Saturday, 11 March brought the much-anticipated Scottish Cup quarter-final between Hibs and Stenhousemuir at Ochilview. The Warriors' ground only held just over 3,500 so that match was also shown live on 'beamback' to Hibernian fans at Murrayfield Ice Rink, of all places, to satisfy demand.

In the build-up to this cup tie, the press and media cast the encounter as a modern-day David v Goliath. They fawned over Terry Christie. They interviewed Adrian Sprott a dozen times. They made much of the fact that Hibs hadn't won the trophy for 93 years. They highlighted the fact that the Warriors already had two big scalps from previous rounds. Not all Scottish sportswriters did this, but most did. In fact, the press did everything except run a headline actually reading 'Hibs are going out'. As far as most of Scotland was concerned, Hibs were really going to 'get it', this time.

The Warriors did put up a decent fight, watched by a full stadium and by a gang of children who had climbed trees next to the stadium, but the home side were completely blown away in the second half, the Hibees crushing them 4-0. All that media hype around the fixture had ensured that Alex Miller and his players knew what a laughing stock they would be if they lost the tie, so they won it, easily in the end. The entire Hibs team played well but O'Neill and Harper were the standouts, tearing the part-timers to shreds. Hibs' goals came courtesy of a Harper brace and a strike apiece for O'Neill and Joe Tortolano. Hibernian were in another semi-final!

The last four teams left in the tournament were Hibs, Celtic, Hearts and Airdrieonians. Hearts had eliminated Rangers in the fourth round and had beaten holders Dundee Utd to reach the semis. Airdrie had beaten Coca-Cola Cup-winners Raith Rovers in their quarter-final, while Celtic had edged out Kilmarnock 1-0 at Hampden in their quarter-final. Hibs were drawn to face Celtic, and would do so on Friday, 7 April, live on TV, at Ibrox, as Hampden technically wasn't a neutral venue while Celtic were playing home league matches there. Hearts would face Airdrie at Hampden the next day. Hibernian were above the two premier sides in the league and had been doing relatively well against them in the 94/95 campaign, so could have been confident against either, while a cup tie against battling Airdrie might have given the Hibees a chance to avenge recent cup exits at the hands of the Diamonds. All four managers at the semi-final stage that year had won the Scottish Cup as players – Tommy Burns while at Celtic, Alex Miller, Tommy McLean and Alex MacDonald while at Rangers.

Three league matches were to be played before the Ibrox showdown against Celtic, with the Cabbage still in with a great chance of UEFA Cup qualification. However, Hibernian's relatively lofty league position masked an uncomfortable truth – Hibs were dull on the road. Up to and including the defeat by Falkirk, the team had played 13 league matches away from home, winning only the August Edinburgh derby. While only four of those matches had been defeats, eight had been draws, five of those ending 0-0. A grand total of six goals had been netted away from home in the league.

New Aberdeen boss Roy Aitken was tearing his remaining hair out on 18 March, as his relegation-threatened Aberdeen side drew 0-0 with the Hibees at Pittodrie. Hibs were repeatedly steamrollered by the Dons in this match, but seven or eight superb saves by Leighton kept the Edinburgh men level and earned them a point. After the match, Alex Miller confessed that his squad needed more defensive steel, and told journalists that he was about to act on that.

Sure enough, utility man Andy Millen swiftly arrived from Kilmarnock in a swap deal for Billy Findlay. Millen had joined Kilmarnock when they were promoted in 1993 and had been a mainstay of the side's survival in the top flight. So much so that Tommy Burns, at one point, wanted to take him to Celtic after he and Billy Stark moved there in 1994. As Killie and Celtic weren't exactly on the best of terms following the saga of Burns's move to Celtic, Kilmarnock's board weren't keen on Millen going there at all, so the player was loaned to Ipswich Town, before Alex Miller swooped to sign 29-year-old Andy. As he could play in both midfield and in defence, he was an ideal signing for Hibernian at the time, particularly as it was no secret that the Hibs gaffer liked to have such utility men in his squad. Dave Beaumont was leaving Hibs to become a police officer, too, so getting another defensive player to Easter Road was crucial. To help make this happen, Billy Findlay left Hibs to join Kilmarnock. The gifted ball player had been playing first-team football on and off for six years, having made 110 appearances for Hibs and with seven goals to his credit. Billy left with the fans' best wishes, seeking regular first-team football.

Millen made his debut on the Wednesday against Motherwell at Easter Road, an encounter in which Hibernian were victorious 2-0 thanks to a brace by Keith Wright. How happy we Hibbies were to see Keith back from injury and playing well again! This match was played at 3.30 in the afternoon as Easter Road's floodlights were gone!

April Fools' Day meant a league trip to Firhill to take on Partick Thistle. While not exactly playing like fools, the green jerseys blew two leads against the Jags and ended up drawing 2-2. Keith Wright gave Hibs a first-half lead, only for Wayne Foster to equalise for Thistle. Kevin

Harper restored the Hibees' advantage in the second period, but Foster again levelled for the Jags, this time from the spot. Mickey Weir was red-carded in the farcical match for stamping on someone. The Firhill horror show wasn't exactly ideal preparation for a massive cup semi-final; then again, with Hibs, you never know what you're going to get next, do you?

Friday, 7 April came and thus began an exodus of fans from Edinburgh and the surrounding areas heading west, to Paisley Road West, more accurately. Hibs fans travelled by coach, by car, by train and even on a small fleet of public Edinburgh LRT double-decker buses which left from Waverley Bridge, specially laid on for the match. In the world that week, the Samashki massacre had just happened during the Chechen Civil War. In the UK, Man Utd and France star Eric Cantona won an appeal against the two-week jail sentence he'd been given for his infamous 'kung fu'-style attack on a racist Crystal Palace fan at Selhurst Park, receiving instead 120 hours of community service, while in Scotland, Edinburgh's telephone dialling code had just been changed from 031 to 0131.

Hibernian's record against Celtic in major semi-finals and finals was then and remains now utterly awful. They seem to have the measure of us when it comes to these types of fixtures and it's a generational thing, a trend which long antedates recent squads and managers. In 1995, prior to this match, they'd won eight out of nine major semi-finals and finals against us since we had defeated them in the 1902 Scottish Cup Final, and they've beaten us in four more since, to date. They'd thumped us 4-1 in the final of the Scottish Cup in the spring of 1915. They'd narrowly edged us out 1-0 in the 1923 final – a match in which Alec Maley managed Hibs while his brother Willy managed

Celtic. The Hoops had thumped us 4-0 in 1965's League Cup semis, in a replay after the first match had ended 2-2. They'd thrashed us 6-2 in the 69 League Cup Final and 6-1 in the 72 Scottish Cup Final. Eddie Turnbull had managed to get the best of Celtic later that year, when his legendary Hibs team beat Celtic 2-1 to lift the League Cup, and then Turnbull's side lost 6-3 to the Hoops in the 74 League Cup Final, despite Hibs striker Joe Harper bagging a hat-trick. The dreadful relegation-doomed Hibs team of 1980, which included George Best, was annihilated 5-0 by Celtic in the Scottish Cup semis, and the most recent Hampden encounter between the sides in 1989 had seen what was a comfortable 3-1 win for the Hoops in the semis of the Scottish Cup. Most of these Hibernian defeats had seen very good Hibs teams of the day lose to very good Celtic teams. This latest 1995 meeting may have been at Ibrox rather than Hampden, but once again, two good, evenly matched teams were about to square off in an epic encounter.

Ibrox being Ibrox and Govan being Govan, a few pubs in the area around Ibrox chose to close on Friday, 7 April. Others didn't, and thus, the open pubs within a few miles of the stadium were fairly rammed and operating a 'one in one out' policy. As a result of this, many fans who wanted a pre-match tipple and whose buses weren't pre-booked into a club had little option other than to drink in the street. The police were surprisingly lenient about this, but there was no real trouble, either, between the fans or from drunkenness in general, other than a few minor public-order offences. Indeed, before the match, a large gathering of Hibs fans stood happily outside the huge Govan Stand drinking carry-outs bought from the adjacent Haddows and nearby Asian shop.

Hibs fans had been allocated the entire Govan Stand and half of the Copeland Road end. Celtic fans had the rest of the stadium, with the exception of Ibrox's newish club-deck on the main stand, which remained closed. Just over 40,000 fans were in attendance, around 15,000 of whom were supporting Edinburgh's finest. Hibs wore the home kit, Celtic were in a largely black strip. The referee was John Rowbotham. Neither side had yet conceded a goal in the 1995 Scottish Cup. Ibrox, the home of Rangers, was a wonderful spectacle that evening, absolutely carpeted in green and white, with little purple specks in the Hibs ends, too.

Adult match tickets for the Hibs v Celtic cup tie cost around £14. Hibs would be without the suspended Mickey Weir and the injured duo of Gordon Hunter and Kevin McAllister. New signing Andy Millen slotted in to replace Geebsy at the back, partnering big Tweed, while Kevin Harper was deployed on the right wing. Wright and Jackson were up front, O'Neill was on the left, Farrell and McGinlay were the engine room, with Mitchell and Miller as full-backs, Leighton in goal. On paper and going by Hibs' and Celtic's league placings at the time, Hibernian were a match for the Hoops, as that season's close league matches had shown. Celtic had very much a half-and-half team, guys from their 'biscuit tin' era like Andy Walker and Peter Grant, alongside newer fellas like towering Dutch hitman, Pierre van Hooijdonk. Whatever happened in this semi-final, it was going to be close, this time.

Celtic threatened early on, Leighton saving well from John Collins. McGinlay, Harper and Wright came close for Hibs in the first half, the latter having an effort cleared off the line by Rudi Vata. Celtic spent most of the first half on the attack, but found the pairing of Millen and Tweed at the back to be a formidable obstacle. Hibs seemed happy to soak it all up and hit on the counter-attack. It was 0-0 at half-time.

Into the second half and Hibs were again pressed back often, yet didn't look like conceding a goal. Two Hibs counter-attacks ended with Harper and then Jackson shooting inches wide of Bonner's goal. Jim Leighton made good saves to deny Collins, Brian O'Neill and Walker. Andy Millen cleared a Willie Falconer effort off the line. And so the two sides slugged it out until the 73rd minute.

As Celtic attacked the Hibs goal at the Broomloan end of Ibrox, Pat McGinlay challenged Paul McStay for the ball just outside the box and referee Rowbotham awarded Celtic … a penalty kick!

Hibs players and the fans couldn't believe it. It had been clearly outside the box. Not quite as blatant an error as the infamous David Syme dodgy penalty in the 91 SKOL Cup semi between Airdrie and Dunfermline, but still a dreadful refereeing cock-up. TV evidence proved that the challenge had been outside the box. As the Hibs players protested in vain, the Hibs fans felt cheated. Fans generally thought that Rangers and Celtic always got the best of refereeing decisions against 'lesser' teams at that time, and they weren't entirely wrong. So, it looked like Hibernian's Scottish Cup dream was over for another year.

Ex-Hibs hero John Collins usually took and scored Celtic's penalties, but striker Andy Walker had grabbed the ball and placed it onto the spot. Green and white Ibrox held its breath.

Jim Leighton hurled himself to the right, brilliantly saving Walker's spot kick. The ball was cleared. The Hibby-filled Govan Stand broke into a loud chorus:

'Scotland's, Scotland's number one, Scotland's number one!' Justice had been done with the penalty save and once more Jim Leighton had proved his excellence. The match stalemated thereafter and ended 0-0. The teams would meet again at the same venue on the Tuesday night, just four days later.

The day after that drawn match, a pitiful crowd of just over 22,000 at Hampden saw Airdrieonians beat Hearts 1-0, with a goal by Steve Cooper. So, whoever won the Ibrox replay would face First Division opposition in the final.

The replay saw Hibernian don that iconic purple and green jersey, while it was Celtic's turn to wear their home kit. Understandably, the crowd was significantly lower because the replay was so soon after the first match. Just over 32,000 fans made it to the match, no more than 7,000 were supporting Hibs, which was nevertheless an impressive support for the Cabbage given the replay's circumstances. Both sides featured virtually the same starting XIs, though Alex Miller did switch to three up front instead of two, Mark McGraw starting in place of David Farrell.

Andy Walker missed a great chance for Celtic early on. Hibernian had a great opportunity to take the lead on 26 minutes, a Willie Miller cross into the box eluding everyone at the near post except Steven Tweed, but the big stopper somehow managed to put the ball wide from four yards, with the goal at his mercy. It was a miss which the Leith side would rue, as Celtic were the better side in the first half. Leighton saved well from a low drive by Rudi Vata. After half an hour Hibs went behind, clever work from McStay and Collins creating space that allowed Falconer to beat Leighton with a low angled finish. Alex Miller's men weren't defending as well as they had in the first encounter, but no defence could have stopped Celtic's second just before the break. John Collins was the scorer, with an excellent long-range chip into the top corner. Celtic led 2-0 at the interval.

Hibs did play a little bit better in the second half. Gareth Evans replaced McGraw after 55 minutes. The Englishman set up Michael O'Neill, whose top-corner-bound effort from 25 yards was superbly saved by Pat Bonner. The fightback continued. On 63 minutes Andy Millen looped a ball into the box which Bonner and Pat McGinlay both went for. The Celtic goalie made a hash of things and spilled the ball. Keith Wright was lurking and duly slammed the ball into the net to make it 1-2. Hibernian threw everything forward in search of an equaliser but were caught on the break, Leighton saving the day once more by thwarting Willie Falconer. Seven minutes from the end Rudi Vata pumped a long ball into the Hibs box and substitute Phil O'Donnell – who had missed the first match – powered an unstoppable header past Leighton. There was no coming back from that for Hibs and it finished 3-1 to Celtic. Hibs hadn't played as well as they had in the first encounter, while Celtic's passing game had improved and had tipped the balance. There was no shame in the defeat and had Tweed been more fortunate in the first half things might have been different. Hibernian were applauded at the end by both sets of fans. The cup dream was over for another year, but Hibs fans could take comfort from having pushed a good Celtic side hard for most of the titanic 180-minute encounter. It was now, once again, a case of getting on with league business.

Hibernian's third trip to Ibrox in nine days came five days after the semi-final loss. It was a Sunday afternoon match against Rangers, which was shown live on STV. It was Rangers' title-winning party and the green jerseys did their best to spoil it, but were put to the sword, largely thanks to a great performance by Brian Laudrup. Ex-Hibs hero Gordon Durie gave the light blues the lead in the first half, but Hibs went into the interval level. Just before half-time, Rangers gave away a free kick 25 yards from their goal at the Copeland Road end. Darren Jackson rolled the ball to Michael O'Neill who smashed a wonderful shot beyond the despairing Billy Thomson and into the net. Ibrox was, for a time, silenced.

The second half saw what may well have been the single greatest performance of Jim Leighton's football career. The goalie made at least nine superb saves to keep the match level, including a superhuman quadruple save that saw him applauded by even the home fans. Hibs eventually folded late on, Durrant and Mikhailichenko scoring to give the home side a 3-1 win.

Saturday, 19 April came and Falkirk visited Easter Road and won 1-0, Steve Kirk being on target. Just 5,440 fans were at this match as there were only two stands in use, Easter Road looking more like a building site than a stadium. On the following Saturday, the Hibees were on Tayside to face managerless Dundee Utd, who were under the temporary charge of former Hibs player Billy Kirkwood. The green jerseys won this match 1-0 thanks to a McGinlay goal, despite having Gordon Hunter red-carded.

With Easter Road's capacity temporarily slashed to around 8,000, 7,146 fans were in attendance for the season's final Edinburgh derby. For once in the fixture, there was more than city bragging rights at stake. Hibs were chasing a UEFA Cup spot, whilst Hearts were in a relegation dogfight. The small Hearts support at this match was crammed into the southern end of the main stand.

Hibs were all over Hearts from the first whistle, employing a crisp, up-tempo passing game, yet it was Hearts who took the lead, ex-Rangers player David Hagen heading them into the lead from a John Colquhoun cross. Hearts somehow led 1-0 at the interval.

Hagen cleared a goal-bound Mickey Weir lob off the line just after the restart, as Hibernian continued to dominate the match. Alex Miller sent Kevin Harper on for McAllister and the sub had an instant impact, sending in a looping cross to the back post, which was headed past Craig Nelson and into the net by Mickey Weir, making it 1-1 after 62 minutes. This match saw a real vintage Mickey Weir performance, the fans' favourite showing great trickery and an enormous appetite to vanquish Hearts. Brian Hamilton then wasted a golden opportunity to restore Hearts' lead, shooting wide when it looked easier to score, triggering a great sarcastic roar from the Hibs fans. A minute later, Mickey Weir set up Keith Wright, who scored his and Hibernian's second. Four minutes later, Hibs fans were in dreamland. Hearts goalie Nelson could only parry a shot from Pat McGinlay, and the loose ball fell to Kevin Harper who slammed the ball into the net to put Hibernian 3-1 up. That's how the match finished, and as the Hibs fans celebrated, the Hearts fans, for the third time that season, had to trudge out of a stadium with Hibee victory songs ringing in their ears. The win meant that Hibernian could still overtake Motherwell and finish second, if they managed to defeat Celtic at Easter Road in midweek.

Another early midweek kick-off on the Wednesday saw Hibs take the lead against Celtic through Kevin Harper, only for that man Falconer to equalise for the visitors, in front of 6,010 fans. The point wasn't enough for Hibs and the result guaranteed second place and the last UEFA Cup slot to Motherwell.

Hibernian's season finale was on 13 May – a trip to Rugby Park to play Kilmarnock. Youngsters Michael Renwick and Darren Dods both made their first-team debuts in green in this typical end-of-season affair, which Hibernian won 2-1. Almost 12,000 fans were at this encounter, as Kilmarnock, rather admirably, let all juvenile supporters in for free. Paul

Wright scored against Hibs again, while the Hibees' strikes came from McGinlay and Keith Wright. Hibs would have had more were it not for the goalkeeping heroics of Colin Meldrum. There was a carnival atmosphere at this match, which was fitting, as the season had indeed been a bit of a rollercoaster for Hibernian.

And so, season 1994/95 came to an end. Rangers had won the league and subsequently qualified for the next season's Champions League. Celtic beat Airdrie 1-0 in the Scottish Cup Final, ending a six-year trophyless run, and got into the Cup Winners' Cup. The League Cup, or Coca-Cola Cup-winners, Raith Rovers were awarded a UEFA Cup slot for winning the trophy, which was the last time that particular tournament's winners were rewarded in that manner. The Kirkcaldy side also won Division One and were promoted to the Premier Division once more. Runners-up Motherwell also got into the UEFA Cup. At the bottom of the table, the new 'three points for a win' system had played havoc with Scotland's top flight established order. Teams who for years had done well simply by avoiding defeat now found that too many draws could be catastrophic. None more so than Dundee United, who finished bottom of the Bell's Premier Division and were relegated. Aberdeen, too, had struggled in season 94/95. They finished second bottom and had to face a play-off against Division One runners-up Dunfermline Athletic, in order to secure their top-flight status, which they ultimately did, crushing Bert Paton's side 6-2 on aggregate. Hearts' battle against relegation had succeeded, just, largely thanks to a 1-0 win over Celtic at Hampden near season's end. Another Scottish side did qualify for Europe. Partick Thistle gained a place in the minor Intertoto Cup via UEFA's Fair Play system. Down south,

England's Premier League was won by Kenny Dalglish's Blackburn Rovers.

It had been an excellent season for Edinburgh's green and white; we finished third. While Easter Road's physical structure had been fluid and constantly evolving as the campaign wore on, fans' fears about lack of atmosphere caused by the new seating arrangements proved to be unfounded. Just two league matches and one cup tie had been lost at fortress Easter Road all season. The quarter-finals of one cup and the semi-finals of the other had been reached. Pat McGinlay had returned, while Andy Millen looked a useful addition to the squad. That annoying winless run against Hearts had been ended in some style, the green jerseys winning three of the season's four derbies. On the down side, form away from Easter Road had been indifferent. Only three league matches had been won away from home, yet only five of them had been lost – two of those to champions Rangers. Lack of goals away from Easter Road had made it an excellent season rather than an historic one. In total, Hibs had scored 49 goals and had conceded 37 in the league. Ever-present Jim Leighton and his defence had kept an astonishing 19 clean sheets in all competitions – there hasn't been a Hibs defence that good since. Asides Leighton and the almost ever-present five of Willie Miller, Steven Tweed, Gordon Hunter, Darren Jackson and Michael O'Neill, seven players, Farrell, Evans, Harper, McAllister, Mitchell, McGinlay and Wright all made around 20 appearances each – consistency of selection was key to the team's success that year.

Hibs drew 17 league matches in season 94/95, won 12 and lost just seven – the same number of league defeats as the champions. It was as close as Alex Miller's Hibernian or indeed any Hibs side since the early 1970s had come to mounting a title challenge. Had season 94/95 been played under the two points for a win system, Hibs would have finished second on 41 points, a point above Motherwell and just eight points behind Rangers. The new points system had not cut down on the number of draws, but it had made the prospect of a draw much less appealing than in previous campaigns. The new ten-team top flight, combined with that new points system, had proved a game-changer, and had already produced more exciting outcomes than the old 12-team 44-match gruelling schedule.

Midfielder Michael O'Neill was Hibernian's top scorer in season 94/95, bagging 14 goals. Darren Jackson had scored 11 goals, despite playing in a deeper role, while Keith Wright had also scored 11, despite missing half of the season because of injury. Kevin Harper had scored eight, while McGinlay had managed an impressive nine. No other Hibs player had scored more than two. Young defender Graeme Love had established himself as a first-team player, if not quite a regular, making 12 appearances. The entire team had been largely excellent all season, but if one player was the best, it was Jacko. Special mention must also go to young Kevin Harper for his role in the campaign as we played half the season without big Keef, so Kevin exploded onto the scene at just the right time. Our best performances had come in two of the three derbies that we won, the victory over Rangers at Easter Road and in the first semi-final against Celtic. By far the biggest horror show of the campaign had come against Airdrie in the Coca-Cola Cup defeat.

While McGinlay and Millen had arrived, two players were gone at season's end. Dave Beaumont gave up professional football to become a police officer with Fife Constabulary, but continued to play junior football with Kelty Hearts. Dave had played for Hibs 80 times since joining from Luton in 1991. He'd won a 1991 League Cup medal with Hibs despite not kicking a ball in the tournament, being an unused substitute in the final, but overall had contributed well to the Hibernian cause. One of his three goals for the club had come against Anderlecht in the UEFA Cup, while it was his knock-on against Hearts which had set up Gordon Hunter's winner at Tynecastle in 1994. Striker Mark McGraw also moved on. The lad had been at Hibs since 1990 but had failed to establish himself as a first-team regular. His best period in the first team had come in season 1991/92 when he had been instrumental in the club's run to the SKOL League Cup Final, particularly in the quarter-final win over Ayr at Somerset Park in which he had been man of the match. Mark had cruelly had to miss that final because of injury and never really regained his place in Alex Miller's match-day plans. That's no slight on Mark's ability; by 1992 he was behind Keith Wright, Darren Jackson and Gareth Evans in the pecking order. That's quite illustrious company to be in, and, as many fans have noted, to be fourth-choice striker in a 90s Alex Miller squad was akin to being on the moon.

McGraw had made 57 appearances for Hibernian in five years, scoring three times. Aged 24 when he left, Mark signed for Falkirk in the summer of 1995, in a bid to play regular first-team football. It's doubtful that his phenomenal scoring record for Hibs reserves will ever be broken. The player is remembered fondly by Hibs fans as a good talented professional who was unlucky with injury and who tried his hardest for the club at a time when there were other great forwards in front of him in the queue for a starting place.

Though Hibs finished third in 2001 and in 2005, Hibernian didn't enjoy as comparatively successful a top-flight campaign as the 94/95 season again until 2017/18 under Neil Lennon. Even then, Miller's 94/95 Hibs remain the last Hibernian side to split the 'old firm'.

And I can't believe you're all I'll ever need
And I need to feel that you're not holding me
And the way I feel just makes me want to scream
Come home, come home, come home …

I KNOW WHAT I'M HERE FOR – STRAITON – BY BOBBY SINNET

'Easter Road, Take me home
To the place, I belong
To the East Stand, To the East Stand
Easter Road, Take me home'

HIBS MOVED into their Easter Road home in 1893, and have remained there ever since. The 1990s were a time of great change to football stadiums; the crumbling concrete terraces showing the wear and tear of stadiums largely unchanged for a generation. The Hillsborough disaster of 1989 followed by the Taylor Report of 1990 created great change, and the requirements to move to all-seated stadia within a time frame of five years. We can, of course, look at Easter Road today, a fine modern stadium completely rebuilt in the last 25 years, first of all with the north and south stands of 1995, followed by the Main Stand in 2001 and finally with the beautiful sweeping East Stand of 2010. However, this wasn't a smooth process and Hibs initially investigated the option of relocation. Several ideas were floated, but the only option the Hibs board looked at seriously was relocating to a greenfield site outwith the city near to the town of

Loanhead – Straiton. It was in early 1992 that then Hibs chairman Douglas Cromb unveiled grand plans for a new 25,000-seat stadium which was to be ready for action by 1994. The timeline seemed ambitious looking back it now seems even more so. Something had to be done though, and the Taylor Report had been the instigation. Easter Road only had one seated stand. Sure, there were benches, and benches could be installed to the concrete terraces, but this wasn't a solution. The new stadium at Straiton was to cost £25m and was 'to rival anything in Europe'. Hibs raised a few eyebrows by openly courting Hearts to join them at the new ground – at this time Hearts were investigating their own options at Millarhill in Midlothian and also a possible stadium on the west side of Edinburgh. Hearts had run into planning problems, and complaining locals. At one point Hearts had even considered moving to Murrayfield, but as history tells us, they continue to reside in Tynecastle in a stadium a little bit smaller than Hibs'.

So, the grand plans were to be submitted to the then Midlothian District Council – and the capital for the stadium project was to come from a consortium, Straiton Ltd, involving the man who had saved Hibs from Wallace Mercer – Tom Farmer. In addition, money was available from the European Community and the Football Trust. It was assumed sponsorship would raise additional funds for the move, too. The consortium planned to gift the stadium to the community through a trust. The 50-acre site was owned by the consortium, and they had already submitted plans for an adjoining 80-acre site which would include housing, retail and commercial development as well as a hotel. The commercial element of the plan was accepted and incorporated in the Lothian Structure Plan – but it was expected that the leisure aspect would be called in for further scrutiny by Lothian Regional Council. Douglas Cromb was keen to emphasise the positives. This would be the third biggest all-seater club ground in Scotland. It would have good transport links, and easy access to the recently completed city bypass. It would comply with all the requirements of the Taylor Report. There would be parking for 2,500 cars and 250 buses. Not only that, a reserve stadium was to be part of the deal, too. It's fair to say that at this point a fair number of fans whilst not entirely keen to leave Easter Road could see that this was perhaps progress to a more functional facility. It might provide the impetus to get Hibs moving forward again after some torrid times. Douglas Cromb was also keen to emphasise the challenges of staying at Easter Road. A feasibility study had apparently shown that developing Easter Road would have limited Hibs to a capacity of 11,000, hindered by an issue with the pitch.

Mr Cromb went on to say at the time, 'Straiton Ltd's offer is too good to turn down. Easter Road is now a grand old lady which we are sorry to leave but we have to look to the future and think of our fans. We will be able to offer them the level of safety and comfort they deserve and I hope we will attract more families. We have always been open-minded about the possibility of sharing. It is up to them [Hearts] but we believe it makes economic sense and that the reservations of both sets of fans can be overcome.'

Hearts were publicly non-committal. Hearts fans were vehemently opposed to sharing under any circumstances. The chairman of the Hibernian Supporters Club, however, struck a more pragmatic note – citing that whilst Hibs fans might prefer their own stadium, a shared stadium might be the best option for all concerned – certainly something the planners would consider when scrutinising not one, but two breaches of the previously seemingly sacred green belt. A

Hibs' fan consultation had been run too, and around 1,000 supporters had backed the club's plans. As time unfolded, the grand Straiton plans failed to materialise. The 25,000 all-seater stadium became an initial development of 12,000 with only two stands built to start with. The fans weren't as committed to this, and voices began to speak out in favour of staying at the club's spiritual home. The community factor, the Leith factor was talked up more and more. The timeline was pressing, and something had to give – and did. In late 1994 Hibs committed to staying at Easter Road, and said that moving to Straiton had been 'laid to rest' and the development of the stands behind the goals would commence.

Work was to begin the following March and be finished a few weeks into the 1995/96 season. There would be restricted capacity at games later in the 94/95 season, and even the strange day that Hibs played an afternoon midweek game because the floodlights had been removed. Hibs came up with a novel, and successful, fundraising scheme, too. Fans were asked to donate £100 to help fund the stadium development. The fans did their part and supported the club in massive numbers. And that is where the Straiton story ends – well, not quite. There is a postscript to this. Out of the blue, in the close season of 2003, it emerged that Hibs and Hearts had been engaged in talks about sharing a stadium at Straiton again. Hibs by this time had also redeveloped the main stand in 2001, whilst Tynecastle had been hastily redeveloped. So, what had caused this revisit? Hearts were in a dire financial state, and Hibs were restructuring their business after costs had been set at a level consistent with the previous television deal, and the new television deal left all the clubs facing shortfalls. Savage business decisions had to be made, and some clubs like Motherwell and Dundee went into administration. It was suggested that the clubs could sell their grounds, clear their debts, and there would be enough left over to build the shared stadium. Nevertheless, the fans were unconvinced this time and implacably hostile to moving. The hibeesbounce.com website in particular rallied support against the move on the basis that Hibs and the community around Easter Road would be far lesser for moving. 'At Easter Road they stay!' was the ingenious tagline. Talk about transport to and from Straiton did little to soften the feelings, and the promise of a new stadium when Easter Road was three quarters complete and looking magnificent didn't sway the fans' opinions either. It didn't help that the general perception was that Hearts needed this move more than Hibs, and had more to gain by leaving Tynecastle. So it was that, after a consultation with fans, in October 2003 Hibs relented and scrapped the idea of moving and committed to staying at Easter Road.'

The Hibs board set up a campaign, 'stand up be and be counted' – and many fans did. The change in manager and style when Bobby Williamson left and Tony Mowbray took over changed things; the upturn in attendances was spectacular. Hearts on the other hand changed owners around this time, as Chris Robinson was desperate to recoup his capital and get out of Hearts. George Foulkes, the then Labour MP, initiated contact between Robinson and a Russian submariner called Vladimir Romanov. Romanov immediately got the fans onside, by insisting that they would stay at Tynecastle and would not be moving. Hearts also completed their stadium, by rebuilding their main stand in 2017. The opening was delayed, as someone had forgotten to order seats, much to the hilarity of opposition fans.

Finally, whatever happened to Straiton? There has been significant development there, with a large retail park that has been extended several times. The development has grown considerably over the last 30 years. Recently there was talk about an indoor arena, and talk before that of a Scottish film studio, which failed because of land tenancy dispute. But yet, the site of the proposed stadium remains undeveloped, despite the pressure for land in Edinburgh and the seemingly relentless push into the Edinburgh Green Belt.

What a life
A trick of light
Then everything returns to the sea
You can have whatever you want
But are you disciplined enough to be free.

DESTINY CALLING – BOSMAN

'Money, get away
Get a good job with good pay and you're okay
Money, it's a gas
Grab that cash with both hands and make a stash
New car, caviar, four-star daydream
Think I'll buy me a football team!'

RIGHT, HERE goes – this is dull but extremely important – a bit like porridge, dull but good for you. Here comes the transfer system part – concentrate!

Before the Bosman ruling in 1995, a football player could only really move between clubs when both clubs were in agreement to the transfer. The two clubs would agree on a transfer fee to be paid by one club to gain the services of that player. In some ways it was like a civilised version of indentured servitude. This requirement for a transfer fee applied regardless of whether the player was still under contract with the first club. Therefore, even players who were out of contract with their club were unable to sign a contract with a new club until a transfer fee had been paid or they were granted manumission papers, sorry, a free transfer by the first club. In other words, players couldn't just leave at the end of their contract and sign for a new club, like they do now, without the consent of the club that they were leaving.

It wasn't a great system; players were virtual serfs, serving at the whim of clubs. The old system meant that clubs rather than players and agents held most of the cards. The old system was sometimes used by clubs to punish want-away players as player wages weren't as high as they are now, so any player viewed as 'troublesome' by his club could simply be dumped into the reserve team until either his attitude changed, there was a reconciliation or his club relented and let him leave. There were countless incidents in British football down the decades of players having their careers stalled, hampered or even ended by this type of dispute. Players' wages pre-Bosman were often made up of a very small basic wage which only became a decent one with the addition of things such as win bonuses and appearance money. If a player was dumped into the reserves, he usually lost a chunk of his pay and, while his club might deprive itself of his services on the field for a time, it didn't really lose any money. Here's how the two systems differed. I've written this as an absurd over-simplification but the basics are there.

In 1980 a talented player at a club is earning £80 per week but can make almost £200 if he plays, the team wins and he scores. He's not getting a game every week for whatever reason: loss of form, an argument with the manager or simply can't get into the team. He has six months left on his contract. The player, exasperated, puts in a request for a transfer. The club manager or the chairman is annoyed at this so the player is banished to the reserves. In the reserves he's not playing and not earning much, essentially wasting his talent, or having it wasted by his club. Even when another team enquires about signing him, his club says no. The player then has two choices. He can patch up the relationship with his club and toe the line, in a bid to get back into the team, or he can wait until his contract expires then hope that his club will do the decent thing and release his registration so that he can sign for another club.

The vast majority of pre-Bosman football transfers were concluded amicably, but there were numerous instances where clubs held on to a player's registration even after his contract had expired, sometimes even dumping the player onto the dole as the out-of-contract player wasn't 'free' to sign for another club. Players were, though, entitled to a free transfer once out of contract if their current club didn't offer them a new deal on at least the same terms that they had been on. One of Hibs' Famous Five even had one such brief dispute with Hibs in the 50s, ending up stuck at the club, unable to play for a time but unable to be transferred.

Later, in instances where the player's club consented to let a player leave but couldn't agree on what the transfer fee should be, the fee would be decided by a tribunal. Players whose contracts expired did often re-sign for the same club on monthly contracts, though, until something more long term could be arranged. Between 1981 and the Bosman ruling, things eased up slightly. Out of contract players could sign for another team but the team that they signed for still had to pay a transfer fee to their former club, effectively still giving clubs a tacit say in where their former players went next. It wasn't ideal at all. British football did at least have that tribunal system from the early 80s onwards, many other European countries didn't. Hibs did well at such tribunals, usually. We signed out-of-contract Darren Jackson and Michael O'Neill from Dundee Utd. United tried for big bucks for both but we ended up paying far less for the players. It sometimes helped us with outgoing transfers, too. Pat McGinlay's move to Celtic in 1993 is a good example of Hibs 'winning' at tribunal – Celtic offered £275k and ended up paying almost twice that for Pat.

Fast forward to 1999. Talented player is earning £3k a week but isn't a first pick for the starting XI. He has 18 months left on his contract when he has a row with the manager and decides he wants to leave. It's an irreconcilable dispute. His club now has a choice. Pay that want-away player over £234k in wages to play reserve football for the next 18 months then watch him leave for nothing at the end of it, or cut their losses and sell the player immediately.

That's the main difference between the two systems; the post-Bosman system that we use today is stacked firmly in favour of players, rather than being designed for the benefit of clubs, like the old one was. The newer system was a great step forward; however, it also gave license to greedy agents to hoover up a large slice of football's wealth, far more than they ever got under the old system. Indeed, it's estimated that almost a third of the money that European clubs have spent on players since 1995 has ended up going to agents. The newer system has also created a minority of whingy cry-baby players who use the Bosman system to hold clubs to ransom, often at the behest of their agents. The old system *had* to change, though. Being a footballer *is* a job and every human being has the right to choose who they want to work for and to decide when they want to look for a new challenge elsewhere.

In short, some disputed transfers have gone from being a case of 'You're not leaving ya wee d..k, it's the reserves for you,' in the early 80s, to 'Get him off the wage bill ASAP!' today.

Jean-Marc Bosman, the player whose court case opened the Pandora's box that is the modern transfer system, was a mediocre Belgian footballer who wanted to join a club in France (Dunkirk) after his contract had expired at Royal Liege in Belgium. He was prevented from doing so by Liege, who demanded £500,000 for the transfer. He had actually played for them against Hibs in the 1989 UEFA Cup, not long before this dispute began. He took UEFA, his club and the Belgian FA to the European Court of Justice and eventually won in 1995. Henceforth, players within the EU were permitted to leave and join another club in another member state when their contract expired, without a transfer fee. Bosman's 'reward' for sticking up for himself and for his fellow professionals in this manner was, well, nothing. He actually became a bit of a pariah thanks to dark forces within football and in the wider European establishment.

The wonderful footballer and Hibernian icon Paul Kane was the first British player to move on a 'Bosman', leaving Aberdeen for Viking Stavanger late in 1995 shortly after Bosman won his case. The transfer system didn't change overnight for everybody. For a time until the late 90s, the Bosman ruling underpinned transfers of players moving from clubs in one EU member state to a club in another member state, but the old system lingered for a short while in the UK domestic transfer set-up as the market transitioned, thanks in part to the fact that many players in the UK were already tied up on pre-Bosman-era contracts and would have to wait until they expired before joining the Bosman stampede. This caused a temporary talent-drain, as many out-of-contract British players left to play in the EU rather than wait for a traditional domestic transfer, and UK clubs later realised that they could sign an EU national for free rather than paying a fee for a British player. The football establishment hated Bosman at first; some clubs tried not to embrace it, and were hostile to it because it had caused a revolution in football finance – it upset the apple cart. Others utilised it early on – look at the free agents from the continent Hearts signed in 1995 and 1996, for example. Hibs didn't fully embrace Bosman until Alex McLeish was the manager. Rangers started to use it more in the 2000s as their money ran low, while Celtic utilised it in their quest to stop their city rivals from winning ten in a row, despite Fergus McCann's initial hostility to the ruling (he once threatened to sue UEFA over John Collins's switch to Monaco).

The Bosman case has had the following general implications for European football clubs:

- Clubs are now required to sign players for longer contracts than previously, if they don't want to run the risk of losing them to a Bosman-type free transfer. That therefore costs clubs much more in player wages than under the old system; though small to medium-sized clubs tend not to shell out larger transfer fees as often now.
- Smaller clubs can't afford to sign players on long contracts. This is particularly the case in relation to young players who are not certain to fulfil their potential.
- Smaller clubs often, therefore, lose young players whom they have brought up through the ranks to bigger clubs on a free 'Bosman' transfer – though there are some safeguards as regards to players under 23, whose clubs can receive a development fee.
- Work permits are no longer needed for foreign players who come from within the EU.
- UEFA's 'three foreigners' rule in its tournaments became illegal on the grounds of discrimination; the same rule was also abolished in Serie A and in other domestic leagues where it was used.

The effect that this has had on some smaller clubs means that they have lost one of their biggest sources of income – selling players they have developed to bigger clubs for large sums of money. This has had the effect of many smaller clubs going into administration or being forced to turn semi-professional or even amateur over the years. The consequences of Britain leaving the EU, as regards to football and Bosman, remain to be seen.

As for Hibs, we've done alright out of Bosman. It has given us a much higher turnover of players and many of our best players over the last 25 years have arrived at Hibs via that transfer system – though our best stars have still been homegrown. We've lost out a few times with players leaving for free, sure, but without Bosman we'd not have had Franck Sauzee or a dozen other cult heroes. Alex Miller and Jim Duffy's spells at Hibs weren't really affected greatly by Bosman, whereas Alex McLeish first became a manager at Motherwell just a year before the ruling, so he was able to use it to his advantage during his time as Hibs gaffer.

One thing Bosman hasn't done is improve player quality. Under both systems, it was equally easy to sign a dud or a genius. One thing Bosman has done well, though, is to make football in these islands far more cosmopolitan, as it allows clubs to significantly widen their recruitment net and bring in players of myriad nationalities and ethnic backgrounds. In a way, thus, Bosman is and was the footballing embodiment of the EU ideal of freedom of movement. That's right, if it wasn't for the EU you'd never have seen le God Franck Sauzee wearing the green at Easter Road. Or, if you prefer, it's the EU's fault that we signed the colossus that was Humphrey Rudge.

Bosman changed football from 1995 onwards, so, it's an important part of Hibernian's 90s story even though we weren't really using it much until near the end of that decade. There you go, that's Bosman for you. It was mostly about workers' rights and it dragged football, kicking and screaming, into the 21st century.

Don't believe the adverts
Don't believe the experts
Everyone will sell our souls ...

GETTING AWAY WITH IT (ALL MESSED UP) – SEASON 95/96

*'We hate Glasgow Rangers, we hate Celtic, too (they're sh*te), we hate Heart of Midlothian but the Hibees we love you, all together, now …'*

AS WITH the previous campaign, season 1995/96 would see Hibernian play their home matches amid very different surroundings. Hibernian didn't play a home league match until mid-September due to snagging work on the two huge new stands behind the goals, which had replaced the Dunbar End and the Cowshed. These impressive new structures had cost between £4m and £5m in total and changed Easter Road forever. The only sad thing about them was the fact that the new south stand at a stroke robbed Easter Road of that beautiful vista of Arthur's Seat that fans used to get if watching from the East Terrace, particularly upon cresting the steep steps to get into that stand. That lovely view was gone now, save for a little bit that you could see at the corner of the south and main stands, which remained until 2001.

At first they were simply called the South Stand and the New North Stand – the latter name doubtless irked some Hibbies who sat in the old north stand in the Main Stand, which was itself quickly renamed. Though the East Stand rightly has the reputation of housing our support's more vocal element, Hibs wouldn't be Hibs without the intermittent booming chorus of 'Hibees' which often emanated from the old North Wing Stand, complete with foot stomping. That, at least, would remain until the turn of the century.

The new North Stand (renamed 'The Famous Five Stand' in 1998) had function suites and other hospitality amenities within it which were supposed to, in time, raise revenue for the football club. The new stands also brought new catering facilities and even some new dishes for fans to try on match days – who can forget the bright green pakora? The new North Stand also provided space for a proper club retail shop – the previous two, one in Easter Road the street and the other in the old Main Stand, had been little more than kiosks. Staffing the new stands also created over 70 jobs.

Easter Road's capacity was thus increased to around 16,500 and would remain roughly so until the old Main Stand was replaced in 2001. Increased capacity meant increased revenue, but in the summer of 1995 the Hibs board made it clear to the fans that there would be no money for Alex Miller to spend on players for the coming campaign, and, unlike in 1994 when the board said the same thing in the summer but then shelled out £420,000 for Pat McGinlay four months later, this time, the board really meant it. All Hibs' cash had gone into the new stands. Most British clubs were in the same boat because of the Taylor Report. Alex Miller would have to make do with what he already had – which wasn't actually a bad thing as Hibs had been largely great the previous season.

The summer of 1995 had been a turbulent one in the world. Serbia's army had slaughtered thousands of innocent civilians at Srebrenica and the Siege of Sarajevo was still in full swing, finally forcing NATO to begin strikes against the Serbs. The USA had just re-established diplomatic ties with Vietnam. In the UK, sitting PM John Major was challenged for leadership of his party, and won, beating blithering Euro-sceptic John Redwood. A long hot summer had seen The Outhere Brothers top the charts for all of July with 'Boom Boom Boom', though as the new football season began the top spot was occupied by boyband Take That with 'Never Forget', who themselves in turn would be knocked off number one by Blur's song 'Country House' – after it won a much-hyped battle with Oasis's 'Roll with It'. At the cinema, *Batman Forever* had been the film of the summer. Liverpool had just broken the British transfer record, paying £8.4m for Nottingham Forest's Stan Collymore.

Champions Rangers spent a lot of money in the close season, bringing in England star Paul Gascoigne for £4.3m from Lazio, Stephen Wright from Aberdeen for £1.5m, defender Gordan Petric for £1.5m from relegated Dundee Utd and Russian striker Oleg Salenko – famous for scoring five goals in one match at the USA World Cup in 1994 – for £2.5m from Valencia. These signings, added to their already strong pool of players, made Rangers virtually unassailable domestically, though one team did almost catch them in the coming season. Rangers' huge spending also sort of justified the relative frugality of clubs like Hibs – there was no point spending big just to finish second or third. In any case, a player named Jean-Marc Bosman was about to change football finance forever.

Elsewhere, Hearts legend Jim Jefferies took over from Tommy McLean at Tynecastle. Jefferies was then best remembered by Hibs fans as having played in defence for Hearts when Hibs famously humiliated the Jambos in 1973, winning the New Year derby 7-0. Jefferies had done enormously well whilst managing Falkirk. Celtic were still managed by Tommy Burns but had moved back to Celtic Park, where renovation work was ongoing. They had added talented German winger Andreas Thom to their side. Sky TV would show more Scottish games in the 95/96 season than ever before.

Hibernian's pre-season warm-ups came in the form of a tour in the north of Ireland, a trip to Fife and two home friendlies against top English sides. Ballyclare Comrades, Cliftonville and Bangor were all easily defeated in Ireland, while in Fife Hibs suffered a 1-2 defeat against Dunfermline Athletic.

Thursday, 10 August brought Middlesbrough to Edinburgh. Bryan Robson's side were newly promoted to England's top flight and had just vacated Ayresome Park to move into their brand-new Riverside Stadium. Though not yet quite the cavalier side which would feature Juninho and Fabrizio Ravanelli, the Smoggies were a solid outfit and featured great players like Fjortoft and Nick Barmby. A Hibs side without O'Neill, Wright and Weir did well to hold the Teeside outfit to a 0-0 draw, with Jim Leighton again proving to be more than worth his salt. Two days later, Queens Park Rangers, also of England's Premiership, came to Easter Road. Alex Miller had often mentioned his search for a 'Ray Wilkins-style' midfielder in the mid 90s, and Wilkins was QPR's player-manager when the two sides met in this pre-season challenge match. Alex Miller gave youth a chance, Chris Reid, Chris Jackson and Graeme Donald all playing from the start. Big Danny Dichio put the Londoners 1-0 up but a second-half brace from Pat McGinlay gave Hibs a deserved 2-1 victory. QPR went on to be relegated that season. Hibernian were 20-1 with the bookies to become league champions. A record 5,500 season tickets were sold for the campaign, an improvement on the total of 3,150 from the previous season, which had also been a record high. The manager was upbeat about the new campaign, telling fans, 'Our hopes and aspirations for the season are high, we hope to challenge for all honours and the players know that we must strive for consistency.'

Hibernian's 1995/96 season began competitively in round two of the Coca-Cola Cup at Easter Road on Saturday, 19 August. Stenhousemuir were once more the cup opponents, their new player-manager was none other than Eamonn Bannon. A Darren Jackson double, one from the spot, and a Pat McGinlay deflected effort were enough to see the Hibees past the Warriors 3-1, Jimmy Fisher netting Stenny's consolation. Such was the laziness displayed by some Hibernian players in this match, however, that Alex Miller kept the players in the dressing room for 45 minutes after the final whistle, giving them one of his famous roastings. Graham Mitchell vanished from the first team with an injury after this match and didn't reappear until January. Stenhousemuir's goalie that day was Hearts on-loan youngster Roddy McKenzie.

Hibs were drawn to play Airdrie away in the next round, but first there was the opening league match to deal with.

The league campaign began, seven days after the win over Stenhousemuir, with the latest trip to Firhill. Darren Dods and Chris Jackson started as wing-backs, while Graeme Donald played in midfield, having begun his Hibs career as a striker. The green jerseys dazzled the opposition for much of this match, Hibernian playing a crisp passing game which the Jags had no answer to. Hibs besieged the home side's goal and would have won by a huge scoreline were it not for the heroics of Nicky Walker in goal for Thistle. Despite every positive of Hibs' performance, the match ended 1-1 and the green jerseys had to come from behind. Andy Gibson capitalised on a rare defensive error from Tweed to put the home side undeservedly in front. The Cabbage's blushes were spared by Michael O'Neill, who equalised with a thumping right-foot shot, and went on to hit the bar twice as well.

The Tuesday came and Hibs fans made the short trip to Cumbernauld to take on Airdrie at their temporary Broadwood home, in round three of the Coca-Cola Cup. Hibs were without Mitchell, Miller and Keith Wright, all were injured, but the home side had their own selection headaches as well. Hibbies made up the majority of the 3,000-plus crowd but it made no difference. Alex MacDonald's men were 2-0 up within ten minutes, thanks to a Tweed own goal and a Jimmy Boyle strike. Hibs were atrocious; every attack was easily mopped up by Tommy McIntyre and Jimmy Sandison at the back for Airdrie. Darren Jackson even missed a penalty. There were bookings aplenty and Kevin Harper was sent off after 70 minutes for a bad foul on McIntyre. Airdrie won the match 2-0 on what was a night to forget for Hibernian. The Diamonds had now eliminated Hibs from cups three times in three years. A week later, ironically, Kevin Harper scored a stunning hat-trick for Scotland under-21s in a 5-0 victory over Finland at Broadwood.

The Saturday brought Hibs fans a trip to Ayrshire and some much-needed cheer after the cup exit. The Hibees thumped Alex Totten's Kilmarnock 3-0 with goals from Gareth Evans and a double from Keith Wright on his return from injury. All goals came in the first half, in a performance in which Hibernian looked back to their old selves, playing with pace, power and passion. Jim Leighton made his 100th appearance for Hibernian the following week at Easter

Road, against his old club, Aberdeen. Duncan Shearer gave the Reds the lead but Hibs earned a point thanks to a superb solo effort by Darren Jackson. It ended 1-1.

A baying horde of over 40,000 Rangers fans awaited Alex Miller's men in their next fixture seven days later. Injury-ravaged Hibs went to Ibrox with a makeshift defence and rode their luck at times, being fortunate to go in level at the interval. Salenko and McCoist both missed good chances. Then, in the second half, Kevin Harper went on a great run and was double-fouled by Petric and McLaren. It happened just outside the box but referee Kenny Clark pointed to the spot. Darren Jackson more than atoned for his miss against Airdrie in the cup by stepping up and sending Andy Goram the wrong way, putting Hibs 1-0 up, to the delight of the Hibs contingent behind the goal at the Broomloan end. Yes, that's right; Hibernian got a dodgy penalty at Ibrox! Somehow, Hibs held on to win the match 1-0. It was Hibs' first win at Ibrox in five years. It would be another ten years before Hibernian beat Rangers there again, with help from a certain Ivan Sproule. The unexpected victory put Hibernian into fourth place in the league.

Sunday, 1 October saw the season's first Edinburgh derby, at Easter Road. It was the first time that Alex Miller and Jim Jefferies went head-to-head in the fixture; 12,300 fans were inside the new-look Easter Road and saw a bad-tempered but entertaining match. Hibs started with a back three and it didn't work at all, Hearts had the better of the first half and led at the interval thanks to a header by big Dave McPherson. Alex Miller reverted to a back four for the second 45 and it steadied the ship. On 60 minutes Hibs equalised when Evans brilliantly squared for young substitute Graeme Donald to hammer the ball home, 1-1. Gary Mackay received his marching orders in the derby once more, this time a straight red card for an unprovoked stamp on Gareth Evans, while it was still 1-1. Hibs went for the jugular and a tried and trusted combination soon had the Hibby faithful on their feet. On 73 mins, O'Neill floated a ball into the box which Keith Wright squared to Pat McGinlay, who slotted the ball past Craig Nelson to put the Hibees 2-1 up. For the first time since the new stands had opened there was real, deafening noise in the ground as the Hibs fans celebrated their lead and taunted the away fans. Not for the first or last time in this fixture, however, Hibs fans had laughed too soon, though thankfully most Hearts fans had already left the stadium when John Robertson scored deep in injury time to give Hearts a draw, which on balance they probably deserved.

On the Wednesday, Stark's Park was the venue as Jimmy Nicholl's Raith Rovers inexplicably routed Hibernian by three goals to nil, two of the goals coming from Colin Cameron. Raith's big striker Ally Graham, though not on the scoresheet, terrorised the Hibs back line that night. On the Saturday Falkirk visited Easter Road, under their new gaffer John Lambie. Hibs had the lead after 30 minutes via a Jackson penalty, then Kevin McAllister scored after 56 minutes, finishing well after a great assist by Harper. Hibs won 2-1. Scott McKenzie had pulled one back for the Bairns after 68 minutes.

Saturday, 14 October saw Hibs return to Glasgow, this time to take on Celtic at Parkhead. The purple-and-green-striped men had the lead after 28 minutes, when Celtic goalie Marshall fumbled a McAllister cross and Kevin Harper reacted fastest, putting Hibs 1-0 up, somewhat against the run of play. John Collins equalised for Celtic a few minutes later. Dutch hitman Pierre van Hooijdonk gave the Hoops a deserved lead after 66 minutes, and the home side could easily have had another three or four, roared on by their fans. Celtic were so busy charging forward that they left gaps. Seven minutes from time, a brilliant through pass from Harper to Evans triggered a foul on Evans by Tom Boyd in the box. Darren Jackson sent Marshall the wrong way from the penalty spot and earned Hibs a somewhat flukey draw. It ended 2-2.

A week later Hibernian were once more back to their very best, against Motherwell at Easter Road. They led Alex McLeish's side 3-0 at the interval, blowing the Steelmen away with a display of total football. A Jackson double and an excellent goal from Wright had it all tied up in the first 45 minutes. John Hendry pulled one back for Well in the second half when Hibs eased off, but this just seemed to bring out Hibernian's inner Hulk, as, angry at having conceded, the Hibees started to play again and went 4-1 up through O'Neill. Hendry did add a late consolation for the visitors but the result was never in doubt.

Saturday, 28 October came and almost 10,000 fans were in attendance for Hibernian's home league match against Kilmarnock. Alex Totten's men put up a real fight but were overcome by Michael O'Neill's strike just before the interval then KO'd in 65 minutes when McGinlay and McAllister combined to set up Keith Wright to head home and to seal a fine 2-0 victory.

A freezing 4 November trip to Pittodrie was next for Alex Miller's men. This match was a tale of two goalkeepers, with Theo Snelders and Jim Leighton both putting in outstanding performances. Keith Wright headed Hibernian into the lead midway through the first half. Aberdeen's new young prospect Stephen Glass rocketed in a 25-yarder to level that match after 53 minutes. Not to be outdone by Aberdeen's teenager, a few minutes later Michael O'Neill weaved his way past three Dons defenders, then when the fourth, John Inglis, stumbled in front of him, O'Neill unleashed a glorious 25-yard effort which beat Snelders all ends up and bulged the net. It ended 2-1 to Hibs. Kevin Harper was magnificent in this match, with him and Glass both showing that Scottish football wasn't all doom and gloom.

That wee run of five matches in which Hibs won four times and drew once propelled the men from Leith into third place in the table, three points above fourth-placed Celtic and just two points behind Motherwell in second.

That week had seen a large amount of negativity about Scottish football in the press, doubtless in part to divert attention from Rangers' recent back-to-back humiliating group-stage televised drubbings from Juventus (4-0 and 4-1) and the Ibrox club's subsequent Champions League exit. In the Cup Winners' Cup, Celtic had demolished Dinamo Batumi of Georgia 7-2 on aggregate only to themselves be hammered by Paris St Germain 5-0 over two matches in the next round. Juventus and PSG both won the respective tournaments, so for Scotland's 'big two' to have lost to them really wasn't that big a deal. The UEFA Cup had been interesting for Scotland's representatives. Motherwell had suffered a humiliating away-goals exit in the qualifying round to Finnish side MyPa. The new-look Easter Road had seen its first European match, but it was Raith Rovers who had been the home side in October. Stark's Park wasn't considered safe for a European tie so Raith played their UEFA Cup home leg against Bayern Munich in Leith. Raith had already eliminated Faroese side Gotu and Akranes of Iceland but lost 0-2 to the German giants at Easter Road then lost 2-1 in the second leg in Munich. The second leg actually saw ex-Hibee Danny Lennon give Rovers a shock lead, beating Oliver Khan with a free kick, in a match in which future Hibees Steve Crawford, Shaun Dennis and Tony Rougier all played. Jean-Pierre Papin had a penalty saved by Scott Thomson in that match, too. Sounds quite surreal, now, doesn't it?

Another reason that there may have been so many negative stories about the standard of Scottish football in the press around late October and early November 1995 was that the SFA think-tank into the state of Scottish football – instigated after Scotland failed to qualify for USA 94 – had just published a report. There was nothing revolutionary about the findings but there was consensus that grass-roots football and youth development needed a major overhaul if Scottish clubs in Europe and the national side were to evolve and keep up with Europe's changing football landscape. All that said, Scotland had just qualified for the Euro 96 tournament in England, finishing second in their group behind Russia, qualifying as the fourth-best runners-up, so it's puzzling why there was such a flurry of media negativity at this time. One final reason may have been the financial panic caused by the recent Bosman ruling – it changed everything.

Wednesday, 8 November brought darkness to Easter Road. Not in the shape of defeat, but in the form of floodlight failure. The match against Partick was called off at the last minute for health and safety reasons when the new lights failed. Hibernian's next match on 11 November produced a humiliating defeat away to bottom side Falkirk. Mo Johnston scored both of Falkirk's goals in this 0-2 defeat. Hibs had now gone seven matches against the Bairns without beating them. Alex Miller's son Greg, a midfielder, made his first appearance in the green jersey during this match. His brother Graeme was also on the books at Easter Road.

On 15 November, while on international duty, Michael O'Neill put in one of the best performances of his career, as Northern Ireland hammered Austria 5-3 in Belfast, in the Euro 96 qualifiers. Michael scored two goals. At the time his ability was compared to that of George Best. His midfield foil for Northern Ireland in this match was future Hibs boss, Neil Lennon, who was then a Crewe player.

* * *

Sunday, 19 November saw the season's second Edinburgh derby, played at Tynecastle at 1pm and shown live on TV as part of one of the first Scottish 'Super Sunday' events, with Rangers playing Celtic at Ibrox shortly afterwards. While Hibs still hadn't signed any new players, Hearts had embraced the recent Bosman ruling and snapped up three out-of-contract continental stars, in the shape of Serie A veteran and hatchet-man Pasquale Bruno, ex-Sweden and Sporting Lisbon striker Hans Eskilsson and ex-Rennes, Marseille and France goalie Gilles Rousset. All three started in the derby and made an impact.

Just over 12,000 fans were at this match. Hibs were without Keith Wright, Mitchell and Harper. Hearts by then had finished the new stand at the School End, now called the Roseburn Stand. It housed home supporters at this match, with Hibs fans still occupying the uncovered, seated Gorgie Road end. The crowd was so low because Hearts were near the bottom of the league at the time. With Hibs flying high, you can probably guess what happened in this match. That's right.

Hearts led at half-time through a John Millar goal. Young Chris Jackson picked an ideal time to bag his first goal in the green jersey, his long-range effort levelling the match after 53 minutes, to the delight of the Hibbies behind the goal. The delight didn't last long, though. Hearts defender Gary Locke clashed with Andy Millen just inside the Hibs box and referee Kenny Clark awarded Hearts a very soft penalty, which Robertson duly slammed into the top right-hand corner beyond the helpless Leighton. Two incidents made headlines for the wrong reasons. Bruno, who fouled his way through the match with relative impunity, was booked for a disgusting tackle on Chris Jackson. Then, in the dying minutes, Michael O'Neill was red-carded for a second booking, and on his way off the pitch gave some cheek to fourth official Bill Crombie, before booting a fire extinguisher up the tunnel. All of this was seen by millions live on TV. Hearts won the match 2-1. The old firm match, played right after it, ended 3-3. For the pubs and police in central Scotland, it was a very busy Sunday.

Six days after the derby defeat, Chris Jackson was again on target for Hibs, this time against Rangers at Easter Road. Unfortunately for Edinburgh's green and white, the Govan side ran riot, scoring four goals themselves to win 4-1. The Wednesday between the games against Hearts and Rangers had seen the postponed match against Partick replayed at Easter Road. Darren Jackson scored but also had a spot kick saved by Nicky Walker; Hibs' other goals came via McAllister and Weir, the latter's coming after great link-up play with 'super' Joe Tortolano. It was an easy 3-0 win. Hibernian entered December still in third place.

Fir Park was the Cabbage's next destination on 2 December, where a fine 2-0 win was recorded over Motherwell. Both Hibs goals came in the second half and both were headers by Keith Wright from crosses supplied by O'Neill, the latter signing off in style before starting a belated three-match ban for his Tynecastle tantrum. The

Steelmen probably could've had a draw but Jim Leighton saw to it that they didn't get one.

Talk of any title challenge from Hibs – a challenge which, in truth, existed only in the heads of some journalists anyway – was virtually brought to an end on Saturday, 9 December at Easter Road when the green jerseys were mauled 0-4 by Celtic. Darren Dods was sent off early on for a nasty foul on Phil O'Donnell. Goals from McNamara, Van Hooijdonk, Donnelly and O'Donnell completed the rout. Another home defeat followed seven days later, this time to Jimmy Nicholl's Raith Rovers. Pat McGinlay gave the Hibees the lead with a cracking long-range effort in the first half, but the Fife side fought back. Inspired by their impressive winger Tony Rougier, Raith equalised through Steve Crawford then bagged a winner through big Ally Graham.

The year 1995 ended for Hibernian with a trip to Ibrox on 30 December, a Saturday. It was first against third. This match is remembered for two things. One is that Hibs were utterly annihilated by a rampant Rangers side; the other is referee Dougie Smith having no sense of humour. Paul Gascoigne was booked in this match. Smith accidentally dropped his cards during the match and Gazza picked up the cards and jokingly showed the referee the red card before handing them back. The miserable referee booked him for the joke. Even the Hibs players couldn't believe it. As for the match itself, Charlie Miller and Gordon Durie had Rangers 2-0 up at half-time, but Hibs hadn't been awful. Rangers won the second half 5-0,; Hibs *were* awful in the second 45. Gascoigne, Salenko and three more Durie goals completed the massacre. It was a sore one for Hibs fans. Your intrepid author went into his work on the Tuesday and was handed a can of 7up by a Rangers fan he

Hibs boss Alex Miller with his assistant, Martin Ferguson and coach Jocky Scott look on as Hibs beat Hearts 2-1 at Easter Road in October 1994.

Darren Jackson, Chris Jackson and Keith Wright celebrate after Jacko has scored the winner against Rangers at Ibrox in 1995.

John 'Yogi' Hughes and Chic Charnley celebrate with scorer Lee Power, during the Hibees' 2-1 win over Celtic in August 1997.

Pat McGinlay celebrates defiantly with Chris Jackson, after Pat had equalised against Hearts at Tynecastle, New Year's Day 1998.

Hearts fans wearing those silly yellow waterproof ponchos at Easter Road in 1994 – some fans in home areas of the ground were issued these, too.

Gordon Hunter tussles with Rod Wallace of Leeds United, during the clubs' 1993 friendly at Easter Road.

David Farrell, complete with cycling shorts, shouts for the ball in a win against Rangers, 1994.

Gareth Evans, in the new away kit, is poised to score the winner against Sheffield Wednesday at Easter Road in 1994.

Michael O'Neill runs riot against his former club, as Hibs crush Dundee Utd 5-0 in season 1994/95.

Pat McGinlay and Kevin Harper celebrate together after Hibs score against Motherwell in the 1995 Scottish Cup.

Kevin McAllister tussles with ex-Hibee John Collins during a hard-fought draw with Celtic at Easter Road in 1994.

worked with. It was Hibernian's worst defeat since 1935, when Airdrie had beaten Hibs by the same scoreline in the league in Lanarkshire, and Hibs didn't receive another such hiding until the 2013 fiasco against Malmo. Though recent poor form and the home hiding from Celtic in recent weeks had made a prolonged Hibernian title challenge sound increasingly far-fetched, it was this 0-7 defeat at Ibrox that killed that challenge utterly.

This defeat to Rangers remains Hibernian's worst modern defeat. The Malmo one had mitigating circumstances and was only a preliminary qualifier, this Rangers doing was a doing we got slagged about, dished out by a team that many Hibs fans dislike. Worse still, the Hibees were due to play a resurgent Hearts at Easter Road just 48 hours later. Many a pundit predicted a New Year derby slaughter; some even suggested that Hearts might finally score seven at Easter Road. How on earth would Alex Miller prepare his players for such a big test, having just so dismally failed another?

New Year's Day came. Easter Road was almost full. Alex Miller only made two changes to the starting XI who had been humped at Ibrox. Chris Jackson and Mickey Weir were dropped, in came fit-again Kevin Harper and Michael O'Neill, who was back from suspension. Hibs had by then lost six of their last eight matches.

Sure enough, Neil Pointon put Hearts 1-0 up after just seven minutes and many Hibs fans began to feel that sinking feeling. It looked like going from bad to worse a few minutes later, when Robertson carved out a chance that only Hans Eskilsson could have missed. Unmarked 12 yards out and with plenty of time and only Leighton to beat, the striker managed to scuff a pathetic shot wide, to howls of derision from the relieved Hibbies in the stands around him. It was just the type of lucky break that Hibs rarely got in the derbies. The miss is now part of Edinburgh football folklore – and it changed the game.

On 28 minutes, McAllister left two Hearts defenders trailing in his wake and crossed to the near post at the Dunbar End. Michael O'Neill got there first and brilliantly headed the ball past the despairing Rousset to make it 1-1. Easter Road erupted.

'Oh Mikey Mikey, Mikey Mikey Mikey Mikey O'Neill!' 'Hail, hail, the Hibs are here, all for goals and glory now …' Suddenly for the Hibs fans, it wasn't such a cold day after all.

Just before half-time, Darren Jackson lofted a ball into the box for Keith Wright; the big striker headed the ball down to Kevin Harper, who smashed a superb volley past Rousset from 16 yards: 2-1 to Hibs!

Pasquale Bruno should have been red-carded in the match for a dreadful knee kick at Keith Wright, but the Italian thug was yet again let off with a booking. In the second half, Rousset made fine saves to deny Millen, Jackson and McAllister. The latter gave Pointon a torrid time for much of the match; Pointon and indeed most of the Hearts team couldn't handle Crunchie at his best. Hibs won the match 2-1 and remained in third place in the table.

It was quite a turnaround, from Ibrox whipping boys to derby-day destroyers in just 48 hours. Jim Jefferies admitted that the better side had won but lamented Eskilsson's horrendous miss. Alex Miller was delighted, but gave a typical response after the match, saying that despite this victory he still hadn't forgotten about the Ibrox result, though he was pleased with his defence in the derby and thought that his team could easily have scored five. Hearts fans who had trooped along to Easter Road expecting an easy victory now had egg on their faces, while Hibs fans had the New Year bragging rights in the capital for the first time since 1989. Near the final whistle, the fans on the East Stand gave the dejected visitors a friendly reminder that Hearts hadn't won a trophy in almost 35 years, belting out a fine chorus of 'What's it like to win fuck all?'

One week after that fine victory over Hearts, the green jerseys were welcomed onto the hallowed Easter Road turf with a standing ovation from the green legions of Hibbies, who had braved the icy-cold conditions to take in Hibernian v Aberdeen in the league. As so often happens with Hibs, a fantastic result was followed up with a very different one.

The manager started with the same XI that had humbled Hearts.

After 11 minutes that man young Stephen Glass made a dash down the left and whipped in a cross which was bundled into the net by Joe Miller to put Aberdeen 1-0 up. Twenty minutes later, Miller this time whipped in a cross which Billy Dodds reached first, his header beating Jim Leighton. Thankfully though, it seemed, Kevin McAllister had cleared Dodds's header off the line. Aberdeen players surrounded referee Willie Young and pressured him into consulting the linesman, which he duly did and then subsequently awarded Aberdeen a goal. Hibs had been robbed and went in at half-time 0-2 down.

Hibs fans spent most of the second half jeering and shouting abuse at the referee. This intensified upon the hour, when Young red-carded Pat McGinlay for a foul on Glass. Young was taunted with several choruses of 'Who's the bastard in the black?'

Hibernian, 2-0 down and reduced to ten men, oddly chose this time in the match to start playing properly. Michael Watt did well to save a choice O'Neill piledriver. Mr Young waved away good Hibs shouts for a penalty.

We had the better of the last 20 minutes but didn't breach Aberdeen's back line until the 88th minute, when a great ball by O'Neill was superbly controlled by Harper, who took the ball on his chest then drilled it past Watt into the bottom corner. There were eight minutes of injury time played because it had been a pretty dirty match and there were seven bookings as well as Pat's red card. O'Neill almost levelled the match in the 94th minute but fired just wide. Willie Young was booed at club-sonic levels when the final whistle went. Though a bad result, the performance hadn't been completely awful.

Hibs' next match was at Rugby Park a week later and it looked for a time like the green jerseys had their mojo back. The Hibees led 2-0 at the interval. Michael O'Neill scored after 21 minutes, and then on 41 minutes came a trademark 'O'Neill cross-Wright header' beauty. The three points looked to be heading back to Edinburgh. Darren Dods was red-carded early in the second half and this changed the match dynamic entirely. A series of defensive errors from the men in green allowed Killie to score through Steve Maskrey, Paul Wright (again!) and John Henry to complete a remarkable comeback to beat Hibs 3-2.

On the Tuesday, a pitiful crowd of fewer than 2,800 souls was at Firhill to see Hibs play Partick. Murdo MacLeod's men provided stubborn resistance and the green jerseys couldn't break them down, the match ending 0-0, largely thanks to some woeful finishing by the visitors and another fine display by Nicky Walker. Another 0-0 draw was played out four days later against Motherwell at Easter Road.

Saturday, 21 January saw round three of the Scottish Cup begin. Alex Miller and his players had a chance to make up for that embarrassing early exit from the Coca-Cola Cup. Kilmarnock were the visitors to Easter Road, on a freezing, snowy day. The pitch was atrocious; Killie boss Alex Totten demanded that the match be postponed. It wasn't, despite police warnings on the radio telling the public to avoid non-essential travel. Killie's team bus was almost two hours late arriving in Leith. For whatever reason, the match went ahead. The first half went how one might expect – 22 men blundering around in the snow while trying to play football. The second half was much the same, save for two moments of brilliance from Paul Wright. On 55 minutes the ex-Hibs striker pinged an unsavable 30-yarder past Leighton to break the deadlock. Nine minutes later the same striker coolly rounded Leighton and chipped home from a tight angle. The Cabbage just couldn't find their shooting boots and it finished Hibernian 0 Kilmarnock 2. Hibernian hadn't been eliminated in round three since 1985 when John Blackley's men lost to Dundee Utd.

The green-clad players were booed off the park by the home fans at the final whistle, but even louder came the chants of 'Miller must go', a ditty scarce heard at Easter Road since season 90/91. Then the fans started to sing 'sack the board'. Just a few weeks earlier the Hibs faithful had been in rapture after beating Hearts. And yet, the uncomfortable truth was that the derby win had masked a seriously bad dip in form. Only three of the previous 11 matches had been won and 25 goals had been conceded, despite Hibs having excellent strikers and a top goalkeeper.

Now, listen carefully, as within the aforementioned run, which culminated in the cup exit, resides the reason that the writing was on the wall – at least in the fans' eyes – for the manager Alex Miller by this time.

Losing that cup tie to Kilmarnock meant that the Hibs fans didn't get a 'something' in season 95/96. Generally, at that time, for Hibs fans to be content the club needed to, in each season, do well in one of the cups and sign a decent new player.

Season 91/92 – Keith Wright was bought for £500,000, we won the League Cup.

Season 92/93 – Darren Jackson bought for £400,000, reached the Scottish Cup semis.

Season 93/94 – Spent over £500,000 on McAllister and O'Neill, reached the League Cup Final.

Season 94/95 – Spent £420,000 re-signing Pat McGinlay, finished third in the league and got to the Scottish Cup semis.

Season 95/96 – No big players signed, fuck all. Airdrie had knocked us out of the League Cup, Kilmarnock had ended our Scottish Cup campaign. For the first time since the dreadful 90/91 campaign, Hibs fans didn't get a 'something'. Yes, we got new stands, but that's not really a 'something' to most Hibbies.

* * *

There were, of course, reasons why there had been no big signings for season 95/96: sound financial reasons. But football fans, often motivated as we are by emotion rather than prudence, need their 'something' to keep them interested and believing. Perhaps Hibs fans had been spoiled with good signings and some moderate success from 1991 to 1995, maybe we expected to do better, maybe it was unrealistic of us to expect things to stay as they had been. But that Kilmarnock defeat really was a sore one. It was made worse by the fact that Kilmarnock got Hearts in the next round, the draw for which, embarrassingly, was held at Easter Road right after the match.

Alex Miller needed to do something to strengthen Hibernian's defence and turn things around. Enter stage left big Joe McLaughlin. Technically, big Joe was Hibernian FC's first 'Bosman' signing, as his Falkirk contract expired in January 1996 and he was then free to simply sign for another club. Hibs didn't need to pay Falkirk to free up his registration. The previous September's Bosman ruling had changed everything. Joe had been impressive for Falkirk in the preceding few years, a Falkirk side whom Hibs toiled to beat – and had enjoyed a good career down south as well at Chelsea and Charlton. He had actually scored Chelsea's consolation goal when Hibs had thumped the Blues 4-1 at Easter Road in a 1986 friendly. At 35 years of age when he signed for the Cabbage, he wasn't exactly a potentially lucrative youth prospect, but he was needed to plug defensive gaps in the Hibs side caused by injuries, suspensions and by poor form.

Saturday, 3 February saw the new signing start against Celtic at Parkhead. In the purple and green stripes, the Hibees played a patient passing game, soaking up Celtic's pressure yet always looking dangerous on the break. Leighton made some great saves in the first half to keep Celtic at bay. The defence was solid. The midfield competed well. Then, after 35 minutes, McAllister sent Keith Wright hurtling through on goal with a clever pass, and Keith squared the ball to an unmarked Jackson in the box, who swept the ball beyond Stewart Kerr to give Hibs a 1-0 lead, which they held at the break.

Celtic came out for the second half all guns blazing, determined to keep their own title hopes alive. Soon after the restart a ball to the back post caused a sickening accidental clash of heads between Leighton and John Collins; both players had to leave the field for treatment. Both had blood pouring from their heads. Alex Miller had no goalie among his three substitutes and also didn't know if Jim would be able to continue after treatment, so Darren Jackson donned the goalkeeper's jersey and gloves and took over. This tipped the balance of the match and Celtic soon carved Hibs open and equalised through Van Hooijdonk. There then occurred a bizarre thing. Jim Leighton was ready to come back on after treatment, so Darren Jackson took off the goalie gear and returned to his position up front. However, referee Mr Roy, for reasons unknown, allowed play to continue while Hibs had nobody in goal. It was farcical; both sets of players obviously wanted the Hibs keeper back on. The law of the game back then didn't actually say that you *had* to have a goalkeeper on the pitch (so our media claimed, anyway). Celtic were in possession and just passed the ball around, looking to the referee, who still wouldn't let Leighton back on. Eventually a Celtic player passed the ball into the empty net and once again the players all looked to the referee. Technically, the goal should have stood, morally, it was a shambles. Mr Roy then reinforced his incompetence by disallowing the 'goal', before letting Leighton return to the pitch. It was still 1-1 and Hibs had some chances to win the game, but ultimately the Hoops came out 2-1 winners, thanks to a thunderous long-range effort from Paul McStay, that not even Jim Leighton could stop. Hibs had played incredibly well but came away with nothing.

The following Saturday a woeful display by Edinburgh's green and white brought a 0-1 defeat at Stark's Park against Raith, who were managerless following the departure of Jimmy Nicholl. Davie Kirkwood scored the only goal with a long-range strike just before half-time. That result saw Hibs slump to fifth in the table, just a point above the Kirkcaldy side who were in sixth. Hibernian ended February with a 2-1 win over Falkirk at Easter Road. Gareth Evans put Hibs 1-0 up, Steve Kirk equalised for the Bairns from the penalty spot, while the winner came courtesy of a last-minute Keith Wright strike. That weekend had seen the cinema release of *Trainspotting*, a screen adaptation of Irvine Welsh's 1993 novel, with book and film both containing references to Hibernian FC.

Sunday, 3 March brought embarrassment to Hibs during a home match against Rangers, shown live on TV. Unlike when the two sides had last met, the embarrassment for Hibs wasn't in the result, which was 2-0 to Rangers, with a Mitchell own goal and a Laudrup penalty deciding the match. The embarrassment came in the second half when a Hibs fan entered the pitch at the home end of the ground and squared up to and assaulted Rangers goalie Andy Goram. Goram himself dealt with the man before police and stewards carted him off for a night in St Leonard's. The fan who entered the pitch was a carer, at the match assisting a disabled Hibs fan. This made the incident even more embarrassing for Hibernian and Douglas Cromb vowed that the pitch invader would be banned from the ground for life. One archive piece I found says that the man eventually received a 12-month jail term, but I've been unable to verify that. Lots of Hibbies disliked Andy Goram back then, but that assault really was taking things too far, much too far.

Alex Miller was allowed to sign another player after the home defeat to Rangers: £125k was shelled out to Chelsea for their left-sided midfielder Andy Dow. Miller had been an admirer of Dow back when the player had burst onto the scene at Dundee in 1993. By 1996 Chelsea were starting to buy top-class European stars so half-decent Scottish players like Andy were surplus to their requirements. The fact that Dow played on the left wing wasn't lost on Hibs fans, who knew that there may have been a chilling of the relationship between Michael O'Neill and Alex Miller since the fire extinguisher incident at Tynecastle the previous November. Around about that time, Leicester City manager Mark McGhee was supposed to have offered Hibs £1m for O'Neill's services. The Foxes' gaffer wanted O'Neill to bolster his midfield at Filbert Street, but for whatever reason, Leicester were rebuked at that time and that move didn't happen.

Saturday, 16 March at Tynecastle was when the final Edinburgh derby of season 95/96 was played. Andy Dow started on the left for Hibs, Michael O'Neill was initially on the bench but played for much of the match as Keith Wright had to limp off injured. This derby was a half-decent game of football which Hibs had the best of for the opening 70 minutes. Andy Dow scored on his debut, when in the second half he put the ball through Rousset's legs at the near post right in front of the Hibs fans on the Gorgie Road end. Michael O'Neill then brought out a world-class save from Hearts' French goalie, a save which marked a change in the game. Had his shot gone in it's likely that Hibs would have murdered Hearts, but it didn't. The home side took heart, no pun intended, and rallied. Hearts had the best of the closing stages and earned a point thanks to a late equaliser from Gary Mackay.

Though avoiding defeat in a local derby is important, to Hibs fans that Tynecastle match did feel very much like two points dropped. Hearts had also crept up the league and were now competing with Hibs for a UEFA Cup place, with Hearts actually having momentum on their side.

Saturday, 23 March witnessed fifth-placed Hibernian travelling to play third-placed Aberdeen at Pittodrie, and Darren Jackson sporting a new pair of bright white boots. They didn't do him much good early on as he blazed a shot from each flank high and wide, after good initial build-up play both times. The away side had the lead after 34 minutes, clever passing between Dow and McAllister leading to Crunchie shooting past Michael Watt and into the top corner to give Hibs a lead, which they held until 72 mins, when Scott Booth headed an in-swinging corner towards the net. Leighton produced a breathtaking save but Billy Dodds was on hand to score with the rebound. The Dons stole a somewhat fortunate victory six minutes from full time, via route one. Gary Smith lumped a high ball forward; Scott Booth got to it first and smartly lobbed the advancing Leighton. Aberdeen won 2-1.

Seven days on from that, Kilmarnock came a-calling to Easter Road; 8,000 or so fans turned out for this one. Hibs led through a Kevin McAllister goal but were hauled level 12 minutes from the end by a goal from that man Paul Wright, again. Though the wee striker hadn't left Hibs under any sort of cloud in 1991, by 1996 it's fair to say that most Hibs fans were utterly sick of the sight of him. He did to Hibs what Darren Jackson did for us against Dundee Utd – put his former club to the sword. Wright's goal was also the 50th Hibs had conceded in the league that season. Jim Leighton was not to blame for that shocking statistic; indeed, without him it would've been even worse. It was ironic that Hibernian had conceded too many goals when they had one of the league's top two keepers. Joe McLaughlin's arrival had steadied the ship slightly but there were multiple problems with Hibernian's defence. Graham Mitchell, Gordon Hunter, Willie Miller and David Farrell had all been out of the side through injury and suspension at various times in the preceding few months. Injuries helped to ruin the season for Hibernian, more so in fact than in any other season under Alex Miller. Indeed, with even Steven Tweed's form having dipped, only Andy Millen was consistently holding it together at the back for the Cabbage. It's ironic that in Alex Miller's last full season in charge, it was the defensive side of the team which was weakest. In any case, the Kilmarnock draw ended Hibernian's hopes of reaching the next season's UEFA Cup. All the fans had to look forward to now was the league run-in, as bit-part players in other teams' endeavours.

Goals from Brian Martin, Willie Falconer and Tommy Coyne helped Motherwell to a very easy 3-0 victory over the Hibees at Fir Park on 6 April, one week after the Killie draw. Well played with confidence, Hibs with indifference. A miserable afternoon for the travelling Hibs support that day was compounded by events at Hampden in the Scottish Cup semi-final between Hearts and Aberdeen. A Hibs fan with a transistor radio in Fir Park's huge Motorola (as was) away stand was relaying the Hampden events to the Hibbies. Hearts had been 1-0 up but Shearer equalised for Aberdeen with three minutes remaining. That pleased the Hibs fans at Fir Park, but then Alan Johnston scored an injury-time winner for Hearts. When news of that reached Fir Park, several Well fans would later claim that they heard a collective groan come from the Hibs fans. And so they did. Trudging out of Fir Park that day as a Hibs fan, having just watched your own team's capitulation then heard that your city rivals had reached their first cup final in a decade, meaning that said rivals had a chance to end their miserable, humiliating 35-year trophyless spell, which in banter terms is really the only thing we, as Hibs fans, had 'on' Jambos then, well, how did you feel? Let's just say, it wasn't great. Our city rivals were on the up, we were going nowhere. The next day, Rangers beat Celtic 2-1 in the other Scottish Cup semi.

Title-pursuers Celtic came to Leith on Sunday, 14 April and, as if by magic, Hibernian rediscovered how to play football. Everything seemed to have gotten back on track. Jim Leighton saved the visitors' two best first-half chances, denying Tosh McKinlay and Van Hooijdonk. Andy Millen, moved up into a midfield-general role, frustrated the Hoops. All was going well until just before the interval. Graeme Love got into a tussle with Van Hooijdonk and lashed out at the Dutchman with his arm, right in front of the referee. Love was red-carded and Hibs were down to ten men. Into the second half and it was actually Hibs who took the lead six minutes after the interval. McAllister floated the ball forward, his pass was headed on by O'Neill to McGinlay, who brilliantly turned his marker and unleashed a magnificent thunderous strike which beat Gordon Marshall and bulged the net just inside the post: 1-0 to Hibs.

Both sides enjoyed their fair share of chances thereafter; indeed to Hibs' credit it didn't seem like they were a man down at all – until fitness became a factor in the last 20 minutes. Right on 70 minutes, Donnelly's cross was met in the air by Van Hooijdonk, who put a powerful header beyond Leighton to level the score at 1-1. Shortly after that goal, McAllister went on a trademark dribble past two Celtic defenders and crossed to the near post. Gordon Marshall was left stranded but McGinlay and O'Neill both got in each other's way while trying to score from the loose ball, and the chance to regain the lead was lost.

Ten-man Hibs were eventually broken seven minutes from the end. Substitute Andy Thom raced past the tiring Hibs defence and squared the ball to Van Hooijdonk, who, unmarked, side-footed home. It was a sore one for Hibs fans, particularly as Thom had appeared to be offside for the winning goal. Hibs had battled well against what was becoming a very good Celtic side but got nothing from the match.

Six days later, Raith Rovers came to Easter Road. Rovers had just signed John Millar from Hearts and the ex-Blackburn Rovers man gave Jimmy Thompson's team the lead with a fine 20-yard drive. Pat McGinlay's powerful headed goal eight minutes from the end spared Hibernian's blushes, but didn't hide an embarrassing truth. Hibs had by then won just two matches in five months. The Raith game also saw Michael O'Neill's final appearance in the green jersey.

Falkirk were under the temporary charge of Gerry Collins when Hibs came a-calling to Brockville one week later, in a match best remembered for both sides' woeful finishing. Paul McGrillen put the Bairns 1-0 up just after half-time but Hibs squared the match a few minutes later, McGinlay scoring after excellent work out wide by McAllister and Evans.

Hibernian's season 1995/96 ended with a relatively easy win over Partick Thistle at Easter Road on Saturday, 4 May. Darren Jackson scored the only goal, late on. In fact, it was the last goal scored in the Premier Division that season. Hibs finished fifth in the table. The defeat didn't do Thistle any harm as they were already consigned to second bottom and the dreaded relegation play-off.

Hibernian's season may have ended against Thistle but for most Hibs fans there was still one big game to come, though most wouldn't have admitted so at the time. That game was on 18 May at Hampden, as city rivals Hearts took on Rangers in the Scottish Cup Final. Few, if any, Hibs fans wanted Hearts to end their 35-year spell without winning a single trophy, but on the other hand, many Hibs fans don't like to see Rangers winning things either. For many Hibbies, being asked who you'd prefer to win that final was like being offered a choice between a shit sandwich and a shite sandwich. In the end, the final was no contest; Hearts were humiliated 5-1 by a rampant Rangers side, ex-Hibee Gordon Durie bagging a hat-trick. Oh how we Hibees laughed!

Aberdeen had won the Coca-Cola Cup back in November, beating First Division Dundee 2-0 in the final at Hampden. Dundee were managed by Jim Duffy. Falkirk finished bottom of the Premier Division and were relegated. Dunfermline won the First Division and automatic promotion to the Premier Division. Murdo MacLeod's Partick Thistle lost their relegation play-off with Dundee Utd 2-3 on aggregate after extra time, so Dundee Utd returned to the top flight at the first time of asking. In Division Three, new club Livingston won the title and promotion in their first season after rebranding and relocating from Meadowbank.

Celtic lost just one of their 36 league matches in season 95/96, yet still finished second, four points behind title winners Rangers. Rangers largely had Gascoigne, Goram, Laudrup and Celtic's 11 draws to thank for that. Rangers got into the Champions League, Celtic the UEFA Cup. Aberdeen also qualified for the UEFA Cup, but by virtue of finishing third, not for winning the Coca-Cola League Cup. Hearts' reward for their 5-1 hammering in the Scottish Cup Final was Scotland's Cup Winners' Cup place, as runners-up.

It hadn't been a great season for Hibernian FC. With hindsight, we should have brought in one or two quality players at season's beginning – after all, we had just finished third in the league in 94/95 and could have built on that, but the stadium finance thing meant that we played the 95/96 'hand' with the cards that we already had. Had it not been for the team's relatively good start to the campaign, though, it could have been a lot worse. Indeed, had the team's form in the season's second half been the norm in its first, Hibs would have spent all season in a relegation dogfight.

There were still many positives. Only one derby had been lost, for the second season in a row. Rangers had been beaten at Ibrox. Darren Jackson had enjoyed another good season, Andy Millen had done exceptionally well, Chris Jackson had established himself in the first team and evergreen Jim Leighton had once again been ever-present and largely brilliant, though only eight clean sheets were achieved by Hibs' defence during the campaign. The two cup campaigns had been a great disappointment to the fans. Hibs had won 11, drawn ten and lost 15 matches in the league; 43 goals had been scored, 57 conceded. That's right; the goal difference was back in the red for the first time since season 92/93.

The squad had been threadbare to begin with and even with the arrivals of Dow and McLaughlin, it hadn't been deep enough to cope with the unusually large number of injuries incurred during the campaign. The team also suffered badly from suspensions in season 95/96, not just from the six red cards received but also from the entire multitude of bookings. Our single best performance of the season had been in the New Year victory over Hearts, while our worst was the 0-7 humping from Rangers two days before that derby – though the Broadwood fiasco against Airdrie in the League Cup and the early Scottish Cup exit at home were sore ones, too. We played reasonably well up until Christmas then were fairly indifferent for the remainder of the campaign – mostly. Jim Leighton, Jacko and Tweedy had been our best players.

Darren Jackson, who played in a deeper role for half of the season, was the campaign's top scorer with 11 to his name. Keith Wright, our centre-forward, despite missing a third of the season with injuries, still managed nine goals. O'Neill and McGinlay had bagged six apiece, McAllister had got four, Harper had scored three. Only five other players scored for Hibernian that season: Chris Jackson got two, Gareth Evans got two, Dow, Weir and Donald got one each. A total of 25 players had been used in season 95/96; 36 would be used the following season.

There were a large number of departures from Easter Road in the summer of 1996. In fact, it was more akin to an exodus.

Michael O'Neill was sold to English Premier side Coventry City, then managed by Ron Atkinson. Hibs received around £670,000 for the talented player, more than twice what Hibs paid to Dundee United for him three years earlier. Technically Hibs lost out on the extra £230,000 they'd have got if they'd accepted Leicester's offer for the player a few months earlier. Then again, O'Neill was out of contract in July 1996 anyway, and with the new Bosman ruling could have left for the continent for nothing, so Hibs did well to get a fee for him at all. Michael was a true Hibernian great during his three years at the club and has become one of the club's 90s icons. He had made 112 appearances and scored 24 goals from midfield in three seasons. His skill, trickery and tenacity won him the love of the Hibernian faithful, and we missed him when he left.

One player whose contract was also up but who left Hibs for hee-haw was big defender Steven Tweed. He used the Bosman ruling to head off to Greece to sign for Ionikos, where future Hibee Craig Brewster was also playing. Tweedy had worn the green jersey 126 times in five seasons since his Hibs debut in 1991/92. He'd scored five times and, like O'Neill, been part of Hibs teams which had played in cup finals and even split the old firm in the league. After breaking into the team midway through season 92/93 he became part of its backbone, and would be hard to replace. A real fans' favourite, Tweedy would have stayed at Hibs if given a modest pay rise. He didn't get one, yet we ended up spending rather a lot of cash to fill the void he left. That was one episode where the fans felt that the board could have done a bit better.

Joe Tortolano's 11-year senior spell at Hibs also came to an end. Joe had made his debut under John Blackley way back in 1985 against Clydebank. Joe played for Hibernian 257 times and scored 16 goals in that incredible career. Sometimes a target for the boo boys when things weren't going well, yet nowadays almost universally loved by the fans, Joe was a talented left-sided player who always gave 100 per cent in a Hibs jersey. He joined Falkirk in 1996. His departure left just two players behind whose time at Easter Road antedated the manager's; those two were Gordon Hunter and Mickey Weir. Joe always comes up in Hibby pub conversations, due to his being sent off in Gordon Rae's testimonial against Manchester United back in 1988 at Easter Road. His offence? A scything tackle on Gordon Strachan.

Graham Mitchell also signed for Falkirk in 1996, ending his near ten-year career at Hibernian. Mitch had been one of Alex Miller's first signings, part of a trio signed at the end of 1986 which also included Dougie Bell and Tommy McIntyre. Graham had made 317 appearances and scored four goals, in a Hibs career in which he won a SKOL League Cup winners' medal, played in one losing League Cup Final and six cup semi-final matches, two of which were won. He also featured in all three UEFA Cup ties the Cabbage played between 1989 and 1992. In modern times, you'll scarce find a player with a better left foot than Graham Mitchell had. Probably the best left-back Hibs have had in the modern era.

David Farrell, too, wouldn't be around for season 96/97, having left to join Partick Thistle. Faz had six years as a first-team squad player at Hibernian, making 95 appearances and scoring two goals. His best season was 93/94. Faz was solid and had bags of ability.

Gareth Evans also moved on, joining David Farrell at Partick Thistle. Signed for just £55k early in 1988 after Hibs had missed out on signing Aston Villa's David Platt, Gazzer had been a great club servant, a handful for opposing defences and was of course a cup winner with Hibs in 1991 and featured in all of the club's big moments during his eight years 'in the green'. Gareth played for Hibs 301 times and scored 38 goals. His departure left Hibernian with just three forwards in the summer of 1996. Perhaps 'GET EVANS ON, MILLER!' was one of the most shouted phrases at Easter Road in the early 90s.

Alex Miller's son, Graeme, a defender, also left Hibernian in 1996 to sign for Berwick Rangers. His brother, Greg, remained at Easter Road.

Seven players had left Easter Road, at least three of whom were left-footed. In fact, if you read out that list of departees it sounds like half a team has been lost, and it had. If season 96/97 was to be any better than the previous campaign, recruits were needed badly. With cash in short supply at most Scottish clubs including Hibernian, that recruitment was going to be a challenge, as a new dawn broke in football.

We're getting away with it
All messed up
Getting away with it
All messed up
That's the living …

WE'RE GOING TO MISS YOU – SEASON 96/97

'We are Hibernian FC, we hate Jam Tarts and we hate Dundee, we will fight wherever we *may be, cos we are the mental HFC'*

THE SUMMER of 1996 was big on sunshine and big on events, too. Dolly the cloned sheep was 'born' at the Roslin Institute, near Edinburgh. The Olympics were held in Atlanta, Georgia. Idiotic drunk Boris Yeltsin was re-elected as president of Russia and the Galileo space probe discovered water on one of the planet Jupiter's moons. In the UK, unemployment was down to 2.1m, a five-year low. Prince Charles and Princess Diana's divorce was settled and South African President Nelson Mandela visited the UK.

In music, the summer had seen 'Killing me Softly' by The Fugees battle 'Three Lions' by Baddiel and Skinner for the top spot throughout, each knocking the other off number one, but by the time the new football season began the UK had a new number one song, 'Wannabe' by some new girl band called the Spice Girls. At the movies, fans were going crazy for *Independence Day*, *James and the Giant Peach* and Disney's *Hunchback of Notre Dame*, or as Hibbies joked at the time 'The Steve Fulton film' – sorry, Steve.

In football, the summer had seen the Euro 96 tournament in England take place. Scotland had been there, with Alex Miller acting as Craig Brown's assistant. Darren Jackson and Jim Leighton were both on the bench for all three of Scotland's matches. Jim was unlucky to lose his place to Andy Goram for the finals, as Jim played in most of Scotland's qualifiers. Scotland had done the country proud. A very strong Dutch side were held to a 0-0 draw at Villa Park. A tight match against England at Wembley was lost 0-2, with Gary McAllister missing a penalty. Scotland did win their final group match, beating Switzerland 1-0 at Villa Park, Ally McCoist scoring the only goal of the game. Scotland and Holland were tied in second place with four points apiece and with the same goal difference. The 'fail safe' tiebreak in that situation was to go to the result from when the two tied teams met, but as that had been a 0-0 draw that was no good, so it went down to goals for, so the Dutch qualified as they'd scored three in the group to Scotland's one. It wasn't the first time that a Scotland side has been eliminated from a big tournament by such a flimsy margin.

Just after Euro 96, Newcastle United splashed out £15m to buy striker Alan Shearer from Blackburn Rovers, at the time a world-record transfer. Most clubs north of the border could only dream of having such an amount to spend. The exceptions were Rangers, who spent £10m in the close season on Joachim Bjorklund, Sebastian Rozental and Jorg Albertz, while Celtic spent just over £4.3m in the summer to sign Paolo Di Canio, Alan Stubbs and David Hannah. Hibs and the rest of the top division could only look on with envy at the old firm's spending.

Hibernian's first signing of the summer was actually a sponsorship deal. A six-figure sum was brought in and

Carlsberg thus replaced Calor as Hibs' main sponsor, beginning a relationship between Hibs and the brewing giant which would last an incredible eight years. Mitre still supplied the team kits, with both the home and away kits simplified – gone were the stand-up collars and both kits had very baggy shorts, as was the fashion in the mid 90s. The home shirt didn't have striped sleeves and was more akin to a traditional Hibs home kit, while the new away kit was all purple with green trim and with hooped socks. The goalkeeper shirts were pretty garish and ghastly, again, as most were at that time. These new adornments would be the last kits that Hibernian FC would wear in the old Scottish Premier Division.

With a new team kit procured, now all that was needed was some players to wear it. The players lost at the end of the previous season needed to be replaced and a new striker was also required.

Enter stage left, Barry Lavety, who arrived from St Mirren in a deal costing Hibs between £200,00 and £300,000. The 21-year-old striker had bagged 49 goals in 150 appearances for St Mirren since bursting onto the scene in 1991 as a teenager. Indeed, he had impressed against Hibs in a 1993 Scottish Cup tie at Easter Road and Alex Miller hadn't forgotten about him. Though a talented footballer, at the time Barry was best known in Scotland for having been caught taking the party drug Ecstasy in 1995 and had been punished by the football authorities and by his club, and had even gone for rehabilitation at the Castle Craig clinic down in the borders. All of that was to be expected for a young role model like Barry, who had made a mistake, but what he probably didn't expect was the media vilification which followed, or the utterly vile abuse he was subjected to from opposing fans in Scotland for the rest of his career over the incident. Taking a couple of Es hardly made the laddie a 'junkie' yet that's the terrace taunt he became subjected to. Hypocritical by many who taunted him with it, as, well, a lot of young Scots took E in the 90s. Barry's E thing also hit the papers round about the same time as the death of a young woman named Leah Betts in England, who died after taking a tablet at a party. The Betts tragedy caused media hysteria UK-wide and to some people Barry Lavety became a means with which to chide Scottish youth over the drug. So, this made Barry a controversial signing for Hibs. However, before and since, Easter Road has always been a place where players who need a fresh start can be reborn, to the advantage of the club, the player and, of course, the fans.

We as Hibs fans since the 80s have been taunted with 'Whores, poofs and junkies' by fans of other clubs, even by a minority of Hearts fans, there were also the AIDS-themed chants from when Edinburgh was the UK's HIV capital in the 80s. The fine film *Trainspotting* in early 1996 had shown these stereotypes to the world so, as you might imagine, when 'ex-drug user Barry Lavety' signed for Hibs, fans of other clubs thought 'well, that's a good fit'. But his E episode aside, Barry was a fine footballer, tall, strong and an excellent finisher. It was hoped that he could take his career to the next level at Hibernian, to everyone's benefit. Alex Miller knew Lavety well – he had actually coached Barry when the player was just 11!

More recruits were needed to bolster Hibernian's threadbare squad. The manager wanted Mark Perry of Dundee Utd but was unable to get him but he did manage to sign United's Scotland B centre-back Brian Welsh for £195,000. A move for St Johnstone's Kevin McGowne was unsuccessful, as was an attempt to sign Falkirk defender

David Weir, who joined Hearts. The left side of the team was down to the bare bones so Ian Cameron was signed from Partick Thistle. The skilful left-footed midfielder had impressed Alex Miller as an opposing player and the deal which brought him from Firhill to Easter Road also saw Gareth Evans and David Farrell head the other way. Other players would join as the season progressed. Europe's transfer market in the summer of 1996 was a bit like an ant hill that someone had kicked over – there were players available everywhere whose deals had expired and who were now free to move to other clubs within the EU, thanks to Bosman. There's a fan folklore story from around this time that Hibernian were offered and refused two young French strikers on loan from AS Monaco, on the recommendation of former Hibs legend John Collins, who was playing there at the time. They were both teenagers who needed toughening up. Their names? Thierry Henry and David Trezeguet. Was the rumour true? Who knows? It might just be one of those horseshit stories that some slaver makes up in the pub that subsequently spreads and grows arms and legs over the years, like when we were linked to David Ginola and Gianluigi Lentini. The story over the years has been attached both to the end of Alex Miller's reign and to Jim Duffy's time, so could well be nonsense. And yet, the John Collins link does make it sound slightly more realistic and tantalising, doesn't it?

Hibernian's pre-season schedule was a busy one. Stirling Albion, Berwick Rangers and Alloa Athletic were all battled away from home in July. A three-match tour of Germany playing against minor teams brought two draws and one victory, against Osnabruck, Kickers Emden and Ottersberg respectively. The latter match was a 5-1 win in which Keith Wright bagged his fifth and final hat-trick in the green jersey; McAllister and Pat McGinlay scored the other goals in that game.

Sunday, 4 August came and English First Division side Stoke City provided the opposition for Hibs' traditional Anglo-Scottish pre-season friendly. A Pat McGinlay rocket after 66 minutes was enough to give the green jerseys a 1-0 win over Lou Macari's Potters.

The 1996/97 campaign would begin with a home match against Alex Totten's Kilmarnock. Hibs fans wanted to forget most of the previous season and hoped that the dreadful mediocrity of that campaign would be replaced with something new, something better, something more akin to the good Hibs side of 1993–95. Hibs really needed a good start in the league and a long run in the Coca-Cola Cup. Talk among some fans that summer had been about how long the manager would last in the job. Some fans wanted rid of the boss, others were prepared to wait and see how the season began, while a few were happy for the gaffer to continue. In workplace and pub conversations around 1996, the question wasn't really 'do you think Alex Miller should leave?' – most fans suspected that he might. The real question, often posed by fans of other teams as well as by Hibbies was 'who will replace him?' – that was a far more taxing question.

The Kilmarnock match on Saturday, 10 August wasn't quite groundhog day for Hibernian. Brian Welsh and Ian Cameron made their debuts. Hibs passed well enough and might have scored three of four were it not for the heroics of Kilmarnock goalie, Lekovic. However, Kilmarnock scored two goals inside five first-half minutes through Ally Mitchell and John Henry. Mickey Weir did pull one back for the Cabbage – his last goal for the club – but in the end Kilmarnock strolled to victory, winning 2-1. Hibs hadn't lost on the opening day of the season since 1992. The team was booed off the park at the final whistle.

At Glebe Park on the Tuesday, Hibs comfortably disposed of Brechin City in the Coca-Cola Cup, winning 2-0. Barry Lavety got one on his debut and Andy Dow scored the other one to eliminate John Young's side. On the Saturday Hibernian travelled to Tannadice to face newly promoted Dundee Utd. The Terrors' Dave Bowman was red-carded after just three minutes for elbowing Keith Wright, but the Hibees still had to fight to win the three points. Kevin McAllister, the smallest man on the pitch, scored the game's only goal after 27 minutes, with a header! Jim Leighton's prowess kept the Hibees in front; in a match that some will remember as 'Leighton v McSwegan', as time and again the veteran goalie thwarted the young striker.

One week later in Edinburgh Hibs faced the league's other newly promoted side, Dunfermline Athletic. Chairman Douglas Cromb took to the PA before kick-off in an effort to reach out to the club's fans; it was well meant but it had no effect. Hibbies throughout the match called for the manager's head and booed the team at the end of what was a dreadful 0-0 draw. The most exciting aspect of this match was the first glimpse of Kevin Harper's new dreadlocks. Barry Lavety picked up an injury as well and didn't feature again in that calendar year due to the injury and a virus. To lose your summer marquee signing so early and for so long seldom augurs well.

Tuesday, 3 September and round three of the Coca-Cola Cup saw a full house of 1,200 at Cliftonhill, as the green jerseys took on Vinnie Moore's Albion Rovers. While the Coatbridge side offered virtually nothing in attack, Hibs made heavy weather of putting them to the sword, eventually winning 2-0. Keith Wright scored in the first half; McGinlay wrapped it up with a strike 12 minutes from time. The draw for the tournament's quarter-finals paired Hibs with Rangers at Ibrox.

The Saturday came and a purple-clad Hibs were in Glasgow to receive an utter hiding from Celtic. It was all over by half-time. McGinlay scored an own goal, Portuguese hitman Jorge Cadete bagged a brace, Brian O'Neill and Van Hooijdonk completed the 5-0 rout in the second half. McGinlay was red-carded eight minutes from the end to compound Hibernian's woes. After the match Alex Miller said that he was about to sign a midfielder, someone who could hold the ball up and make a pass.

Midweek, Coventry City came to Easter Road, providing opposition in Gordon Hunter's testimonial match. A crowd of 5,355 fans made it along. Sky Blues' player-assistant manager Gordon Strachan played a half for each team. Richardson put the English side in front but a rare Willie Miller goal levelled things before the break. Scotland youth player Paul Telfer restored Coventry's advantage after the restart but Keith Wright equalised after 65 minutes. Gordon Strachan scored the winner with a penalty, Hibs winning 3-2. Ex-Hibee Steve Archibald played for Hibs in this match. He was player-manager of East Fife at the time and declared himself injured for his own team's Challenge Cup tie, played the very next evening. East Fife lost that match and their angry chairman sacked Archibald as a consequence. England and Rangers veteran Ray Wilkins guested for Coventry City in Geebsy's testimonial, too; this appearance at Easter Road wouldn't be his last.

Hibernian signed Ray Wilkins on a one-month deal after that Coventry match. On the same day they also gave an extended trial to 24-year-old German midfielder

Thorsten Schmugge – Alex Miller's first continental signing, of sorts. The latter player would soon be forgotten. Ray Wilkins, when signed, was 39 years old and would make his Hibernian debut against Raith Rovers on Saturday, 14 September at Easter Road, his 40th birthday. His playing career had been impeccable; almost 700 matches spanning a career in which he starred for Chelsea, Manchester United, AC Milan, Rangers, Paris Saint Germain and QPR. He also had 84 England caps. His experience would be a great boon to the younger lads at Hibs, the man was a class act as a player, had done okay as a manager and while at Hibs was well liked and popular with players and staff. However, many Hibs fans greeted his arrival with despair. Many fans took it as a personal insult from the board or the manager; that's how high temperatures were among the supporters at that time.

Alex Miller had a few times in the preceding few years stated his desire to sign a Ray Wilkins-type of player – the fans never dreamed that they'd actually sign the ageing veteran. At 30 he'd have been out of Hibs' reach financially, at 33 or 34 he might've done a good job for Hibernian. At 40, his arrival certainly raised a few eyebrows. There were stories that he wasn't even training with the squad and was only turning up on match days. There were stories that he was being paid a handsome wage. Whether these stories were true or not matters not now, 25 years on. But, his time at Hibs coincided with a period of dreadful mediocre, unacceptable performances by the team. The team had been poor before Ray arrived and got worse still. Ray Wilkins was a nice guy and a footballing legend; he just came to Hibs at the wrong time.

Ray's Hibs debut against Raith at Easter Road saw him make an impact. He had a calming influence on the team in what was a pretty dreadful match. The Hibees won the match somewhat unconvincingly 1-0, thanks to a Steve Kirk own goal. The fans were not appeased and gave the players and the board repeated verbal blastings throughout the match. The Easter Road faithful were near the point of rebellion and it was at this Raith match that you could feel change was in the air; the fans weren't just on the manager's back any more, they wanted him gone. Hard to imagine that this club and its manager had, a mere 17 months earlier, managed to split the old firm and got close to winning the Scottish Cup. That week, a new play opened at The King's Theatre called *We Are The Hibees*, a light-hearted production about the Hibs story. It was written by Raymond Ross and starred Una Maclean and Hibee actor turned weatherman Lloyd Quinan. Believe me, by then we needed something light-hearted to take our mind off the team.

Wednesday, 18 September at Ibrox was Coca-Cola Cup quarter-final night. Hearts had knocked out Celtic after extra time at Tynecastle the night before. Hibs fans no doubt wanted an Edinburgh 'double' and fancied their chances against a Rangers team which was without Brian Laudrup, but deep down the hardy few fans who travelled to Ibrox that night to watch Hibernian must have known what was coming.

A crowd of 45,104 fans packed into Rangers' ground; as usual the small Hibby contingent was housed in the Broomloan lower. Hibs were at more or less full strength. Gordon Durie fired the home side in front after 29 minutes. Peter van Vossen, the striker who had tormented Hibs while playing for Anderlecht in 1992, added two more in the second half. With the exception of the goalkeeper, Hibernian were very, very poor, especially in midfield where the battle was ultimately lost.

Ray Wilkins in his prime would've had to have been at the top of his game to match Gascoigne, McCall and Albertz – at 40 years old he was all at sea; he simply couldn't compete physically and was too slow. It should be noted that McGinlay and the rest of the midfield were bulldozed that night as well, every individual battle was lost. The Hibs players in the second half at times looked like a schoolboy XI, milling around in a sort of mob while the Gers sprayed passes. In the 87th minute and at 3-0 to Rangers, Richard Gough hauled down substitute Chris Jackson in the box and Hibs were awarded a penalty. Darren Jackson stepped up and smacked the ball over the bar. That was typical of the evening's performance from the green jerseys. Albertz added a fourth for Rangers in the last minute to make it end 4-0. Hibs were out. It was a cowardly performance by most of the players and it was a humiliation for the fans. Having spent the better part of two hours in Ibrox watching their beloved team being torn apart like warm bread, all the while being serenaded with sectarian abuse and pelted with various missiles from the home fans, the Hibs fans in the Broomloan were to have one final insult thrown their way.

Towards the end of the match furious Hibs fans were singing 'Miller must go', among other things. Their exasperation turned to rage as, while they were singing about the manager they wanted rid of, his newest signing was applauding the opposing support, warmly clapping them as he left the field to be replaced by Chris Jackson. He didn't do that to annoy the Hibs fans; he did it because he was a polite guy who used to play for Rangers and because some of the home fans were saluting him. His reasons mattered little, though. Applauding the opposition's fans after that opposition has just humiliated your own team in a match where you yourself have played poorly really isn't on – and it made an already pissed-off Hibs support even angrier.

Surprisingly, after this midweek massacre, on the Saturday Hibs went up to Aberdeen and managed to beat the Dons, winning 2-0. Keith Wright and Darren Jackson got the goals. In post-match interviews both strikers stated that the manager had the full support of the players. Thorsten Schmugge made his one and only appearance in the green jersey in this match, and then went back to the continent. Hibs' next game was against Hearts at Easter Road.

Saturday, 28 September 1996. In the world that week, an Islamist rebel group in Afghanistan captured the country's capital, Kabul, routed its army and took over the country's government; they were known as the Taliban. A North Korean submarine ran aground on the South Korean coast and most of its crew were shot as spies. In the UK, BBC2 first broadcast a new home-improvement show called *Changing Rooms*, while in politics, Chelsea's vice-chairman donated £1m to the Labour Party; at the time, the largest individual donation ever made to Labour. Demi Moore was causing many an embarrassing trouser bulge in cinemas, in the movie *Striptease*, while comedy lovers were lapping up Eddie Murphy's performance in *The Nutty Professor*. In music, The Fugees were at number one in the singles chart again, with 'Ready or not' – a song sampling Enya, while indie rockers Kula Shaker's album *K* topped the album charts.

Hearts, in sixth place, came to Easter Road to play Hibs who sat fourth in the table. There was a strange atmosphere inside Easter Road, akin to the scene in the movie *Gallipoli* just before the final attack – in other words, we knew we were going to lose, but we as fans couldn't prevent it. In all, 14,271 fans were in attendance. It was time for the Hibs players to stand up and be counted. They didn't. Instead, Hibs fans watched on helplessly as their heroes gave up and rolled over to a very ordinary Hearts side. The visitors were 3-0 up at half-time, Colin Cameron scored two and Robertson got one. Three chants emanated from the away end.

'So fuckin' easy, oh this is so fuckin' easy.' 'You're so shite it's unbelievable.' 'Miller must stay.'

Hibs did improve a bit in the second half and even pulled one back through a Darren Jackson penalty, but it was too little, too late. As soon as the first Hearts goal went in, you could almost feel the collective feeling of 'For fuck's sake, here we go again' from almost every Hibby in the stadium. Hearts won 3-1. Such a timid surrender at home in a derby was the straw which broke the camel's back for the fans, though at this match most of their ire was directed at the players who had let them down, as many fans already knew that the defeat meant that there would be changes coming. The defeat allowed Hearts to go level with Hibs on points and above Hibs on goal difference. Hibs were sixth in the table after the match. Alex Miller managed Hibernian in 40 Edinburgh derbies; he won just seven and drew 15. The 22-match winless derby run from 1989 to 1994 he had ridden out because his team was largely good against the other teams in the league and had been successful in the cups. This time, one derby defeat (and a cup humiliation at Ibrox) was about to end Alex Miller's reign, just two months short of the tenth anniversary of his taking over the Hibs hot seat. He remains to this day Hibernian's longest-serving modern manager.

* * *

Alex Miller was one of the great Hibernian managers, nothing can change that. Here's what happened next. The manager had already had the dreaded 'vote of confidence' from chairman Douglas Cromb back on 13 September before the Raith Rovers match at Easter Road. Letting Alex go would've been hard for Mr Cromb as he had an excellent relationship with his manager, forged during and after the 1990 Hands Off Hibs period. Mr Cromb and the great Kenny McLean were the two Hibbies who'd gone to see Tom Farmer CBE (as was) in 1990 to ask the Kwik Fit business tycoon to step in and prevent Wallace Mercer's attempted takeover of Hibernian. Miller had stuck with Hibs throughout that turmoil, too.

The boss resigned on the Monday after the Hearts defeat. He said that he had done so for the sake of his players, so that they didn't have to play amid such an exasperated atmosphere at home any longer. He acknowledged that the fans' hostility towards his continued presence on the touchline was having a negative effect on the players. He made his statement, he went and said goodbye to the players and staff, and departed as a Hibernian great. The boss was dignified to the last.

Miller's resignation was greeted with almost universal relief by the Hibernian faithful. Coach Jocky Scott was placed in temporary charge of the first team. Early speculation about Miller's replacement at Hibs saw many names bandied about, including Alex Smith, Jocky Scott, Murdo MacLeod, Ray Wilkins, Billy Kirkwood, Steve Archibald and Terry Christie. Whoever Hibernian chose to replace Miller, they would have to be at least as good a manager, if not better. Filling the role adequately would be a taxing task; after all, there was no guarantee that the new guy would do any better than his predecessor. Hibernian would be relegated within 19 months of Alex Miller's departure.

No words, all's been said and done
No more words, all's been said and done
Here's a mirror with your name on
Singing, 'We're gonna miss you when you're gone'

TOMORROW – THE JOCKY SCOTT YEARS

'Walk on, walk on
With hope in your heart
And you'll never walk alone'

AS FAR as an ideal experienced manager to fill a temporary void left by a departing club icon went, first-team coach Jocky Scott certainly had the goods. After a decent playing career with Dundee and Aberdeen, Jocky then enjoyed a good managerial career, best known for his time in charge of Dundee, Dunfermline and as co-manager of Aberdeen.

He'd been Dunfermline manager when Hibernian had beaten the Pars in the 91 SKOL League Cup Final. He'd arrived at Easter Road in 1994 as a coach. Now, he stepped into the breach at Hibernian's time of need. Martin Ferguson, brother of Alex of Manchester United, remained as coach for a short time, too.

Jocky was christened by the Hibs fans 'Jock the Janny' because of his caretaker status. The Janny had a stiff test in his first match in charge – Rangers were due at Easter Road and the Govan men hadn't lost a domestic match yet in the campaign.

Saturday, 12 October saw just fewer than 13,000 fans come along to Easter Road to see the first non-Miller Hibs side since November 1986 in action. At first it seemed like nothing had really changed. Rangers went 1-0 up after just nine minutes with an Albertz free kick. The visitors should really have gone 2-0 up on 25 minutes but their Danish striker Erik Bo Andersen missed an open goal from six yards – an even worse miss than Hans Eskilsson's. The atmosphere within Easter Road that day was strange, as if a great weight had been lifted from the fans' shoulders, and the fans' renewed backing helped the players.

A week earlier Darren Jackson had bagged his first goal for Scotland, scoring a wonderful solo effort in a 2-0 win over Latvia in Riga, in a qualifier for the France 98 World Cup. Hibs, and Jackson especially, came out fighting in the second half against the Gers.

A seemingly renewed, and shooting down the slope, Hibernian came at Rangers after the interval. Darren Jackson headed just wide from a Chris Jackson cross. Good work by Ian Cameron created a chance for Chris Jackson, but again, the ball went just wide. Kevin Harper was the next one to shoot wide as once again Hibs carved open the champions' defence. In the 57th minute Darren Jackson was upended by Bjorklund amid another green cavalry charge, and referee Stuart Dougal pointed to the spot. The foul was actually just outside the area but that didn't matter to Jacko, who took the spot kick himself and placed the ball high into the corner beyond Goram's reach: 1-1. The Hibs fans were overjoyed and that eerie 'roar' that you get at Easter Road right after an initial goal celebration enveloped the ground. You know it – it's shouting, chanting, growling, snarling, it's '*come on the Hibees*', it's '*gerrintaethem*' and it's a roar that once you've heard it you'll never forget.

With the fans singing 'Oooh ah Jacksona' and then producing that magical roar, Hibs quickly won the ball back after Rangers restarted. Ray Wilkins played a wonderful through pass which completely wrong-footed the entire Rangers defence – a world-class pass, which was dummied by Jacko just inside the box, so that Kevin Harper could roll it out wide to Willie Miller. He, in turn, lashed the ball towards the six-yard box where Graeme Donald gleefully smashed it over the line to give Hibernian a 2-1 lead. It was a marvellous team goal, and it showed what Wilkins was still capable of at times, when given enough time on the ball.

Hibs were on the verge of a famous victory, then in the 84th minute Laudrup and Gordon Hunter got tangled up inside the D on the edge of the Hibs box. Geebsy did foul the Dane but did so outside the box; however, the two remained tangled up until inside the box, when Laudrup hit the deck. As ever, the Rangers fans behind the goal howled for a penalty, and they got it after Dougal consulted his linesman. Hunter was booked for the foul; Willie Miller was booked for moaning to the referee about it. Jim Leighton now faced Brian Laudrup from 12 yards, with the red, white and blue horde behind the goal, waiting to cheer the equaliser. Laudrup's penalty came back off the crossbar and Albertz ballooned the rebound high and wide. The Hibs fans cheered loudly, in a 'get it right up ye' style, towards the away end. Stuart Dougal then stunned everybody by ordering the kick to be re-taken. He cited encroachment into the box by Andy Millen as the reason and yellow-carded him for the offence. Hibs fans lambasted the referee and the Hibs players protested in vain. Hibbies were used to being on the wrong end of 'honest mistakes' from referees when playing Rangers but, on this occasion, Mr Dougal may have got it right, but fans in the ground didn't know that.

This time Laudrup hit the target with his penalty but Leighton hurled himself to his left and produced a magnificent save to keep Hibs 2-1 up. The ball was cleared, then came two chants from the East Stand.

'Scotland's, Scotland's number one, Scotland's number one!' 'Who's the bastard in the black?' Hibs won the match 2-1 and returned to fourth place in the table, above Hearts. The team had played superbly in the second half. Darren Jackson had the light blues' defence chasing shadows. Ray Wilkins had calmed things down in the middle of the park and had created the winning goal. Young Chris Jackson hadn't given Rangers' midfield a moment's peace, putting in his best performance in the green. If Jocky Scott had wanted the job on a permanent basis, he certainly didn't do himself any harm with this fine win as boss. Ajax manager Louis van Gaal was at Easter Road that day to watch Rangers, as his side were due to play them in Europe. He said this about Hibernian in an interview after the game: 'Hibs were the team with all the spirit. They fought hard, were very aggressive and after half-time Rangers found them a real problem.' In midweek, after the Rangers match, several first-team players were quoted in the press saying that they'd like Jocky Scott to get the job on a permanent basis. Now, I can't recall a single interview with any footballer playing under a caretaker boss where the player has said 'Oh no, we don't want him to get the job', that wouldn't happen. On the other hand, the vitality and drive shown by the team against Rangers indicated that the players wanted to play for Scott, so who knows what the players' real thoughts were? That week, some papers began to report that Hibs' main target to fill the manager's role was Motherwell gaffer Alex McLeish, though if Hibs went for the ex-Aberdeen and Scotland ace, they'd have had to pay Well compensation of some sort.

The search for a manager went on in the background while Hibernian's fans, players and coaches soldiered on.

A week later, a large travelling Hibs support made the short journey to Fir Park to play Motherwell. They were elated when a fine Kevin Harper goal put Hibs 1-0 up. Then on 25 minutes, Leighton sprinted from his box in a race with Well's John Hendry to reach a through ball. The ball was caught by a gust of wind which gave Hendry the advantage and he attempted to lift it over Leighton while both men were 35 yards from goal. The ball came off the goalie's hands and referee Jim Fleming gave Leighton a red card for handling outside the area. Jim wasn't exactly renowned for being booked or sent off, but off he went, leaving his gloves on the turf. For a time, no Hibs player wanted the gloves. Darren Jackson didn't want them again. Willie Miller had gone in goal against Airdrie back in 1992 after John Burridge had been red-carded, even saving an Owen Coyle penalty, but he didn't get the gig this time. Eventually Andy Millen bravely picked up the gloves and took over in goal. Chris Reid was in the stand but hadn't been named among Jocky Scott's three substitutes. Hibs, being 1-0 up yet a man down, formed a ring of steel around their stand-in goalie and did an excellent job of protecting him. Millen made three excellent saves and injured two of his fingers in the process. Hibs held on until the 74th minute, when Shaun McSkimming eventually beat Millen, his goal earning the Steelmen a 1-1 draw. Millen later said that he'd never been in goal before and would never do so again. Jocky Scott's after-match interview was unintentionally hilarious.

The Janny clearly needed a thesaurus, as every answer he gave contained the word 'magnificent'. Still, a win against Rangers and a draw away from home under such circumstances augured well for his chances of getting the manager's job.

Hibs played Celtic next at Easter Road on Saturday, 26 October in the league. The visitors led 1-0 at the interval through an Andy Thom strike, and got another three goals in the second half through Thom, Donnelly and Van Hooijdonk. Hibs were terrible. Wilkins and Cameron were overrun in midfield. Only Kevin Harper up front looked dangerous, yet everything good he and his team-mates did was easily dealt with by Alan Stubbs at the back for Celtic. The 0-4 defeat was a reality check for Hibs fans as it showed that the club's stagnation on the park wouldn't be solved simply by a managerial change. Chris Reid deputised for the suspended Jim Leighton in this match; it was Chris's first appearance in a competitive first-team match since February of 1993, three and a half years earlier.

The ease with which Celtic had broken Hibernian's defence brought about a most curious event. Hibernian, without a permanent manager but in need of defenders, paid £250,000 to Celtic for central defender John 'Yogi' Hughes. Alex Miller had been an admirer of the player – who was from Edinburgh and was a Hibs fan – since Hughes had been at Falkirk. Now, caretaker Jocky Scott brought Yogi home to Easter Road. The player went straight into the team for Hibernian's Friday night match, live on Sky against Kilmarnock at Rugby Park on 1 November. A bumper crowd of 10,872 made it along to the game, encouraged no doubt by Killie's slashing of entry prices.

Alex Totten's men took the lead after 15 minutes, John Henry flicking home after good attacking play by Paul Wright. Kevin Harper levelled for the Hibees soon afterwards with a flick of his own which flew past Meldrum. Four minutes later, Jim McIntyre restored Killie's lead with an excellent 25-yard curling effort which Leighton could do nothing about. After 30 minutes Killie goalie Meldrum had a rush of blood to the head and was rounded twice by Darren Jackson far from goal. Jacko then rolled the ball to Andy Dow 20 yards from goal and Dow coolly chipped the ball into the goalie-free net to make it 2-2. That man Paul Wright scored a fantastic 30-yard screamer just after half-time to put Killie 3-2 up and Alex Totten's men got the match's sixth and final goal five minutes later, courtesy of an unfortunate own goal by McGinlay. Killie won 4-2. Hibs didn't play very well while Kilmarnock were excellent. Hibernian had now conceded eight goals in two matches. Jim McIntyre had been part of the Airdrie side that knocked Hibs out of the League Cup in 1995, now he had become a pest for Hibs at Kilmarnock, too, and would be a nuisance to Hibernian FC in big games later in his career as well.

With the next match being a derby at Tynecastle, Hibs acted to strengthen the team further. In came 30-year-old defender Rab Shannon from Dundee Utd and Finnish defensive midfielder and trialist Juha Riippa. The latter would only play once for Hibs, while the former would make just six appearances in the green before later moving to Australia, despite reportedly costing Hibs £100,000. The derby was played on Saturday, 16 November. Many Hibs fans asked aloud 'Who?' when Tynecastle's announcer read out Riippa's name. Hearts were looking for a morale-boosting home derby win prior to their upcoming League Cup Final against Rangers. They didn't get it. Fans were treated to a veritable bloodbath with a multitude of fouls, bookings and even a red card for John Hughes. Hearts had the better chances but Hibs held on stubbornly, doing their best to atone for their tame derby capitulation back in September. Jocky Scott played for a draw and got one.

Hearts' mascot Hearty Harry at this match was a celebrity of sorts – at half-time the mascot took off its head and there was a beaming Ally McCoist for all to see. He was warmly cheered by the Hearts fans and booed by the Hibs fans.

Scotland's Coca-Cola Cup Final was played the next week at Celtic Park, as Hampden had closed once more to have a new main stand built to replace the rickety old one and wouldn't be reopened until 1999. Hearts, desperate to end their long embarrassing trophyless run, threw everything at Rangers and put in a courageous performance, inspired by their star man, Neil McCann. It made absolutely no difference and Rangers beat them 4-3 and lifted the trophy.

The Jambos' Cup Winners' Cup campaign that season had fallen flat on its face at the first hurdle, Red Star Belgrade eliminating Hearts on the away-goals rule. In the UEFA Cup, Celtic made it through the qualifiers but were hammered 4-0 on aggregate by Hamburg in round one. Aberdeen reached round two, where they lost to Danish cracks Brondby. Rangers made it to the Champions League group stages again but finished bottom of their group.

Saturday, 23 November brought Aberdeen to Easter Road on league business. Hibs played reasonably well but on that day Jackson and Harper up front had no strikers' chemistry between them. Jackson did beat Nicky Walker in the Aberdeen goal but his angled drive came back off the post. Leighton saved well to deny Windass and Dodds. The match was settled by one goal, Bulgarian international Illian Kiriakov and Billy Dodds linking up well to set up Dean Windass for the winner.

Alex McLeish's Motherwell were the opposition at Easter Road a week later. The Hibees went in front after 35 minutes, with a beautifully simple goal that began with a Leighton clearance, headed on by Wright to McAllister, who flicked it to Darren Jackson who smashed a volley past Scott Howie. Hibs had the better of the first hour; the Steelmen bossed the later stages. The difference between the sides was the skill, pace, vision and determination of Jackson. In injury time, Jacko received the ball in Motherwell's box and lofted the ball over Jamie Dolan, only to be hauled to the deck by him. The striker took the penalty kick himself and Hibs won the match 2-0. Ray Wilkins signed a month-long contract extension after this match.

Saturday, 7 December meant another visit to Ibrox for the green jerseys – back to the field of screams. Hibernian's last two visits to Govan had brought about 0-7 and 0-4 defeats and dreadful performances. What Hibs produced at Ibrox on this cold December Saturday was, for a change, quite excellent, if ultimately fruitless. Jocky Scott went with three strikers and a game plan to hit Rangers on the break. With 21 minutes on the clock the Hibees had the lead. Dogged determination from Jackson took him to the byline, drawing Goram from his goal. Jacko then clipped the ball to Keith Wright on the six-yard line and Hibernian's number nine fired home. Rangers had the bulk of possession in the first half and missed a few chances. Derek McInnes and Laudrup asked questions of Hibs' midfield. Then, on 31 minutes, Scott Wilson surged forward for the Gers and Hibs stood off him. Wilson passed to Ian Ferguson who blasted a low shot from the edge of the box which deflected off Hunter and slipped agonisingly beyond Leighton's grasp and into the bottom corner to make it 1-1. Four minutes before the interval, Rab Shannon cleverly switched play to Willie Miller, whose diagonal ball to the back post was met by Jackson, whose downward header beat Andy Goram all ends up. The Rangers fans behind the goal sat stunned: 2-1 to Hibs. Into the second half and Leighton did well to keep out a long-range effort by Rangers' speedy left-back David Robertson. Hibs hit back straightaway, Wright shaving the post with a low drive after giving Gough the slip. At the other end, Ian Cameron made a goal-line clearance as the home side pressed forward. The Cabbage were pegged back to 2-2 with 19 minutes remaining, Laudrup crossing for McCoist to head home from short range. Three minutes later McCoist scored again, prodding home a loose ball after Leighton had saved well from Gascoigne, making it 3-2 to Rangers. With seven minutes left, Laudrup started and finished an impressive move that put the Gers 4-2 up and ultimately decided the match. With five minutes left, Andy Millen launched the ball forward from his own half. It went all the way to the Rangers back post and was headed past Goram into the net by Pat McGinlay. Keith Wright almost snatched a dramatic late equaliser but was fouled when shooting and the ball went inches wide. The home fans had been furious throughout the match – they had expected an easy win and needed the three points as they were hoping to win the title again and equal Celtic's nine in a row record. Instead, Hibs had come to Glasgow and given them a real fright. Darren Jackson had gotten injured early in the second 45 and was a great loss on the day, as he had terrorised the Rangers back line and looked hungry. Had he played on, Hibs would have gotten at least a point. As it was, the fans had to make do with a courageous, battling performance against a very strong side, with no reward.

However, the team's performance in this match showed that the players did indeed want Jocky Scott to become the boss long-term.

Meanwhile, Hibernian's search for a manager continued; it's fair to say that it took too long. Silly names entered the fray as possible contenders, such as Kenny Dalglish and

Gordon Strachan, which was made-up nonsense from reporters. In reality, Strachan had just taken over as manager at Coventry City and had hired Alex Miller as his number two on the same day that Hibs lost 4-3 at Ibrox.

On the Wednesday after the Rangers game, Hibs travelled to East End Park to take on Bert Paton's Dunfermline. Marc Millar put the Pars in front, Darren Jackson equalised via a rebound from a Keith Wright shot, but then Craig Ireland's late lob gave the struggling Fife side a victory. On the Saturday, Dundee Utd were the visitors to Edinburgh. Kevin Harper was able to fire the Hibees into the lead after 20 minutes, thanks to a great pass by Andy Dow. John Hughes and Keith Wright were judged to have fouled Lars Zetterlund just before the break and Andy Maclaren scored the resultant penalty. The match finished 1-1. John Hughes was just back from a four-match suspension following his red card in the derby and was sent off again in this match, too, incurring another ban, five matches this time. His red card against United was a bit harsh but even still, the team needed him. His high number of disciplinary points had been carried over from his time as a Celtic player. Willie Miller was booked against United as well and that triggered a ban for him. Hibs were becoming very short-handed.

Celtic tried to buy Darren Jackson from Hibs on 15 December. Douglas Cromb said that there was no way that the player could be sold at that time. Jackson still had 30 months left on his Hibernian contract and it would have been lunacy for Hibernian to part with this special player at any price at that time; he was needed more than ever.

Saturday, 21 December brought a short trip across the Forth to take on Raith Rovers. One-time Hibs player Iain Munro was now in charge at Stark's Park. This match was eye-bleedingly bad for the first hour. A really typical drab Scottish battle. The Hibees did up their game towards the end, though, and ran out comfortable 3-0 victors, courtesy of a brace from Jackson and a goal by McGinlay. That win hauled Hibs from seventh in the table to fifth, but in a ten-team division that was a deceptively weak position, in reality just seven points off the bottom and five away from the second-bottom relegation play-off spot.

Jocky Scott, or at least someone at Hibs, then decided to sign Aberdeen's experienced midfielder Brian Grant for £75,000. He was a Dons legend and had won both of Scotland's cups while a 'red' but had fallen out of favour at Pittodrie back in the summer, after some kind of late-night drinking binge during Aberdeen's Austrian tour. He was aged 32 when he signed for Hibs so he wasn't exactly a future prospect – Hibs needed him to produce the goods straightaway. He made his debut on Boxing Day against Kilmarnock at Easter Road. Kilmarnock had a new manager by then, Bobby Williamson. Young Graeme Love was recalled to the first team for this match as around one third of Hibernian's squad was ill with some sort of sickness and diarrhoea bug. The weakened Hibs team lost out to Kilmarnock 0-1, Jim McIntyre scoring the match's only goal just before the break. The Hibees were booed off the park once more. It was yet another 'bad day at the office' for the green jerseys. Hibs almost beat Aberdeen at Pittodrie two days later. A fine Darren Jackson solo effort had the Hibees in front until the 95th minute, when sub Duncan Shearer scored to earn the Dons a draw. It was Scott's last match in charge of Hibs and he left the team where it had been when he had taken over from Alex Miller, sixth in the table.

Jocky Scott managed Hibernian for 13 matches. He only won three of them, drawing four and losing the other six. The highlights had been the two performances against Rangers. The rest hadn't been very good at all. Strangely, the club had spent almost half a million pounds on players during his short reign. While Jocky hadn't done enough to earn the job, the players and other coaches had wanted him to get it. So, it was reported, had chairman Douglas Cromb. There had been two changes behind the scenes at Easter Road. Hibby Tom O'Malley had been promoted from board member to the newly created position of vice-chairman, while Lex Gold had become a director. Mr Gold had been a journalist and a civil servant and at the time was also director of Scotland's Chamber of Commerce. He had played for Rangers briefly in the 1950s and said that he became a Hibs fan in the 60s. Newspapers at the time said that Mr Gold was a close associate of Hibernian's owner, Sir Tom Farmer. The same papers at the time (most notably *The Herald*) thought that Mr Gold didn't want Jocky Scott to be the manager, because he reportedly preferred to find someone completely new, untainted by the old regime – a fresh start for the club.

I see you falling
How long to go before you hit the ground?
You keep on screaming
Don't you see me here?
Am I a ghost to you?

SOMETIMES – SEASON 96/97 CONTINUED

'Ooh ah, Jacksona, say, ooh ah Jacksona, ooh ah, Jacksona, say, ooh ah Jacksona!'

ON 30 December, that new manager was appointed. Enter stage left Jim Duffy, manager of Dundee, who at the time sat third in the Division One table. He had a reputation as a manager who liked to play good solid football and who wasn't afraid to give youth a chance. He could also manage on a budget and was considered one of Scottish football's hottest managerial prospects. He had led Dundee to the 1995 Coca-Cola Cup Final, which they had lost to Aberdeen, and he had just led Dundee to the semi-finals of the same tournament again, where they had lost to Hearts. In truth there hadn't been many better options available to Hibs after their pursuit of Alex McLeish came to nothing. However, Duffy was young for a manager at 37, was energetic, upbeat and genuinely wanted to make a difference at Hibernian. Hibs fans at the time probably remembered him best from his playing days at Dundee. Duffy played in the Dundee side which beat Hearts on the last day of season 85/86, when Albert Kidd's double robbed Hearts of the league title. Duffy was also taunted by Hibs fans about his lack of hair when a player. Whenever Hibs were beating a Dundee team with Jim Duffy in it, Hibs fans sang 'Baldy, baldy, what's the score?' That wasn't personal in any way – opposition players were always goaded about their appearances. Lack of hair, silly haircuts, mullets, facial hair, etc. all made players easy banter targets for fans, as did players' weights – who can forget the chants of 'Sumo, Suumoooo' which were roared at opposition players and match officials in the 90s who were a bit on the portly side? Such light-hearted terrace banter, eh? Such was football. Now Hibs fans and their new manager looked to the future together.

That future was to begin on New Year's Day of 1997, with an Edinburgh derby against Hearts at Easter Road. The new manager was flown in to Easter Road on board the Kwik Fit Flyer, a traffic observation helicopter belonging to Hibs owner Sir Tom Farmer. Entrances don't get much more dramatic than that. And so, the Jim Duffy era at Hibernian began. How did it go?

The derby on 1 January was an utter embarrassment for Hibernian and a disastrous beginning to Duffy's Easter Road tenure. Hearts took the lead after 32 minutes with a trademark Robertson goal in front of the Hearts fans. Before the break the green jerseys were reduced to ten men when Andy Millen received a second yellow card and his marching orders for a foul on Hearts' new striker Jim Hamilton. One of Duffy's last acts as Dundee boss had been to sell Hamilton to Hearts, while back in 1996 the Dees had also sold Hearts Neil McCann. Both players, ironically, now played a part in ruining their old boss's first match as Hibs gaffer. In the 64th minute Hamilton put Hearts 2-0 up, prodding home a Cameron cross from close range. Three minutes later, a bungled clearance by Leighton fell to the feet of Colin Cameron, who fired into the empty net to make it three. Hamilton got his second and Hearts' fourth in the 87th minute, rounding off what was a miserable Wednesday afternoon for Hibs and Hibbies. It was worse than the tame surrender against Hearts back in September; in fact, it was Hibs' heaviest derby defeat in 35 years, since Walter Galbraith's side had lost 0-4 to Hearts at Easter Road in September 1962. An inauspicious beginning, then, for Mr Duffy, though, in his defence, his team had played for an hour with ten men and he was working with players who had been signed by two previous bosses.

Saturday, 4 January, just three days after the derby thumping, brought another early test for the new manager, as Rangers travelled to Easter Road. They had just been hit with the same sickness and diarrhoea bug as had ravaged the Hibs squad at Christmas time and consequently had to field a severely weakened team against Hibs. Ray Wilkins, who knew that he was playing his last match for Hibernian, said in the press that clubs like Rangers had a disproportionate advantage anyway due to the larger, better squad that they had, so the illness call-offs shouldn't be used as an excuse if the Ibrox side were to have a bad day in Leith and drop points. It's actually really cool that a guy like Ray played for Hibs at all in his career, no matter what you may think of his contribution to the team at the time. Like George Best when he came to Hibs, his best days were behind him. George Best showed a few flashes of brilliance at Hibs but was otherwise mediocre and part of a very poor Hibernian team very much on a downward trajectory. The same could be said of Wilkins at Hibs. With both players, looking back, it's just kinda cool that we had these world-class players at all!

Against Rangers, the Hibees had the best of the first 30 minutes and actually took the lead after just eight minutes through Kevin Harper, though Bo Andersen levelled for the away side just four minutes later. The match did seem headed towards a draw, Rangers improved but at no time did Hibs look to be on the back foot. The match was decided by Brian Laudrup and Jorg Albertz in the second half. Leighton and Laudrup both went for a through ball, Laudrup went flying and the referee gave Rangers a penalty kick, despite Leighton's furious protests that he didn't touch the Dane, protests which saw the goalie booked. Up stepped Albertz to take and score the penalty, so Rangers won 2-1.

A Hibs move to sign Ireland international striker Owen Coyle from Dundee Utd ended up not happening and the striker joined Motherwell instead – that move could've been a real game changer for Hibs had it been successful. Instead, Raith Rovers defender Shaun Dennis was Jim Duffy's first signing and the big stopper made his Hibernian debut against Motherwell at Fir Park on Saturday, 11 January. Dennis was very much a Scottish centre-back in the old-school style. He was strong, 6ft tall and ferocious in the tackle, though not the quickest. Shaun would one day play an important part at Hibernian, but in another era.

McSkimming put Well 1-0 up after 20 minutes then an unfortunate Gordon Hunter scored an own goal just four minutes later. Andy Dow did pull one back for the Hibees just after the break but the Steelmen held on to win 2-1. Shaun McSkimming liked a goal against us; sometimes I wonder if we might have been better off signing him and Jim McIntyre, and re-signing Paul Wright, just for damage limitation!

The big tests kept coming for Jim Duffy and Hibernian. The next Saturday brought Hibs to Parkhead. That week had seen more transfer activity. Kevin McAllister had already left Hibs and returned to Falkirk for a nominal fee the week before. Duffy had also added left-back Jamie McQuilken, 22, to the squad, bought for £100,000 from Dundee Utd, as well as acquiring 27-year-old utility man David Elliot from Falkirk, presumably as part of the McAllister arrangement. Both players started against Celtic, as did Alex Miller's son, Greg. Keith Wright, Shaun Dennis, Darren Jackson and Rab Shannon were all injured, John Hughes was free from suspension but also injured. A Hibs line-up almost unfamiliar to the fans went up against a Celtic side who were still trying to catch Rangers. Celtic took 48 minutes to wrap up the match, with goals from Brian McLaughlin and a brace from Van Hooijdonk. Kevin Harper did pull one back for the purple-clad Hibees after 63 minutes but just five minutes later a Jorge Cadete strike put the match beyond the visitors. Hibs lost 4-1. The match bore witness to Mickey Weir's las-ever first-team appearance for Hibs, Duffy bringing the wee magician on after Celtic's fourth went in.

That drubbing dragged Hibs down to eighth in the table – third bottom in other words – with 23 points, just four more than bottom club Raith and two more than ninth-placed Motherwell. Some welcome relief from the league campaign was needed and it came on the Thursday night at Easter Road, as Aberdeen came calling in the Scottish Cup.

Just fewer than 10,000 fans were at this tie, and the match was showned live on TV. It was a nervous encounter as both sides seem terrified of losing, but the atmosphere heated up three minutes after the interval when Greg Miller turned a Darren Jackson cross past Michael Watt to put Hibs one up. The Dons equalised on 70 minutes through Scott Booth and went in front six minutes later, thanks to a good 25-yard shot from Dodds. Easter Road roared to encourage the Hibees and the players' heads didn't go down. Three minutes after Dodds's goal, Pat McGinlay connected with an excellent Andy Dow cross and levelled the tie, to the delight and the relief of the home support. It finished 2-2 and the match would have to be replayed.

Five days later, 15,464 fans were at Pittodrie for the replay. Hibernian were without injured players Wright, Hughes and Shannon, while Darren Jackson played with an injury. The match finished 0-0 after extra time and was a somewhat drab affair, repeating the pattern if not the result of the first match. Jacko didn't last the whole 120 minutes because of his injury so when the cup tie went to penalty kicks, Pat McGinlay stepped forward to take the psychologically important first penalty. Pat scored: 1-0.

Stephen Glass scored for Aberdeen: 1-1.

Big Shaun Dennis sent Watt the wrong way: 2-1.

Joe Miller's kick was easily saved by Leighton: still 2-1.

Ian Cameron fired low to Watt's right: 3-1 to Hibs.

Billy Dodds sent Leighton the wrong way: 3-2.

Brian Grant, against his recent employers, blasted his kick past Watt and saluted the Hibs fans: 4-2.

Up stepped big Duncan Shearer. If he missed, Aberdeen were out. He hammered the ball straight down the middle and Leighton saved brilliantly with his legs! The Hibs fans to his left erupted in rapture and a gleeful Leighton ran towards them. However, the celebration was interrupted, as Leighton was called back by the referee and linesman. They said that he had moved off his line too early and ordered the kick retaken. Shearer scored: 4-3.

Young Kevin Harper strode forward. He had just turned 21. He had the hopes of the green half of Edinburgh on his shoulders and to date it was the most important single kick of his career.

His penalty went in off the post. Hibs won the shoot-out 5-3, amid glorious celebrations among the travelling Hibs support. The victory had been achieved by an under-strength Hibernian team and had shown that Hibs still had strength and character. Little if any decent football had been on display in the preceding 120 minutes, but that mattered not on that freezing January night. Jim Leighton had once again produced the goods in a shoot-out and all five Hibs spot kick takers had scored. Hibs were drawn to play Celtic in the next round, at Easter Road. The big tests kept coming for this 'under new management' Hibernian FC.

There were two more league matches before the cup's next round. At Easter Road on Saturday, 1 February Hibs drew 1-1 with bottom club Raith Rovers – a Davie Kirkwood own goal for Hibs, a fine Danny Lennon long-range volleyed goal for the visitors. Another new player made his Hibernian debut in that match, 33-year-old midfielder Chic Charnley. The manager knew Chic quite well and gambled by bringing him to Easter Road in a bid to invigorate the squad, a squad ravaged by injuries and suspensions and which was suffering poor form. Charnley was signed on a pay-per-play basis as he was walking a disciplinary tightrope, one match away from a lengthy ban. His disciplinary record was dreadful; by the time his football career ended he had been sent off 17 times. He'd had 13 clubs prior to Hibs. He was also a little bit unfit when he signed. However, the veteran did have ability, vision, passing and shooting prowess and that type of natural skill which only some players have and which can't be taught. It was midfield creativity that Hibs sorely lacked at the time so Duffy took a chance – after all, Hibs were now in a relegation battle. Saturday, 8 February saw Hibs fight out a 0-0 draw up at Tannadice. Charnley played quite well, while McGinlay was red-carded in the last minute. The two draws saw Hibs climb to seventh.

Celtic came to Edinburgh to play Hibs in round four of the Scottish Cup on Monday, 17 February. The match was shown live on TV. The Hibees were without the suspended Pat McGinlay and Willie Miller, while Darren Jackson, who had missed the last two matches, still carried a knock but played. Keith Wright was back from injury and started on the bench. There were 16,000 fans in attendance. Darren Jackson put in one of his best shifts in the green jersey in this match, constantly making life difficult for Malky Mackay and Alan Stubbs at the back for the Hoops. In fact, the whole Hibs team played very well. They went behind to a Phil O'Donnell goal after 16 minutes but didn't give up. Seven minutes from time, a long ball into the Celtic box saw Celtic goalie Stewart Kerr and Alan Stubbs get in each other's way as the howling wind caught the ball. Jackson pounced and was lining up to score when Mackay clattered into the back of him. Jacko hit the deck and the referee awarded Hibs a penalty. Jackson took the kick himself and beat Kerr, earning Hibs a deserved 1-1 draw and another crack at Celtic in a replay. Tommy Burns admitted that his team had been lucky to escape with a draw.

Hibernian warmed up for the cup replay in Glasgow by playing a league match in the same city, on Sunday, 23 February. This match was on TV and there were 47,618 fans in the stands. Hibernian gave a good account of themselves but once more were no match for the light blues. Laudrup and an Albertz penalty had Rangers 2-0 up and on easy street. Shaun Dennis, who had conceded the penalty, made amends by heading a Jackson flick into the net at the other end to pull things back to 2-1. Goram saved well to deny Hunter, Harper and both Jacksons. David Elliot was sent off and Rangers sealed their 3-1 victory with yet another Laudrup strike. The Dane is probably the third-best foreign player to have graced the Scottish league in the last 30 years, after Franck Sauzee and Henrik Larsson.

Though the performance at Ibrox in front of a large hostile Glasgow crowd was good, the result wasn't. Hibernian hadn't won a league match since before Christmas. However, Hibs fans wanted to play Rangers again soon, as the cup draw had decided that whoever won the cup replay between Celtic and Hibs would be rewarded with a home tie against the Gers. That replay came three days after the defeat at Ibrox. A crowd of 45,880 fans were at Parkhead to see a purple-clad Hibs well beaten by a ruthless, composed Celtic. O'Donnell and Di Canio got the goals; Hibs fought the physical battle well but lacked a cutting edge. Jim Duffy gave a Hibs debut to 17-year-old Stuart McCaffrey in this match, such were the team's injury and suspension woes. The cup dream was over for another year; now the Hibs had a relegation battle to focus fully on.

Keith Wright, back from injury and looking sharp, scored Hibernian's goal on Saturday, 1 March at Easter Road against Motherwell. The goal was a typical Jackson-Wright effort, just after half-time. Tommy Coyne equalised for the Steelmen 13 minutes later, though, and the points were shared. Keith was again on target a week later, scoring the only goal of the game against Dunfermline at Easter Road, after 11 minutes. It was Jim Duffy's 13th match at the helm and his first victory (over 90 minutes) in the Hibs dugout. Barry Lavety returned from his long layoff, as a late substitute. The win kept Hibernian third from bottom, level on points with Motherwell who were above them on goal difference. Hibs had 29 points, second-bottom Killie had 24, bottom club Raith had 23. There were still seven league matches to go and 21 points to play for. Hibs were in danger, but every side below fourth in the table was potential relegation fodder with that number of points still to be won.

The season's final Edinburgh derby came on Saturday, 15 March at Tynecastle, watched by 15,136 fans. It was the last Tynecastle derby at which Hibernian supporters occupied the Gorgie Road end of the stadium. It was a bad-tempered affair again. Though there was no 'doing' this time, Hibs still lost. In the seventh minute Chic Charnley made a schoolboy error and gave the ball away, Neil McCann promptly raced forward and scored at the Gorgie Road end: 1-0 to Hearts. There was some friction between Keith Wright and Gilles Rousset in the second half, which resulted in the Hibs fans booing the French goalie for around 30 minutes. This defeat left the Hibees joint second bottom with Motherwell, with the Steelmen two goals better off. Hibs had 29 points still, bottom club Raith still had 23.

The team was now in serious danger of ending up in the relegation play-off, or even of finishing bottom and going down automatically. To counter this threat, and to boost Hibernian's attacking options, the manager spent another £200,000 on a deal to sign Dundee duo Paul Tosh and Lee Power, with whom he had worked at Dens Park. Tosh was 23 and could play up front or on the wing and he'd bagged 19 goals for Dundee in four seasons. Power, aged 24, was a 6ft-tall Irish striker who had only joined Dundee that season. He was a product of Norwich City's youth system and had been a Norwich first-team player between 1990 and 1994. That was when Norwich had a really good side and Lee had often been on the bench for the Canaries as they already had two big strikers who were first-choice picks, in Chris Sutton and Efan Ekoku. He had been a hot prospect as a youth and was involved in Norwich's famous 1993 UEFA Cup run when they knocked out Vitesse Arnhem and Bayern Munich, before losing to Inter Milan.

He'd been around the clubs a bit since leaving Norwich but was certainly no dud. The manager's initial signing targets had been Manchester City's Gerry Creaney and Morton's Derek Lilley, but Hibs couldn't match Gerry's wages nor meet Morton's £500,000 asking price for Lilley. The manager was also trying to sign an unnamed Scandinavian midfielder.

The urgency with which the two forwards were signed was partly because Darren Jackson was suspended for the next two home matches, which were must-win games for Hibernian. The first of these games was played against Aberdeen on Saturday, 27 March. The Dons were thirsting for revenge after the cup exit to Hibernian on penalties. The two new forwards started for Hibs, so did Barry Lavety. After six minutes, Charnley whipped in a free kick which was headed down in the box by Darren Dods to Pat McGinlay, who lashed the ball past Derek Stillie to give Hibs the lead. Both sides had chances in the first 45: Lavety even had a goal chopped off. Eight minutes into the second half the Dons drew level; their goal was scored by teenager Michael Craig, nephew of Aberdeen assistant boss and one-time Hibs caretaker boss, Tommy Craig. Charnley and Lavety soon combined to set up McGinlay for Hibs' second goal. On 71 minutes it was all over when McGinlay whipped in a cross which was volleyed home by debut-boy Tosh to seal a 3-1 win for Hibernian. The win was just what Hibs needed and most of the 9,669 fans went home pleased. Hibs had gotten the goals needed but the true stars of the day were McGinlay and Charnley, who ran the midfield like two best mates having a summer kickabout against wee boys. Indeed, it was puzzling just how that poor Aberdeen team was above Hibs in the table, on evidence of that performance.

The second must-win home match was against Dundee United. Tommy McLean's men were on a 17-match unbeaten run when they came to Easter Road. Hibs employed the long-ball game. Hibs fans generally don't like to watch that but on this occasion it was highly effective, eventually. In the 71st minute United's Steven Pressley brought down Lee Power and referee Mike Pocock pointed to the spot. Chic Charnley took the kick and scored: 1-0 to Hibs. Pressley was red-carded for the foul on Power and Dundee Utd kind of collapsed after Chic scored the penalty. Pat McGinlay added a controversial second just eight minutes later, bursting into the box and beating Sieb Dijkstra from ten yards to put Hibs 2-0 up and end the match as a contest. The ref had initially blown for offside but his assistant's flag stayed down and the goal stood. After the 2-0 win, Jim Duffy confessed that problems with the Easter Road pitch had compelled him to employ long-ball tactics. The back-to-back victories had pulled Hibs up to eighth in the table with 35 points, five more than ninth-placed Motherwell and 11 clear of basement boys Raith. Just four league matches remained so the team was now virtually assured of avoiding automatic relegation and had a decent cushion in the quest to avoid the play-offs.

A trip to Fife was next for the Cabbage on Saturday, 12 April. Against Dunfermline at East End Park the green jerseys found themselves a goal down after 11 minutes. A Derek Fleming cross was nodded past Leighton by Gerry Britton. After 30 minutes of trying to pass the ball, the Hibees tried route one instead, and the results were instantaneous. When the Pars' defence made a hash of dealing with one long ball, Darren Jackson pounced and was ready to score, but he was brought down in the box by Andy Tod. Pars fans screamed 'cheat' and booed as Jacko waited to take the resultant penalty, but those fans were silenced when Jackson's penalty bulged the net. It finished 1-1. Hibs would have lost had Jim Leighton not produced two world-class saves in the second half. When asked after that match if he thought Hibs were too good to go down, Jackson pointed out that two years earlier people had thought Dundee Utd had been too good to go down, but added that he was glad that Hibs' fate was still in their own hands. Chic Charnley was booked in this match, triggering his long suspension – Hibs would be without him for the remainder of the season, including the play-offs, if they ended up in them. That same day, Motherwell hammered Raith Rovers 5-0 at Fir Park, effectively relegating the Kirkcaldy side as Raith's goal difference was -36: even if they had pegged Motherwell back in the last three games they'd have been down on goal difference. Motherwell's emphatic victory also cut their deficit with Hibs to three points and gave them a goal-difference advantage, though Hibs' point had raised them to seventh, with Kilmarnock on the same number of points as Hibs sandwiched between Well and the Easter Road side.

At Rugby Park a week later, Bobby Williamson's men battered Hibs in the first half and wasted three excellent chances. Unfortunately for Hibs, Paul Wright had already fired Killie into the lead after just 15 minutes. The visitors did eventually equalise, Barry Lavety heading in a Jackson corner, with help from a deflection by Ray Montgomerie. Hibs did improve in the second half and forced two good saves from Lekovic. However, once again, it was industry and effort which got Hibs something from the match, not skill or invention. Killie were now unbeaten in seven and Motherwell drew that day, meaning that with two games remaining Motherwell were in the relegation play-off spot, with Kilmarnock and Hibs three points above them. Hibernian's main problem now was that one of their remaining two matches was against Celtic. Hibs fans who for weeks had been expecting the team to drag itself clear of the mire now began to realise with far more clarity the precariousness of their team's situation. Hibs could go down!

The Hibs v Celtic match was at Easter Road on Sunday, 4 May. Tommy Burns had just been sacked as Celtic boss. Hibernian FC needed its players to stand up and be counted. They did try hard – harder, in fact, than they had against some 'lesser' teams – but were behind after 12 minutes to a Cadete goal. Lee Power did pull Hibs level after 35 mins, with a rare type of goal scored as a result of an indirect free kick, after Celtic's goalie Marshall had picked up a back pass. Di Canio restored the visitors' advantage before the break with a dipping shot. In the 65th minute Celtic got their third and final goal, that man Cadete scoring again as the Hibs defence crumbled. Asides a late chance for Lee Power, that was that. Celtic won 3-1. Elsewhere that day, Motherwell pulled off a shock 2-0 win over Rangers at Ibrox! So, with Hibs having one league match to go, they were third bottom, level on 37 points with Kilmarnock in the play-off spot below them, but the Hibees were three goals better off. Motherwell, now in seventh, also had 37 points but were eight goals better off than Hibs.

There was a problem, though. Kilmarnock also had a game in hand, which they drew 0-0 with Celtic on 7 May at Parkhead. That point allowed Killie to leapfrog Hibs and Motherwell into seventh.

On the last day of the league season, all Jim Duffy's Hibs team had to do to avoid remaining in the play-off spot was beat relegated Raith Rovers at Stark's Park, and hope that Kilmarnock and Motherwell also dropped points.

They both did drop points. Killie drew with Aberdeen at Rugby Park and Motherwell drew with Dunfermline 2-2 at Fir Park.

Pat McGinlay scored for Hibs after 20 minutes at Stark's Park. Sadly, Peter Duffield had given Rovers the lead after just six minutes. It finished 1-1 and Hibernian were into the two-legged relegation play-off. Their opponents? None other than their big-game bogey team, Airdrieonians, Division One runners-up.

The Raith match was a debacle, Hibs were dreadful. After the match, Darren Jackson spoke to the media. 'This must be soul-destroying for our supporters who have been tremendous. They deserve better.' He was right, but was perhaps hard on the old heads – Darren Jackson, McGinlay and Leighton by then must have had sore shoulders from carrying Hibernian for so long.

Jim Duffy had this to say: 'I am devastated, and that is not overstating my feelings. I feel so sorry for our fans that they have to endure the play-offs. We have two games to save our season and ensure they have Premier Division football next season.' Suddenly, mid-table stability under Alex Miller didn't sound so bad at all. After this match the press more or less in unison announced that Darren Jackson would be leaving Hibernian if the club was relegated. For Hibs fans, the phrase 'No shit, Sherlock' surely sprang to mind when hearing that one. It was already known that Joe McLaughlin, Keith Wright and Gordon Hunter were leaving at the campaign's end regardless, as were a number of other players. Some were leaving simply because it was time to move on and because the manager wanted to inject new blood – he had inherited at least ten players aged over 30. There were rumours among the Hibs fans that at least one of the players was leaving because of a long-standing personality clash with the manager; whether true or not and what player that might have been matters not now, almost 25 years later.

Hibernian FC had been sixth in the table when Alex Miller's reign ended back in September. They had still been sixth in the league when caretaker Jocky Scott had left. Jim Duffy had come in and won just three of his 20 matches in charge, four if you include the win on penalties against Aberdeen. It was a dreadful run, but the manager was largely spared any serious criticism because he was working under difficult circumstances, with players signed not only by himself but by two predecessors. The team had also been hampered by injuries and suspensions, but Hibernian actually ended the season with one of the largest first-team squads the club had ever had. Alex Miller's team towards the end had been likewise hampered by injuries and suspensions, yet that team, with a smaller squad, had never been near the bottom two of the league. Hibs fans gritted their teeth and got ready for their heroes to go into two head-to-head survival dogfights against a team Hibbies both hated and rated. Duffy's mix of old heads and new blood would fight the good fight together one last time, as for many of them, no matter the outcome, it would be their last battle while under the Hibernian standard.

Make no mistake; these two encounters were among the most important matches in Hibernian's rich history. Cup finals, title deciders, derbies and European matches are very important, but they're important in a positive way. To lose this tie would have been far from positive; it would have been catastrophic for Hibs and for Edinburgh. Of course, on the odd occasion in the deep past when Hibernian have been relegated after a league season, there have been consequences, but these relegations came from being utter pish for a whole league season, or, if you prefer, the fans saw it coming, kind of like being diagnosed with a chronic illness. In 1997, though, the club's history hinged on just 180 minutes of football, so relegation then would, for the fans and the club, have been more akin to being hit by a bus than being diagnosed with a progressive illness.

The first leg was to be played on Saturday, 17 May at Easter Road. In the world that week, IBM's computer 'Deep Blue' made history by winning a chess match against world champion Garry Kasparov. The New Labour government in the UK banned tobacco advertising in sports, Olive were at number one in the UK charts with a re-release of their 1996 song 'You're Not Alone', while at the flicks the horror thriller *The Relic* and the brilliant comedy *Beavis and Butt Head do America* were among the choices. If you recall the moronic, inane way that the two protagonists in the latter liked to laugh, imagine that laugh now – that's basically what most Scottish football fans at the time were doing at the prospect of Hibs going down. We needed to stay up to save ourselves, but us staying up would see a lot of fans of other clubs with egg on their faces, too, if we managed it. They wouldn't be laughing any more.

When match day came, 15,308 fans were at Easter Road. Jim Duffy called on the old guard for this vital match; Leighton, Hunter, Jackson, Wright and McGinlay as well as returned skipper John Hughes – who hadn't played since December – provided as good a backbone as Hibernian could muster. Dow, too, was an experienced head.

From the kick-off this was a bruising, intense battle of a match. With so much at stake it could scarce have been otherwise. As well as their veteran players, the Diamonds had skilful guys like Paddy Connolly and John Davies and had a decent goalie in Andy Rhodes. Alex MacDonald's team had knocked Hibs out of cups three times in the previous five years and accordingly showed no fear. To survive these matches, Hibernian would need to both outplay and outfight the Lanarkshire side.

After 14 minutes of flying tackles and aggression, ex-Hearts man Gary Mackay scythed down Darren Jackson some 20 yards from goal. As Jacko himself got ready to take the free kick, Hibs fans' heads turned to see big Yogi Hughes running up into the box, looking like a heavyweight boxer. The Hibbies in the stands roared encouragement and the noise level inside the ground intensified. Jacko's free kick went to the back post and was destined for Yogi's head; however, Airdrie striker Steve Cooper saw the danger and leapt to head the ball away first. Cooper's header flew into his own net past Rhodes and Hibernian had a precious 1-0 lead. You could hear the relief among the home fans as they celebrated the goal. The scrap continued until half-time with few further chances for either side.

Airdrie looked a better side in the second half while most of the Hibs team, though committed, seemed to be tired. Hibs should have had a penalty for a Sweeney foul on Jackson, but referee Jim McCluskey wasn't interested. Indeed, he chose to ignore a lot of fouls in the match, seeming to adopt an attitude of 'If you both want to be this dirty, go ahead.' There were still five bookings in the match, though. Davies got away with what looked like a head-butt on Jackson. The second half saw an agitated Jim Duffy and his assistant, Jackie McNamara senior, both bouncing around on the touchline, kicking every ball with their charges. Jim Leighton never had a save to make. Andy Rhodes wasn't very busy, either. With 15 minutes to go and the team clearly tiring, Duffy threw on Lee Power and Barry Lavety. Power should have earned a penalty when he was hacked down in the box but the referee let it go. The introduction of the two big fresh strikers gave the green jerseys a new injection of energy and helped ensure that Hibernian held the lead. The only real downer for Hibs was the sending-off of Gordon Hunter for a second bookable offence. He was a big loss for the second leg; however, he had done all that he could to ensure that his team, for whom he had played for almost 14 years, took a lead into the second leg. It was Gordon's last match for Hibernian, so he went out in style. Hibs' 1-0 win meant half the job was done, but there's many a slip twixt the cup and the lip.

For the second leg on Thursday, 22 May at the Diamonds' temporary home, Broadwood Stadium in Cumbernauld, Jim Duffy made two changes to the line-up from the first leg. Brian Grant was recalled, because of Hunter's suspension. Keith Wright dropped to the bench, replaced by Power, who had looked dangerous against the Diamonds at Easter Road. Tiny Broadwood was packed with 7,560 fans including a relatively vast Hibernian contingent.

Up until this match, there had been two relegation play-offs in Scotland's top flight. In 1995 Aberdeen had retained their top-flight status by hammering Dunfermline over two legs, while a year later, Division One Dundee Utd had won their two-legged tie against premier Partick, relegating the Maryhill men.

This time, Hibernian got off to the worst possible start. Jamie McQuilken's clearance after 90 seconds was controlled by Forbes Johnston, who crossed into the box. Leighton and Hughes suffered a terrible mix-up and Paddy Connolly was on hand to put Airdrie 1-0 up. Hibernian's hard-earned advantage was gone!

After 34 minutes, Brian Welsh handled a Johnston shot in the box and the Diamonds were awarded a penalty – all was going to pot! Up stepped Steve Cooper to take the spot kick. Cooper was out to make amends for his own goal at Easter Road; his penalty gave Airdrie a chance to really bury Hibs. Cooper blasted his spot kick about six yards over the bar, to a huge derisory roar from the Hibs fans and Hibernian were spared. Hibs' best chance in the first half came from Lee Power, but the big striker couldn't get enough power into his shot after good work by Darren Jackson gave him a chance.

Hibernian fans in the stadium at half-time doubtless prayed for divine intervention. As it happened, their prayers were answered just 22 seconds after the restart. Andy Dow passed to McGinlay in the box and the midfield powerhouse was fouled by Jimmy Sandison. The referee gave a penalty and up stepped Darren Jackson to level the match and put Hibs back in front in the tie. Midway through the second half, Davies handled a Tosh cross in the box and referee Young again pointed to the spot. Jackson was just as clinical with the second penalty as the first and Andy Rhodes had no chance. The score was 2-1 to Hibs on the night, 3-1 on aggregate. Three minutes after that, a superb defence-splitting pass by Brian Grant put Paul Tosh through on goal. Tosh burst into the box and pulled the trigger but Rhodes was able to save. The Englishman could only parry, though, and Tosh scored with the rebound. That one move was probably both Grant's and Tosh's best contribution to the Hibernian cause.

That third Hibs goal sent Airdrie heads down, their own play collapsed as did their morale. You could see it in their body language and hear it from their silent fans. Soon afterwards, Sandison elbowed Pat McGinlay in the face and was sent off. Jim Duffy wanted this victory sealed and his team's safety secured so he sent Keith Wright on to replace McGinlay.

While 'new boys' Grant and Tosh had made the third goal, Hibernian's fourth was down to two Alex Miller-era stalwarts. Darren Jackson – Hibernian's star man on the night – crossed for substitute Wright, who headed home in that special way that Keith Wright did. Hibs were 4-1 up on the night, 5-1 up on aggregate. It was fitting that the final goal, which secured Hibernian's safety, was scored by Keith Wright in his last appearance in the green jersey that he so loved. He was a Hibby, his arrival at Easter Road in 1991 had begun the club's on-field revival and won Hibs a cup. Now, with virtually his last touch of the ball before leaving, Keith had ensured the top-flight survival of Hibernian. The Diamonds did score one more goal, Kenny Black converting a last-minute penalty, but it was scored to the sound of Hibernian victory songs and was ultimately futile. Alex MacDonald's men had tried hard in the first leg and for part of the second, but in the end, Hibs had too much ability for them. Hibernian won 4-2 on the night, 5-2 on aggregate, and were saved from relegation. The newer Hibs players had played their part, as had the manager to a degree, but make no mistake, this two-legged tie, tortuous to the fans, was won by Alex Miller's 'old guard' – Hunter, Leighton, Jackson, McGinlay, Wright. These 90s Hibs icons gave their all over the two legs so that Hibernian could survive. They left the field at Broadwood to chants of 'HIBEES, HIBEES, HIBEES'. Before this tie, Airdrie were Hibernian's bogey team. Since then, Hibernian haven't lost a match to any incarnation of that club for 25 years.

The Hibs fans celebrated and rightly so; it was a monumental victory. Though many fans now had concerns about the manager, most accepted that the new boss could only really be judged once he had built his own team. The play-off system wasn't very fair on the lower-league sides, for one reason. The runners-up in the lower division might have played very well all season and perhaps deserved promotion, yet the second-bottom team from the league above might have been absolutely mince all season but then got off their backside at the eleventh hour and started playing well again in the play-off. That's more or less what happened in both the 1995 and 1997 play-offs. Just as well for Hibernian in 1997 that they had some good players who stepped up to the plate when it really mattered. Not long after the play-off win, the author Irvine Welsh joked in a snippet in *Loaded* magazine, 'Having just watched my team avoid relegation following a play-off against Airdrieonians, I'm giving up football. I'm going to be like everybody else and support Manchester United next season'

And so, season 96/97 came to an end. Hibs were safe, Raith Rovers went down, while St Johnstone were promoted from Division One as champions with a record 80 points. Rangers had won the Coca-Cola Cup; Kilmarnock lifted the Scottish Cup, beating Falkirk 1-0 at Ibrox with a goal from that man Paul Wright. Rangers won the league again, equalling Celtic's 'nine in a row' record, and qualified for the Champions League. Killie went into the Cup Winners' Cup, Celtic and Dundee Utd to the UEFA Cup.

Hibernian played 36 league matches in season 96/97, under three managers. Nine were won, 11 drawn and 16 were lost; 38 goals were scored, 55 conceded – that's relegation form. Three of those nine victories were won under Alex Miller, three under Scott and three under Duffy. The 15 matches in all competitions against our 'big three' opponents, Hearts, Celtic and Rangers, had brought one win, two draws and 12 defeats. Both cups had seen the green jerseys eliminated by one half of the old firm.

Darren Jackson, Pat McGinlay and Jim Leighton had been the season's best players by far. Only one would remain at Easter Road after the summer. That would have consequences. In all competitions, Jackson was the season's top scorer with 14, nearest to that total was Keith Wright with six but Keith had missed almost half of the season with injuries. McGinlay had managed eight goals, Kevin Harper got five, Andy Dow scored three, Paul Tosh had two and eight other players scored one goal each. The team's best performances of the season had been in the two matches against Rangers in which Jocky Scott led the team, and in the second leg of the relegation play-off against Airdrie, under Jim Duffy. Low points included the League Cup thrashing at Ibrox, the derby defeat just after it, the New Year derby hammering and that absolute farce at Stark's Park at season's end.

At the end of May, chairman Douglas Cromb stepped down. He'd been at the Hibee helm since 1991 and was a good Hibs man. He had overseen the club's revival, a cup win and the start of Easter Road's transition to modernity. He was replaced as club chairman by director Lex Gold, a man with a wealth of business experience. Gold would be assisted in his new role by a certain Rod Petrie, a merchant banker who was now managing director of Hibs, having come to the club four months earlier. Douglas Cromb remained on the board. Sir Tom Farmer was still our owner.

Big changes came to Hibernian in the summer of 1997. In fact, as the club looked to try something new, there were many changes. Some were off-field, some were on-field. By far the biggest news was all the departures. Some players would turn out to be irreplaceable, others would not.

Jim Leighton left Hibernian to rejoin the team where he made his name, Aberdeen. Aged 35 when he joined Hibernian in 1993, Jim made 178 appearances, missing just one match in four seasons. He came to us at a time when we needed an experienced goalie and he needed a chance to revitalise his career, so, it worked out well for Jim and for Hibs. Countless times his heroics were the difference between one point and three, between a loss and a hammering and between ignominy and pride. As Hibs fans, we were blessed in the 80s and 90s to have had such fine goalkeepers. His greatest performances for Hibernian were probably a choice between the April 95 defeat at Ibrox, or the quarter-final at Firhill and semi-final at Tynecastle in 1993's League Cup, though there are literally too many great performances to choose from. Jim also regained the Scotland number one jersey while at Hibs and went on to play in all three matches at World Cup France 98, thus fulfilling the Hibbies' 'Scotland's number one' chant.

Darren Jackson was transferred to Celtic in a deal, said to be worth around £1.2m, in the summer of 1997. He ended up as part of the legendary Celtic team which stopped Rangers winning ten titles in a row and he was also a vital part of Scotland's 1998 World Cup team, famously playing Brazil's Dunga off the park in the tournament's opening match. At Hibernian, Darren just got better with every passing season after his transfer from Dundee Utd in 1992. In his first season in the green Jacko was as famous for being caught offside and for getting booked for dissent as he was for scoring goals, but as time went on, he matured and became very much the beating heart of the Hibs team until his departure. He was often played in a deeper role between 1995 and 1997 and this made him into an even better player. Jacko became a Scotland player while at Hibs and is a 90s icon to Hibs fans. Back in the day, he was the man opposition fans loved to hate and that just made us love him more. He got stick from us when later he played against us for other clubs, but remember that old saying, 'You cannot hate someone you first did not love,' and we never *really* hated him when he left, anyway. Jacko wore Hibernian green 206 times and scored 59 goals, 14 of which were spot kicks. We fondly remember his days in the green, that collar sticking up, the net bulging, and that iconic chant: 'Ooh ah Jacksona, say, ooh ah Jacksona!'

With a World Cup to come in 12 months' time, it was easy to see why Jackson and Leighton may have felt that they stood a better chance of featuring for Scotland at the finals if they were at clubs who were doing better; for Jacko it would be his first World Cup, for Leighton it would be his fourth and last.

Keith Wright's time at Hibernian ended in the summer of 1997, aged 32, when he moved across the Forth to join Raith Rovers, as part of the deal which brought Raith's Trinidad and Tobago winger Tony Rougier to Easter Road. Keith had of course joined Hibs from Dundee for £500,000 in the summer of 1991 and his goals had helped to revitalise Hibernian. He scored in every round of our 1991 SKOL League Cup-winning campaign and was an excellent foil for Darren Jackson when the two teamed up one year later. Keith is a Hibby and the fans loved him, not just because of his goals, but also because he played with a smile on his face and always gave 100 per cent – even in matches where the team struggled. He did gain one international cap while at Hibs, in a friendly against Northern Ireland at Hampden. Strong, skilful, fast and good in the air, Keith was probably our last great old-school number nine. Like Jackson and Leighton, he is a Hibernian legend and proved impossible to replace. Keith made 234 appearances for Hibs, scoring 76 goals. Also, like Jackson and Leighton, he gave all to the Hibernian cause until his very last match.

Midfielder Ian Cameron also joined Raith Rovers in the summer of 1997. He was a talented player but came to Hibs at the wrong time. He'd played 22 times in the green jersey. Andy Millen headed for Stark's Park that summer, too. Andy never played for Hibernian again after his red card in the 1997 New Year derby. He had played 60 times in just over two years at Easter Road and had been a useful signing due to his adaptability, able to play almost any position. He kept playing top-level football in Scotland until the age of 41 and is seen as being a model professional footballer. Ray Wilkins had left Hibs in January 1997 and retired from playing almost immediately. He had a long and successful coaching career, most notably at Chelsea. He sadly died from an illness in 2018.

Mickey Weir was another big name to have left Easter Road since the change of manager. Michael played for Hibs 247 times in a career spanning 14 seasons in total – with a short stint at Luton Town in 1987 the only wee break in his service. He scored 35 goals in that illustrious career and probably created 100 more. An old-school style Scottish winger, quick, skilful, intelligent and fierce, his best performances in the green jersey probably came in 1991 when he played like a man possessed to help Hibs win the SKOL League Cup. Mickey would have more Hibs appearances to his name were it not for injuries which limited his career; in fact, he often played through the pain barrier for Hibernian. A true Hibernian great, Mickey joined Motherwell in 1997.

Another winger that left Easter Road in early 1997 was Kevin McAllister, rejoining Falkirk. 'Crunchie' had played for Hibs 126 times in three and a half seasons, scoring 15 goals and setting up countless others. Like Weir, he was one of those Jimmy Johnstone-style wingers who possessed the type of natural footballing talent which just can't be taught. There's an old Hibby fan folklore story that Kevin asked for a transfer just six weeks after joining Hibs in 1993, because he felt that the boss was trying to make him into a wing-back! Whether true or not, he stayed and was one of Hibernian's best players in the mid 90s.

Brian Grant would remain at Easter Road until early 1998 but made only one further start for Hibernian and five substitute appearances before leaving to join Dundee. He made 24 appearances for Hibs in total. Rab Shannon's Hibs career was ruined by injury and he missed the whole of season 97/98 and played just one match in 98/99 before moving to Australia to play for Newcastle Breakers.

Another Australia-bound player was club legend Gordon Hunter. Geebsy had been at Easter Road for 14 seasons in which he had played 409 matches, scored eight goals, been sent off five times, won one cup, played in two more cup finals and wore the green in Europe. Like Mickey Weir, he had been first blooded by manager Pat Stanton back in 1983 and had seen it all at Easter Road. Tough in the tackle, quick over short distances and good in the air, he would, like so many others, prove very difficult to replace. Gordon left to join Canberra Cosmos. He's best remembered for his derby winner at Tynecastle in 1994. Once Geebsy left, there were no players left at Hibernian who'd been there before Alex Miller's arrival in 1986.

Jamie McQuilken only played one match for Hibernian the following season, leaving to join Falkirk, having played for Hibs just 13 times. Graeme Love also moved on, joining Ayr United, with 41 first-team appearances to his name for the Cabbage.

Gone, too, was big Joe McLaughlin, with 20 Hibs appearances under his belt. He went to Clydebank.

Youngster Paul Riley completed the exodus from the first-team squad, joining Brechin City.

So, having lost half a team at the end of season 95/96, virtually another whole team's worth of players had departed by the summer of 1997. Jim Duffy now had a summer in which to rebuild his team. There was no blank canvas. He would use a combination of free transfers and traditional deals to supplement the squad of players that remained at the club, though his only real 'old heads' were Pat McGinlay and Willie Miller – much would be expected of those two in the next campaign, probably too much, with hindsight.

However, the summer of 1997 would see a radical shake-up of Hibernian FC on the pitch. Jim Duffy built his team to play up-tempo attacking, cavalier football, passing through the middle, racing down the flanks – that's what we as Hibs fans craved and had asked him to do, even though that wasn't really his preferred managerial style. To that end he would add players that he thought would fit into that new attacking philosophy. There's a story that Jim even went as far as to break Hibernian's traditional links with various youth football clubs in the Lothians, in favour of his own preferred scouting networks. Mr Duffy certainly wasn't a shrinking violet and was going to do his utmost to mould a new Hibernian, an attacking Hibs team which could wow the fans and which would top the table, unlike anything Hibs fans had seen since the 1970s. So, did he manage it? The answer is, actually, yes, for a time, he did.

There's a storm outside
And the gap between crack and thunder
Crack and thunder
Is closing in
Is closing in …

BITTER VIRTUE – SEASON 97/98

'Hibernian, Hibernian, ra ra ra, Hibernian, Hibernian, ra ra ra …'

THE SUMMER of 1997 saw the UK bask in sunshine and in optimism, as the New Labour government began to tackle issues like poverty, unemployment, NHS and school underfunding and peace in Ireland. A referendum loomed in Scotland, one which would ask Scots if they wanted to have their own parliament restored. For many, it was a time when anything seemed possible, a new beginning.

J.K. Rowling's first Harry Potter book *The Philosopher's Stone* had just been published. The UK had just handed back control of a small piece of land it had seized from China over a century earlier, that land being the territory of Hong Kong. Scientists had finally confirmed that all of humanity was of African descent, and the fashion guru Gianni Versace had just been shot dead. As the new football season loomed, 'I'll Be Missing You' by Puff Daddy & Faith Evans topped the singles charts, while many Britpop fans eagerly awaited the imminent release of the third album by indie rockers Oasis, entitled *Be Here Now.* Cinema-goers were going mad for Will Smith and Tommy Lee Jones in *Men in Black*.

In football, a number of English teams left their historic home grounds for new stadiums. Sunderland went from Roker Park to the Stadium of Light, Derby County swapped the Baseball Ground for Pride Park, while Bolton Wanderers were about to leave Burnden Park for their new home, The Reebok Stadium. In Scotland, the coming Scottish Premier Division title race would see Walter Smith's multimillion pound Rangers team try to make it to ten titles in a row, while a 'not as rich as Rangers but richer than every other team' Celtic, under new boss Wim Jansen and his assistant Murdo MacLeod, would do what they could to prevent Rangers reaching that milestone. That title race would dominate the media coverage of the season like never before. It would, however, be the last 'Premier Division' title race, as plans for Scotland's top clubs to resign from the SFL and set up their own money-spinning breakaway top flight, the SPL, were well underway – copying what England's top clubs had done in 1992 when they formed the Premiership.

At Easter Road, the first big announcement of the summer wasn't a new player arriving, it was a media deal. Hibs chairman Lex Gold announced a deal with SMG to show 30-minute 'Hibs Club Programmes' at Easter Road prior to matches. The shows, dubbed 'electronic fanzines', would also be shown on the doomed Sky Scottish channel, which was available on Telewest cable and Sky TV. They were presented by Peter Martin.

Jim Duffy needed to add to the squad. One signing target was said (by the press) to be Bolton's Finnish striker Mixu Paatelainen, but Hibs were *supposedly* priced out of the deal. The manager felt that many clubs and agents knew that Hibs had money to spend and were thus inflating their asking prices accordingly and he actually had a good point. In dire need of a replacement for Darren Jackson, the boss signed Millwall striker Stevie Crawford. The 23-year-old forward was still a hot youth prospect and had bagged 12 goals in 42 appearances for the Lions in England's third tier. Hibs paid £400,000 to bring him from The Den to Easter Road. He had won the Coca-Cola Cup and played in the UEFA Cup while at Raith Rovers prior to his move south. Much was expected from that young man in his first season at Easter Road. One of his old team-mates from Raith, Tony Rougier, was also now a Hibee, having come to Leith as part of the deal that took Keith Wright the other way. Rougier, 26, was a skilful winger with natural talent, just the sort of player Jim Duffy wanted. The big Trinidad and Tobago man had impressed against Hibs for Raith on several occasions. He wasn't exactly noted for his defensive qualities, but in the new Hibernian era, that wasn't an issue. To quote one excited Hibs fan early in Rougier's Hibs stint, 'He just needs to look at a full-back and they shite themselves.' Hibs also had former Metz striker Stephane Adam on trial in pre-season, but the player joined Hearts instead. Though the striker would make history in Gorgie, he ended up rinsing Hearts for hundreds of thousands of pounds in inflated wages, too. However, Hibs losing out on the player to Hearts at the time brought much mirth to the Jambos and kind of put down an early marker for the two clubs' widely contrasting seasons ahead.

The defence may not have been the manager's priority but he still tried to strengthen it, bringing in veteran defender Jean-Marc Adjovi-Bocco from French side Lens. The player was almost 34 years old but must have had something to offer as Hibs had been in competition with Kilmarnock and Motherwell to get his signature. He had made nearly 200 appearances for Lens in a six-year career there so was an experienced pro. Though right-footed, he preferred to play left-back or left centre-back. The African from Benin would achieve cult-hero status at Hibernian, though mostly for his flamboyant appearance and for being a genuinely nice guy, not for his footballing prowess. Jim Duffy also tried to get youngster Grant Brebner from Man Utd, but the move didn't happen then.

With Jim Leighton gone, many Hibs fans felt that it was time to give Chris Reid a real chance with the number one jersey. Chris was a product of our excellent youth development system and was a good goalie, but his chances at Easter Road had been limited due to the presence of Andy Goram and Jim Leighton in front of him in the pecking order. By the summer of 1997 'young Chris Reid' was actually 26 years old and had been Hibernian's backup goalie since he first deputised for Andy Goram in December 1989. To be a backup goalie for so long back then was no sign of failure, like it is today. Guys like Les Fridge, Cammy Duncan, Colin Scott, Alan McKnight and Michael Watt were all good goalies. The case for Chris Reid being Hibernian's number one for the 1997/98 season was a strong one. After over eight years of learning under Goram, Burridge and Leighton, now was the time for Chris Reid to make that number one shirt his own. The apprentice who had learned from the best was due a proper chance to show what he could do. He at least deserved that. He even played in the pre-season games.

Instead, at the last minute before the season began, the manager signed an unknown goalkeeper from Iceland for £200,000. He was a big name, but only in the sense that his name contained a lot of letters. Olafur Gottskalksson, 29, was a backup goalie for Iceland's national side and arrived from Keflavik, though he had played for a few of Iceland's top clubs. He was 6ft 3in and said to be a good shot-stopper

– that's always been a puzzling description of goalies: have you ever heard of a successful goalie that isn't that great at stopping shots? No matter.

These new signings supplemented the players Duffy had inherited from the previous managers and his own signings from the previous campaign. The new-look side would play a number of pre-season matches.

Mourneview Park in Lurgan was the Hibees' first destination, where they hammered Glenavon 6-0. Rougier scored twice, John Hughes got one while the old manager's son Greg Miller scored a stunning hat-trick. Portadown were then beaten 2-1, Pat McGinlay bagging a brace. Dungavan Swifts were annihilated 6-0 and Ards were beaten 3-0. Having toured Ireland undefeated, the Hibees then headed to the highlands, where Keith were beaten 4-2, goals coming from Scott Bannerman, Greg Miller and a brace from Lee Power. A weaker Hibs XI – which included youngsters Kenny Miller and Tom McManus and had coach Tom McAdam in the dugout – was thumped 5-0 by Peterhead at what was supposed to be the last match at Peterhead's Recreation Park. That last match aside, pre-season for Duffy's new-look Hibs was going extremely well.

Monday, 28 July brought Gordon Strachan's Coventry City side to Easter Road for the traditional home friendly against a top English team, and top they certainly were. The English Premiership side dominated the match and limited Hibernian's attacks to a few long-range efforts which never really troubled their goalie, Steve Ogrizovic. The Sky Blues won the match 2-0 thanks to two second-half goals, one from future *Homes Under the Hammer* presenter Dion Dublin, the other from the superb winger John Salako.

Sunday, 3 August amid glorious sunshine saw Hibernian's new campaign begin in earnest with a home match against

Celtic. The match was live on TV and the visitors wore a horrid bumble-bee type kit. All of the new signings were pitched in by Jim Duffy, including the new goalie. From the start, Hibernian moved and passed the ball well; it seemed that the lack of invention which had plagued the team in the previous campaign was gone. After 24 minutes, Rougier got the better of Alan Stubbs and crossed low into the box, where big Lee Power was waiting to shoot the Hibees into the lead: 1-0.

The lead lasted just three minutes, as Malky Mackay bundled home a Simon Donnelly cross at the other end to level the match. A few minutes later, Chic Charnley, putting in possibly the best performance of his career, unleashed a shot from 30 yards which beat Gordon Marshall but then rattled the junction of the post and the bar. It was 1-1 at half-time. Celtic's new signing from Feyenoord, an attacking midfielder named Henrik Larsson, replaced Andy Thom after 57 minutes and made an immediate impact. With 25 minutes to go, Stevie Crawford was unlucky not to score, his shot hitting the post. Hibs were by far the better team and wanted the victory. At the other end, Darren Jackson had a goal-bound shot cleared off the line by Brian Welsh, to jeers from the Hibs fans. Just 15 minutes from the end, new-boy Larsson misplaced a pass and the ball fell to Chic Charnley 20 yards from goal. The by-then 34-year-old unleashed an unstoppable drive to put Hibs 2-1 up and that's how the match ended. The fans chanted, 'CHICO, CHICO, CHICO.' All of Hibernian's new signings played well, while the not-so-new boys were also terrific. McGinlay and Charnley dominated the midfield, fans could even hear Charnley shouting 'Here, here', the veteran demanding the ball throughout the match and playing with a smile on his face. Hibs had secured a fine opening-day win, and their first victory over Celtic at Easter Road since April 1993. Every Hibs fan left that stadium with a smile on their face; it was a big win and no mistake. It brought such optimism to the Hibs faithful. That embarrassing perilous relegation play-off against Airdrie just three months earlier seemed like an age ago. Jim Duffy and Hibs rightly received plaudits for the victory. Hibs fans were happy again.

The following Saturday in the Coca-Cola Cup, Hibs faced Alloa at Easter Road. Once again, the free-flowing expansive football of Hibs was a joy to behold and once more McGinlay and Charnley dominated the midfield. Hibs went 1-0 up after nine minutes with a superb dribbling solo effort by Barry Lavety. After 29 minutes, going down the slope, Chic Charnley took a shot from around 60 yards which beat Wasps' goalie Mike Monaghan to put Hibs 2-0 up. Sadly, there were no cameras at this game so Chic's goal from his own half has been lost to all but those who were there. A vintage McGinlay volley of an inventive Crawford back-heel just after half-time put Hibs 3-0 up and on easy street. Alloa's veteran striker Willie Irvine – scorer of a hat-trick for Hibs against Chelsea in 1986 – pulled one back for Tommy Hendrie's men late on, after a bungle by Gottskalksson, but it mattered not, Hibs won 3-1 and were through. It had been a dazzling display of brilliance from the green jerseys.

Two matches against Dundee Utd at Tannadice followed, the first in the league, the second in the 'Cola' League Cup. On Sunday, 17 August, the Terrors led Hibs 1-0 at the break thanks to a Robbie Winters goal. Hibs had still been playing very well and had looked dangerous through Power, Harper and Charnley. After 66 minutes Hibs got a lucky break when Maurice Malpas was red-carded for a foul on Jimmy Boco. It seemed harsh to both sides, but off he went. Hibs turned the screw and got an equaliser through Paul Tosh and would have won the match but for some heroics by Sieb Dijkstra in the United goal. It ended 1-1. Tosh's equaliser was a rare type of goal – one which came from an indirect free kick resulting from an opposition back pass to the goalie.

Three days later in the Coca-Cola Cup, the teams faced off once more. Barry Lavety's fine 20-yard shot gave Hibs the lead inside two minutes and once more Hibs looked a confident, swaggering side. Gottskalksson was away on international duty so Chris Reid deputised and managed to keep Dundee Utd out until the 88th minute, when Lars Zetterlund equalised to send the tie into extra time. Reid made a mistake early in the first period of extra time, allowing a 35-yarder from Gary McSwegan to beat him, so the tie ended Dundee Utd 2 Hibs 1. Chic Charnley had blasted a penalty high and wide just four minutes after McSwegan's goal. Hibs were out, somewhat unfortunately.

Any thought of a cup-exit hangover was banished on the Saturday, as Hibs demolished Kilmarnock 4-0 at Easter Road. Killie had Ray Montgomerie sent off. Goals came from Crawford, Lavety, Willie Miller (via a deflection) and a peach from Pat McGinlay, scored from around two yards closer to goal than Charnley's one against Alloa in the cup, and also scored down the slope. Charnley and Pat even had a wee debate after the strike, Chico leading Pat back to the spot where he had scored from to show him the difference. That fantastic long-ranger from Pat *was* caught by the cameras. Once again in that match, Hibernian's football was beautiful: fearless, skilful, attacking, dangerous. The win put Hibs top of the league, a point above Rangers. Suddenly, the media was full of talk about Hibs winning the title. There was even talk of Chic Charnley being called up to the Scotland squad! Jim Duffy's revolution seemed in full swing. Next up was the season's first Edinburgh derby.

Hearts were mid-table when they came to Easter Road on Saturday, 30 August and 15,565 fans came along. All week long, the papers had been full of glowing articles about Hibs, about Charnley and about how Hibs were *really* going to give it to Hearts, this time. Jim Jefferies sent his team out to stop Hibs and they actually found it rather easy. Hearts man-marked Chico and neutralised him, and Hibs had no response to that. Hearts won the rather dull encounter 1-0 thanks to a clever chip from Neil McCann. The most exciting aspect of the match was a touchline 'handbags' incident between Jackie McNamara and Hearts' assistant boss Billy Brown. Not for the first or last time, a good Hibs team had fallen flat on its face in a local derby, but the loss wasn't the end of the world – Hibs still topped the table. That derby was supposed to have been at Tynecastle, as the first derby of the previous season had been played at Easter Road, but the clubs sensibly agreed to swap the venues for the season's first two derbies around, so that Hearts' new stand at the Gorgie Road end would be ready in time.

At Hibs' next home match on Saturday, 13 September against Dunfermline – which was a top-of-the-table encounter as the Pars were joint top with Hibs on seven points – Chic Charnley and his fellow green jerseys ran riot, bagging five goals, Charnley with two, Crawford, Lavety and McGinlay getting the others. The Pars had led 1-0 through a Millar penalty and scored the match's last goal through Stewart Petrie, but those goals were an irrelevance, scored because Hibs were too busy attacking. Hibs won 5-2. Here, Duffy's Hibs team reached its high-water mark, its perfection, its zenith, even. Leaving aside the goalie, we had Jimmy Boco confidently spraying out passes from the back, we had Tony Rougier playing in a free role, terrorising defences, we had the two young strikers Lavety and Crawford getting on the end of things, Dow looked inventive and hard-working, the defence was okay and in the middle we had Chic Charnley and Pat McGinlay playing like two best pals in a kickabout at the height of summer. There was swagger, there was skill, there was hard work, and there was even some genius. The Hibs team of late summer and early autumn 1997 was often a joy to watch and it excited the fans, got some memorable results and rightly was widely acclaimed at the time. It gave Hibs fans the feel-good factor and made us proud of our team again. For that brief Indian summer, Hibernian FC was reborn, like a beautiful green and white butterfly, emerging from the chrysalis of monotony, playing confident, swaggering entertaining football. For a good few weeks, we as Hibs fans admired that butterfly. Of course, there's one sad thing about all butterflies – they don't last for very long …

Hibernian's next two matches both brought 1-1 draws. Tony Rougier scored in a share of the spoils at Fir Park, while Stevie Crawford was on target a week later against St Johnstone at Easter Road. Hibs weren't quite as good in those two matches but still looked a decent outfit. Over 10,000 fans were at the home matches against St Johnstone and Dunfermline, which shows just how reinvigorated the team and the support was. Little did we know that our 5-2 win over Dunfermline in September would be our last victory for four months.

Jim Duffy's brilliant Hibs team disappeared during a match on Saturday, 4 October 1997 against Rangers at Easter Road and was never seen again. Prior to this match Hibs had slipped to third in the table, two points behind Rangers in second and three behind league leaders Hearts.

Pat McGinlay gave Hibs the lead after 29 minutes but the Gers equalised through Negri. Barry Lavety gave the green legions more to cheer about before the interval, at which point Hibs led 2-1. Stevie Crawford headed Hibs 3-1 in front just after the restart and put the Hibbies into dreamland; it seemed that anything was possible. The green jerseys had the champions at their mercy, but then it all turned on one bad decision. Pat McGinlay was on the attack for Hibs again after 50 minutes when he was bundled to the ground by Gascoigne right in front of referee Bobby Tait. The referee, said by some to be a Rangers fan, did nothing and Rangers charged forward and immediately earned a free kick, from which Gascoigne scored. Albertz and Negri scored another two in the next seven minutes to put Rangers 4-3 up and that's how it ended. Hibs fans couldn't believe that they had lost this match; neither could the players, or the manager. The defeat, snatched from the jaws of a great victory, was a psychological blow from which that group of players never recovered and was a reality check which showed the Hibs faithful that maybe season 97/98 wasn't going to be so easy after all.

Before that 4-3 win over Hibs, Rangers had just been eliminated from the UEFA Cup by Strasbourg, losing 2-4 on aggregate. Strasbourg's team had included Freddy Arpinon and David Zitelli. The latter had scored the goal at Ibrox which had sealed Rangers' exit. The Gers had already been knocked out of the Champions League in the qualifiers by IFK Gothenburg that season. In the Cup Winners' Cup, Kilmarnock had overcome Irish side Shelbourne but had then been eliminated by Nice. In the UEFA Cup qualifying round, Celtic won 8-0 on aggregate against Welsh side Inter Cabletel FC, while Dundee Utd racked up an extraordinary 17-0 win on aggregate against Andorran side Principat.

United lost in the next round to Trabzonspor while Celtic went one round further, overcoming Tirol Innsbruck before being eliminated by Liverpool on away goals.

Sunday, 12 October brought some relief from the domestic agenda, as Hibs were the guests at Tynecastle for Craig Levein's second testimonial match. Over 8,500 fans came along, dwarfing the fewer than 3,000 figure that had turned out for his first one two years earlier. It cost £10 for adults, £2.50 for concessions. Both sides fielded reasonably strong teams, Hibs also had John Collins, John Leslie and Kevin McKee in the squad. The Hibees won the match 1-0, thanks to a late goal by a young fella named Andy Newman. That match was actually shown live on the old analogue 'Edinburgh L!VE' cable channel, which thus added an Edinburgh derby to its impressive array of programmes, which also included quality shows such as *Topless Darts*, *Strip Mastermind*, *What's In The Box* and *Spanish Archer*. John Collins received a standing ovation from both sets of fans during that match, as the day before at Celtic Park he had been outstanding in Scotland's 2-0 win over Latvia, which had secured Scotland's place at the 1998 World Cup.

* * *

League action resumed, and it was time to see how much damage the Rangers defeat had done to the confidence of Jim Duffy's Hibs. Saturday, 18 October brought a trip to Pittodrie and a 0-2 reverse. The following week the Hibees were in Ayrshire, losing 2-1 to Bobby Williamson's Kilmarnock. New signing Bjarni Larusson, a 21-year-old Icelandic midfielder who would only ever play for Hibs seven times, was on target in the Rugby Park defeat, a match in which Kevin Harper was red-carded. A week later Dundee Utd came to Easter Road and spanked the Cabbage

3-1, Stevie Crawford netting the green jerseys' consolation. In those three defeats a worrying pattern emerged in Hibernian's displays, as the other teams in the league had clearly sussed out how to stop Hibs and Charnley. Hibs would start brightly, then disintegrate, with performances characterised by bad luck, poor defending, goalkeeping errors and misfiring strikers – all the ingredients required for relegation.

The Edinburgh derby on 8 November at Tynecastle was the first big derby where Hibs fans occupied the new Roseburn Stand at the old School End. A crowd of 16,739 was there. The Hibees did put up more of a fight in this match than in their previous three but ultimately got the same thing from the match – nothing. High-flying Hearts won 2-0 with a goal in each half, Robertson in the first, Jose Quitongo in the second. A week later Stevie Crawford scored again but it was to no avail as the Hibees went down 2-1 to Dunfermline at East End Park, having Willie Miller sent off. A grim 1-0 defeat away to St Johnstone was next.

That run of seven consecutive defeats left Hibs joint second bottom on 12 points with Motherwell, Hibs being four goals better off than the Steelmen. Aberdeen were bottom with 11 points. Hibs did look to be back to winning ways on Saturday, 29 November against Motherwell in Edinburgh. They led through a Darren Dods goal until the last minute, when Gottskalksson made an error which gifted Owen Coyle a goal and Motherwell a precious point. After his many errors, Jim Duffy finally dropped Gottskalksson after his Motherwell howler and put Chris Reid in goal. The defence became less nervous but was still poor. It's a shame that Chris had to wait until the team was at rock bottom before he really got his chance.

Sunday, 7 December brought a trip to Ibrox and an expected thrashing for the men in green. The thrashing didn't materialise, though the Hibees still lost 1-0. Chris Reid's heroics prevented another Ibrox mauling for Hibs, though on the whole the team did play fairly well that day. The only good news for Hibs fans in late 1997 came when Pat McGinlay signed a new three-year deal. He had been out of contract and had been signing monthly deals. He'd been offered lucrative contracts by Rennes, Metz and Strasbourg but in the end decided to remain at the club he cherished.

Jim Duffy was desperate for a striker who would score goals. So desperate, in fact, that he had 17-year-old Kenny Miller on the bench for a couple of games and even gave him his debut. A more immediate solution arrived in the shape of veteran striker Andy Walker, who came in on loan from Sheffield United. The 32-year-old had been a prolific goalscorer both at Celtic and at Bolton Wanderers and it was hoped that his goals would have an immediate impact and fire Hibs back up the table. His Hibs career got off to the best possible start at Easter Road on Saturday, 13 December, as he scored a brace in a 2-2 draw against Aberdeen. A week later Hibs were thrashed 5-0 at Celtic Park and then, on the day after Boxing Day, Duffy's men ended the calendar year with a pathetic 0-1 loss at home to Kilmarnock. There's a story, not just fan folklore as it also made it into *The Herald*, that hardly any Hibs first-team players bothered going to the club's annual Christmas party in 1997, and that the reason was that, sometime in December, an understandably frustrated Jim Duffy inadvertently let it be known that everybody except Stevie Crawford was available for transfer. The manager had supposedly circulated a list of his 'for sale' players to other top Scottish managers via agents, and some

Hibs players found out. If the story is true, one can see how it might have unsettled and annoyed the players. It sounds similar to what Malpas and Butcher supposedly said to the Hibs squad in 2014 – that didn't work out well at all, did it? If it isn't true, then file it under 'nonsense Hibs stories from Glaswegian papers' along with 'Joel Cantona for Hibs' and 'Hibs hire witch doctor to break derby hoodoo', and move on. That's football.

It seems possible that by the end of 1997 there may have been tensions between some players and the boss, or just tensions in general because things weren't going well. Whether there were tensions or not, the boss really should have been sacked before Christmas, with the benefit of hindsight. Hibernian ended 1997 as bottom side in the table, with Aberdeen above them, two points better off. The Leith men didn't have to wait long for their next big test, the New Year derby. Hearts were flying high, real title challengers sitting second in the table, just two points behind leaders Rangers. Papers talked a lot that week about how this might finally be Hearts' chance to score seven goals in the fixture, while commentators and pundits predicted another easy derby win for the maroon side of Edinburgh. To be blunt, at the time, Hibs were shite while Hearts were really good – there was only going to be one outcome – or was there?

If there was friction between the players and the manager, they put it aside for the sake of the fans when they faced Hearts on Thursday, 1 January 1998. If there wasn't friction, the team simply got its act together. At first it looked as if the media's predictions would come true, as Hearts were 2-0 up in just ten minutes, Steve Fulton bagging both goals in a first half where Hearts were the better side. Chris Reid kept the score down. The 17,564 fans crammed into the new-look Tynecastle saw a very different second half, as the green jerseys, far from resorting to damage limitation, came out fighting. Andy Walker pulled one back after 51 minutes and then Pat McGinlay scored the equaliser with 23 minutes remaining. After that, the Hibs fans goaded Hearts' goalscorer Steve Fulton for much of the match's remainder, with that famous Edinburgh derby chant about his striking appearance, all meant in jest, of course. 'So fuckin' ugly, oh you are so fuckin' ugly, so fuckin' ugly' to the tune of 'Guantanamera', the Cuban revolution anthem, originally written by the wonderful poet, philosopher and revolutionary, Jose Marti. The tune is probably one of the most sung ditties at football of the last 50 years. The Fulton song remained a fixture of the derby as long as Fulton was at Hearts. Hibs fans would chant it for long periods, even when we were losing. Eventually, in August 1999, Fulton was booked at Easter Road for reacting to the chant and it was changed to 'Booked for being ugly, you've just been booked for being ugly!' The Hibbies' taunting of Fulton actually had its roots in our 1989 Scottish Cup semi-final mauling by Celtic at Hampden. They ragged-dolled us 3-1 that day and their teenage winger Steve Fulton destroyed our defence in the first half with his pace and skill – Hibbies didn't forget that. Fulton – nicknamed 'Baggio' by the Jambos as he was actually quite good – was never a dirty player; indeed, his only booking in the derby was the one in 1999 that we just looked at.

Hearts fans that had turned up expecting a cricket score left the stadium with egg on their faces, while Hibs fans in the stadium were elated. Maybe this superb fightback would turn around their season? The draw kept Hibs bottom but narrowed the gap between Hibs and Aberdeen to one point, while at the other end, Hearts went down to third, their dropping of two points saw them leapfrogged by Celtic. Was this 2-2 draw against Hearts a good result for Hibs? In the short term, as in the week after the match, yes it was, as there'd be no slaggings from Jambos when the fans went back to school/work after the festive holidays. Longer term? To this day most Hibs fans agree that while it was good to avoid defeat in the derby with such a spirited fightback, the draw probably bought the failing manager a reprieve, giving him an extra few weeks to turn things around, or if you prefer, a few more weeks in which Hibernian would struggle, with ultimately dire consequences.

Hibernian had gone 15 matches and four months without a victory of any kind when Bert Paton's Dunfermline came to Easter Road on Saturday, 10 January. Such a woeful run wouldn't curse Hibs again until the reign of Terry Butcher in 2014. Hibs did stop the rot that day, albeit temporarily, winning 1-0 with a Stevie Crawford goal. There were more than 10,000 at that match. Almost unbelievably, the fans didn't abandon the team in any great numbers. Just fewer than 10,000 were at Easter Road a week later as the Hibees were again defeated, losing 0-1 to St Johnstone. On 22 January Billy McNeill was appointed as director of football at Hibernian FC. The legendary ex-Celtic player and manager was brought in at Jim Duffy's request so that Duffy could concentrate fully on the first team. The appointment was seen as quite a coup, though, by then, many fans had already had enough of the manager, and the boss himself had even joked in media interviews that his coat was 'on a shoogly peg'.

The Scottish Cup offered Hibernian an opportunity to escape from their depressing league campaign. Raith Rovers came to Easter Road for round three on Saturday, 24 January and turned things from bad to worse for Hibs, the manager and the fans. One might ponder what Billy McNeill made of his first sight of the team he was supposed to help. It was barely a team. At one point, Darren Dods and Willie Miller squared up to each other on the pitch. Dods was red-carded in the match. The green jerseys were woeful, lacking invention, effort and passion. Raith Rovers had all three of those qualities and won the match 2-1, ex-Jambo John Millar getting both Raith goals. One wonders what Keith Wright, wearing the yellow and blue of Raith on the pitch, thought of the green and white shambles around him. Pat McGinlay scored a fine goal in the match, for what it's worth. Hibs were out. Jim Duffy's time was running out, too.

Duffy is a good manager and a good football person who came to a massive club and tried to do something different. It didn't work; that's football. Nobody ever doubted his commitment, his passion or his genuine desire for Hibernian to do well. His Easter Road odyssey came to an end after Hibs were destroyed 6-2 by Motherwell at Fir Park on the last day of January 1998. Almost typically, Hibs had raced into an early lead with goals from Lavety and Crawford, only to be pegged back to 2-2 by half-time, then bulldozed with a further four goals in the second half. Hibernian simply crumbled. Brian Welsh was sent off but that really made no difference. Ironically, one of Well's goals was scored by none other than Mickey Weir. One newspaper headline the next day simply read 'NEXT STOP BOGHEAD'. (For younger readers, that was Dumbarton's old stadium.)

Jim Duffy was sacked after that defeat. He'd led Hibs for 26 matches that season, just five had been won. His overall Hibernian statistics were poor: 48 games managed, ten won, 15 drawn, 23 lost.

Here's how our 97/98 campaign fell apart.

The goalkeeper, Ole Gottskalksson, had a poor first season. He only kept one solitary clean sheet, he made costly errors which cost Hibs points and he seemed to make the defence nervous. One joke often cracked by both Hibs and Hearts fans during season 97/98 went like this: 'Hibs got a goalie from Iceland; they'd have been better off trying ASDA or Tesco!' Chic Charnley's form nosedived after the 3-4 defeat by Rangers and he never recovered it, although, this was partly because, after Hibs had played every team once, they all knew how to stop him second time around.

Jimmy Boco, for all his flamboyance and likability, was a liability for much of the season, often playing opposition players onside and being caught ball-watching at crucial moments, again, costing the team goals and points.

The two main strikers Lavety and Crawford did well to get nine apiece in all competitions by season's end, despite being starved of service, but, in all honesty, Crawford was no Darren Jackson, and Basher, try as he might, was no Keith Wright.

Andy Dow had tried his best, while the only players that really didn't let the fans down were Willie Miller, Pat McGinlay and Darren Dods. Three men can't keep a team up. Our injury problems in central defence didn't help, either.

The simple truth was and is – Hibernian signed a large number of Division One standard players in the year 1997, so, it's not surprising that Division One was exactly where the club was heading.

Live in awe
Love your life
It's yours to live
Regret forgive
Make more mistakes
Regret forgive
Accept everything

LA PETITE MORT (GONE BABY GONE)

'Hibernia, we are the Hibs of Edinburgh …'

BILLY MCNEILL took interim charge of the team for the first match after Jim Duffy was sacked, a 0-3 capitulation against Aberdeen at Pittodrie. Chic Charnley made his last appearance for Hibs in the match, coming off the bench. That defeat left the Hibees rooted to the bottom of the table, five points behind Motherwell in ninth. Billy McNeill made it clear that he didn't want the manager's job. Names bandied out by the media to succeed Jim Duffy included St Johnstone's Paul Sturrock, Tommy Burns and Jimmy Nicholl. In the end, Hibs went for the man that they had initially tried and failed to get when Alex Miller had left in 1996. This time Motherwell let their manager speak to Hibs and Alex McLeish was thus appointed as Hibernian's new boss. He had worked wonders with Motherwell and of course it had been his team who had sealed Jim Duffy's fate with that 6-2 Fir Park mauling.

The new gaffer assured the Hibs squad that they all had a fresh start. He also identified four players to the board that he felt, if signed, would help keep the club up. The first was Bryan Gunn, the ex-Aberdeen and Scotland goalkeeper. He arrived on a loan deal from Norwich City and was thrown straight into the first team for Eck's first game in charge, a home match against Rangers. The goalie was 34 years old and was just what Hibs needed. When he arrived, the defence was averaging around three goals per match conceded – Gunn cut that to just over one. Despite a Barry Lavety goal and a courageous performance against title-chasing Rangers on Saturday, 21 February in Edinburgh, Hibs still lost 1-2.

Next came a 1-1 draw with Dundee United on Tayside in which Yogi Hughes scored, then a narrow 0-1 defeat by Celtic at Easter Road. A Tony Rougier penalty up at McDiarmid Park helped the Hibees earn a crucial point against St Johnstone, then on Saturday, 21 March the new manager got his first win as Hibs boss, when his charges beat his old club Motherwell 1-0 at Easter Road thanks to a Lavety goal. David Elliot was sent off in that match. Hibs' next match was against Aberdeen at Easter Road. In the side that day were two of the other players McLeish had spoken to the board about – 20-year-old midfielder Grant Brebner, on loan from Manchester United, and 29-year-old midfielder Justin Skinner, who came in from Bristol Rovers. Skinner added a bit of much-needed steel and experience while Brebner brought some much-needed youth, enthusiasm and ability to the Hibs squad. McLeish was unable to obtain his fourth signing target, Mixu Paatelainen. The match with Aberdeen was a hard-fought 1-1 draw. Hibs remained bottom; six points behind ninth-placed Dunfermline with six matches still to play and 18 points up for grabs. McLeish's arrival steadied the ship and the new boss and his signings had restored Hibernian's backbone – though the team still faced likely relegation. After all, McLeish was a manager, not a fucking magician. The team's next two matches were against Rangers and Hearts.

At Ibrox on April Fool's Day, a midweek game, the Hibees went down to a 0-3 defeat. They didn't collapse but were still well beaten by the Gers. Saturday, 11 April brought the season's final Edinburgh derby. Prior to the match, Hearts were very much still in the title race with Celtic and Rangers and sat third in the table. Celtic had 66 points, Rangers had 63, Hearts had 62 but both Rangers and the Jambos had two games in hand on the Parkhead side. Hearts had also just a week earlier qualified for the Scottish Cup Final, after beating Falkirk 3-1 at neutral Ibrox. They would face Rangers in the final. A double-chasing Hearts team coming to Easter Road to play a relegation-fodder Hibs side, who by then were seven points adrift at the bottom – surely another easy Hearts derby triumph was on the cards?

That Saturday in Leith, Edinburgh's high-flying establishment team were looking for a victory to boost their title hopes. Hibs, meanwhile, were fighting for league survival. Hearts fans were confident and had every right to be. Hibs fans were scunnered, both at their own team's plight and at the prospect of Hearts finally actually winning something, yet still, Hibbies came along to the match carrying much hope. McLeish's arrival had improved the team but hadn't really improved its predicament. Defeat in this derby would have meant almost certain relegation for Hibernian.

The first half was very much a typical 'salt n sauce' affair, bruising, physical, nervous even, with both teams scared to make mistakes. Throughout the first half the Hearts fans goaded the Hibs fans with, 'Going down, going down, going down …' Hearts looked liveliest in the second 45 but the first chance of that period fell to Lavety, who aimlessly thumped the ball high and wide, to howls of derision from the away fans. They weren't laughing after

56 minutes, though, when Lavety beat Rousset to give Hibs the lead. The Hibs fans were overjoyed and the away fans became oddly silent. Jefferies threw on veteran John Robertson and the wee striker got his final Edinburgh derby goal, pinging a free kick past Gunn at the Dunbar End. The Hibs fans and players did not lose heart. 'HIBEES, HIBEES, HIBEES,' was the rumbling chant which echoed around the Leith 'San Siro'. Ten minutes from full time, substitute Kevin Harper beat Rousset at the home end of the ground to put Hibs 2-1 up and that's how it ended. There was an outpouring of joy from the stands at the end, real emotion, as if that win had been some sort of miracle. At the end, John Robertson, who'd just played in his last derby, shook the hand of every Hibs player and coach, expressing his wishes that Hibs should stay up. Results elsewhere that day meant that Hibs had reduced the gap with Dunfermline from seven points to five. The result also seriously dented Hearts' title challenge, though like in 1986 it wasn't points dropped against Hibs which deprived Hearts of the title, they blew it themselves. Nevertheless, Hibs' win over Hearts gave Hibbies a great sense of having unleashed a Parthian shot at their city neighbours. In a wider sense, this famous derby victory also opened up a new possibility to Hibs fans, a possibility that, in fact, Hibs might not go down at all. We could catch Dunfermline – we could survive!

Seven days later came a relegation showdown with Dunfermline at East End Park. That day, you'd have thought that there was a cup final being played in Fife as the Forth Road Bridge was rammed with cars and buses all sporting flecks of green and white. There were 12,749 fans at this match, the majority of whom were supporting Hibs. It was like a home match for the green jerseys. The game was a typical relegation battle, not pretty at all. The Pars went

1-0 up just after the break via an unfortunate own goal from Grant Brebner. Hibernian's newfound battling spirit kept the match alive. Deep into injury time, Hibs got a corner. Bryan Gunn even came up for it; there was virtually no standing room left in the box. On that beautiful Saturday afternoon, thousands of green-clad fans stood, praying, willing the ball into the net. Sure enough, up popped big Brian Welsh to nod the corner past Westwater to make it 1-1. The scenes at the end were more akin to a cup-final win than a basement battle. Every Hibby who was there remembers that goal. That goal kept Hibs up for another week. Results elsewhere that day also meant that while Hibs were still five points behind Dunfermline, Motherwell and Dundee Utd were now just one point above the Pars. With three matches to go, Hibs could still pull off a great escape.

On Saturday, 25 April, Hibs were at Parkhead to face Celtic. Before the match, McLeish made a comment to the media saying that he hoped the referee would be strong. At kick-off when the Celtic players did their huddle, Hibernian's purple-clad players formed a line together, facing down the huddle. It wasn't quite the New Zealand rugby haka but it symbolised the team's renewed togetherness. That togetherness saw Hibs in good stead that day as the purple jerseys fought, fouled, tackled and ran themselves into the ground, earning a precious point and a 0-0 draw. The home fans were very angry at their own players, while at one point, McLeish and Celtic assistant Murdo MacLeod were dismissed from the technical area for a 'handbags' incident. It was a gutsy, belligerent performance from Hibernian.

Unfortunately, Dunfermline won their own match that day and secured their safety. With two matches left Hibs needed to win twice and hope that other results went their way. Motherwell and Dundee Utd were both five points above Hibs. Hibernian's next match was at home to Dundee Utd.

May of 1998 saw a massive earthquake in Afghanistan kill over 5,000 people. The European Central Bank was established and the Good Friday Agreement, which halted the long civil war in Northern Ireland, was approved by a referendum on both sides of Ireland's border. 'Turn Back Time' by Danish popsters Aqua topped the singles chart, while cinema fans were enjoying *Deep Impact* and *Wild Things*.

On Saturday, 3 May 1998, in front of 13,413 fans, Hibernian's valiant attempt to stave off a third relegation came to an end. They led Dundee Utd at half-time thanks to a Grant Brebner goal and were the better side, but when midfield general Justin Skinner went off injured in the second half, Hibs lost their shape and the Terrors struck back ruthlessly. A double from Swede Kjell Olofson was enough to give Utd a 2-1 victory and to send Hibs down. There were tearful scenes at Easter Road. Pat McGinlay and John Hughes seemed the most hurt. The damage had really been done during Jim Duffy's reign, though, and the fault was not McLeish's. Indeed, he was looked upon as the ideal man to restore Hibs to the top flight at the first time of asking.

The last match of the season was at Rugby Park, where Hibs got a 1-1 draw, Stevie Crawford scoring. A huge crowd in excess of 12,000 was at that game as Kilmarnock were letting youngsters in free again. Hibs ended season 97/98 bottom of the league on 30 points, Motherwell were second bottom on 34. Hibs had only won six games in the league, losing 18 and drawing 12. They had scored 38 goals and conceded 59. Crawford and Lavety were joint top scorers on nine. Just two of 12 matches against Rangers, Hearts and Celtic had been won. Once again, our best player had been Pat McGinlay. Our best performances that season came in the early home wins over Celtic, Kilmarnock and Dunfermline, all under Jim Duffy, and in the April derby win under Big Eck. There were many lows, the lowest probably being the early Scottish Cup exit and the 3-4 loss at home to Rangers – the latter for psychological reasons.

Celtic won the Coca-Cola Cup and the league championship, stopping Rangers' quest for a historic ten consecutive titles. Hearts, who had a great season, finally ended their embarrassing 36-year run without winning anything, when they beat Rangers 2-1 in the Scottish Cup Final at Celtic Park. For Hearts to end their barren era at the same time Hibernian were relegated was a sore one for Hibs fans, but with McLeish at the helm most were confident of coming straight back up. Hibernian's place in the top flight was taken by Division One winners Dundee. At least fans had Scotland's appearance at the World Cup in the summer to look forward to, before that great adventure in the First Division would begin. It had been a sad season for Hibbies, but even before relegation had been confirmed, there were already green, green shoots of recovery at the club for all to see. Hibernian would live on, would fight on, would persevere, and would be back.

* * *

While Hibernian and their fans were licking their collective wounds in the summer of 1998, a few guys with Hibs connections spent some of the summer on a short trip to France. That trip was of course to the 1998 World Cup finals, at which Scotland were playing. Alex Miller was Scotland boss Craig Brown's assistant, while Darren Jackson and Jim Leighton would also play a big part. On

10 June 1998 at the Stade de France in front of 80,000 fans, Scotland played Brazil in the tournament's opener. Jim Leighton had won back the number one jersey for the finals, while Jackson also started. Both players did well. Scotland narrowly lost 2-1 in the curtain-raiser, Brazil scoring with an own goal and with a header from a corner – not the types of goal one normally associates with the samba stars. Scotland did draw level at one point when ex-Hibs player and future Hibs cup-winning manager, John Collins, coolly stroked home a penalty kick. Scotland went on to draw 1-1 with Norway then were surprisingly beaten 3-0 by Morocco, so were eliminated from the tournament at the group stages once more. That was the last Scotland team to reach a major tournament for more than two decades, until Steve Clarke's side qualified for Euro 2021, and the genius coach Alex Miller was instrumental in getting us there.

You wanted freedom
But now that she's gone
There's no depth to the song
The song that you're singing …

MOVING ON – THE GREAT ADVENTURE

'Walk on through the wind
Walk on through the rain
Though your dreams be tossed and blown'

CHAIRMAN LEX Gold resigned when Hibs were relegated. He left to take up a role at the SPL, the new breakaway body which governed Scotland's new top flight. He was replaced as chairman by vice-chairman Tom O'Malley. The millionaire and philanthropist Brian Kennedy made noises about his desire to buy the club in the summer of 1998, but didn't. For season 98/99 the SPL would replace the old Premier Division as Scotland's top league. It had a lucrative Sky TV deal which brought more money into Scottish football than ever before and would show more live matches than ever before. From sponsorship deals to Sky and terrestrial TV and radio revenue, the new SPL would bring in almost £70m in revenue in four years – the preceding four years had brought in just £10m. It was a revolution. Scotland's top flight was about to be Americanised, with squad numbers, Opta stats, an online presence, big foam hands, big gulp colas and that song 'Inside' by Stiltskin – among other things. For Scotland's top clubs, it was, financially, feeding time. There were a few other changes. The number of substitutes for SPL matches was increased to five. A new under-21 league was created for the SPL and periphery clubs, partly at the behest of Sky. It aimed to nurture future talent and thus ensure that Scottish football remained an attractive product to TV companies, so only three 'over-21' players could play in each match in that new youth league.

That league ran from 1998 to 2004 and would indeed help to produce a golden generation of Scottish youth players, particularly at Hibs, though it's interesting to note that the golden generation spawned by that under-21 league didn't improve the rapidly diminishing Scotland national side, which, ironically, didn't qualify for a major tournament from the time the SPL and under-21 league were first created in 1998 until late in 2020, when they won their place at Euro 2021.

Hibs were actually the turkeys who voted for Christmas as regards to the new SPL breakaway league, as we voted for it, even though we wouldn't be in it for its inaugural season. There were some half-hearted attempts by some people, mostly other clubs' managers and journalists, to have that season's relegation cancelled and to expand the top flight to 12 teams instead of ten – which happened for season 2000/2001 anyway – but nothing came of them. Hibernian FC had been sick, so it took its medicine and dropped down a division. The 1997/98 relegation play-off didn't happen; it had been cancelled long before the season ended. That was perhaps just as well, as Falkirk finished second in Division One, and had they beaten second-bottom Motherwell in a play-off they would have been refused promotion anyway, because of the SPL's controversial '10,000 seats' rule. Hibernian did receive a six-figure 'parachute payment' for going down, which softened the blow of missing out on the lucrative first season of the new SPL. That cash would prove vital to Alex McLeish and to Hibs in the coming campaign.

As you might imagine, there were a lot of departures from Hibernian in the summer of 1998, though even more players actually left as the new 1998/99 season began, too.

Pat McGinlay could've left, but he stayed. He was easily Hibernian's best player at the time. If there was an award given for 'Hibs player of the 90s' then Pat would surely be a top contender for the gong. Asides his short spell at Celtic, Pat wore the green of Hibernian 374 times between his debut in 1988 and his swansong in 2000. He scored 79 goals from midfield, won the SKOL League Cup, played for Hibs in Europe, was part of the last Hibernian team to split the old firm and was to be pivotal in the club's First Division promotion campaign of 1998/99. Hibs were lucky to have him. He'd actually begun his Hibs career as a full-back, but a performance in midfield as a substitute against Royal Liege in 1989 showed that he could play anywhere. One wonders if Hibs could've split the old firm in 2000/01 had Pat been given one more season in the green.

One player who had wanted to remain at Easter Road following his successful loan spell was goalie Bryan Gunn. He signed a two-year contract with the club. However, he fractured his leg in pre-season training and ended up moving back down to Norwich. The injury forced him to retire from football. His son, Angus, is a goalkeeper for England under-21s at time of writing this book. Chris Reid was another goalie to leave Hibs in the summer of 1998, signing for Hamilton. Chris had played for Hibs 42 times over a nine-year spell as a first-team player. He was a good keeper who was perhaps unfortunate to have been at Easter Road when the club had other, even better goalies. Gunn and Reid's departures meant that Ole Gottskalksson would be given the number one jersey for the team's Division One campaign, and with it a chance to redeem himself for his costly errors during the relegation season.

Kevin Harper would only play a cameo role in Hibernian's First Division campaign. He played three times in the green early in season 98/99 before heading south to sign for Jim Smith's Derby County in a deal worth around £300,000. In his first match for the Rams he scored against Liverpool at Anfield, right in front of the Kop. Kevin had played for Hibs 116 times in just over five years as a first-team player. He'd scored 18 goals, three of them in victories over Hearts. He was undoubtedly one of the brightest attacking talents to come out of Easter Road's youth system in the 90s and would be missed. We loved him.

After new contract negotiations, Willie Miller chose not to play First Division football and joined newly promoted Dundee instead. Willie was a fine right-back and remains a 90s icon to Hibs fans. Willie played for Hibs 287 times in a great career spanning nine seasons in the first team. He won the SKOL League Cup at Hibs and played in the 1993 cup final as well and was a big part of the club's other 90s achievements. He scored three times for the first team. He should really have been given a testimonial.

Most of Jim Duffy's signings were gone by the autumn of 1998, the notable exceptions being Gottskalksson, Shaun Dennis and Stevie Crawford. David Elliot played eight matches for the Cabbage in the First Division, then was transferred to Partick Thistle. Andy Dow left in the summer of 1998 to join Aberdeen. Chic Charnley ended up at Clydebank. Chris Jackson moved to Stirling Albion, having made 80 appearances for Hibs over a five-year spell in the first team. Chris had been a product of our youth system and helped win the BP Cup in 1992 but would come back to haunt the Hibees in a 1999 Scottish Cup tie while a Stirling Albion player, scoring one of the Binos' goals in a cup shock. Greg Miller signed for Livingston, while Lee Power went to Ayr United. Brian Welsh signed for Stenhousemuir, while Tony Rougier was sold to Port Vale early in the 98/99 season, having played for Hibernian 49 times, scoring four goals. Jimmy Boco retired, having made 33 appearances in the green jersey. Paul Tosh made just one appearance in season 98/99 before joining Raith Rovers. Graeme Donald had moved to Stirling Albion, having made 46 appearances in the green jersey between 1992 and 1998, while big Darren Dods moved to St Johnstone, having made 70 appearances for Hibernian in the preceding four seasons. Thus, 15 players left Hibernian between the end of season 97/98 and the autumn of 1998. Some were big names who would be missed, some were not.

These departures left Alex McLeish with a very small first-team squad. If one excludes those players who would start the season at Hibs but would move on after it began, the new manager was left with Ole Gottskalksson, John Hughes, Pat McGinlay, Michael Renwick, Justin Skinner, Shaun Dennis, Stevie Crawford and Barry Lavety, plus some youth players. That's a situation akin to what Alan Stubbs had to initially work with in the summer of 2014. If Hibs were to be promoted, new blood would be needed.

One bright spot of the tail end of season 97/98 for Hibs had been the excellent performances of on-loan youngster Grant Brebner. Hibs fans really hoped that the talented midfielder, who was a Hibby, would return to help the club's push for promotion. The fans were to be disappointed when the Man Utd player opted to join Tommy Burns at Reading instead. Alex McLeish pressed on with his recruitment.

In came Australian attacking midfielder Stuart Lovell from Reading. He had scored 59 goals for Reading in a seven-year stint down south and would become an important part of the Hibernian team for the next three years. One can divide the rest of the 1998 recruits into two categories: those who made a difference and those who didn't. For the latter category, we had Austrian pair Peter Guggi and Klaus Dietrich. The former, who had played for Rapid Vienna in the 1996 UEFA Cup Winners' Cup Final, made just ten appearances in the green then left suddenly following a tabloid sleaze scandal article about him. Dietrich would play just one full match for Hibs. Veteran midfielder Paul Holsgrove joined from Darlington but would only make 20 appearances in the green, half of them being as a substitute. The less said about defender Derek Anderson's six-match Hibs career, the better. The other, better signings would come later, as the season wore on.

(Author's supplementary note: 'Derek Anderson's short disappointing Hibs stint in the first division' has become part of that era's Hibs folklore. I've left it in this story for narrative purposes – everyone remembers 'that' game v Ayr and Derek's errors in it. In truth he was a fine solid defender. When Hibs signed him from Ayr he had a minor injury. He initially played four matches of which we won three and drew once, but his injury got worse over those games. Derek wanted to earn a long-term deal at Hibs so he played on through the pain barrier. The injury caught up with him in his fifth and last start for Hibs, away to Ayr in October 98, when his compromised fitness led to him being led a merry dance by Ayr's Glynn Hurst and Andy Walker in the first half. He was substituted at half-time because of his injury and made just one more substitute appearance for Hibs, then was allowed to move to Morton to find a regular first-team spot, as by then Hibs' central defensive pairing was fixed as Hughes and Dennis. Derek is now head of youth development at Morton.)

For the new 1998/99 season Hibernian's main sponsor, Carlsberg, remained. However, French sportswear giant Le Coq Sportif took over from Mitre as the club's kit sponsor. The new strip was baggy, green with white sleeves and a green trim, a trendy mix of the style of the 1982–86 France kit, the 70s Bukta-style Hibs kit and general 90s bagginess. The away kit was similar in essence but its colour was yellow with green trim. We only wore that away kit a couple of times as the players didn't like it.

The pre-season matches began with a three-game tour of England. Port Vale were beaten 2-1, while Telford United and Macclesfield Town both held the Hibees to 0-0 draws. West Ham United came to Easter Road on Thursday, 23 July. Harry Redknapp's men had just been relegated from England's Premiership and travelled north to face Hibs with a very strong team which included John Hartson, Eyal Berkovic and a young Frank Lampard. Ian Wright was injured and missed out. Scott Mean gave the Hammers the lead in the first half. Hibs forced a number of great saves from Shaka Hislop and might have won the match; however, the green jerseys had to settle for a draw, Stevie Crawford scoring a late penalty to tie the match at 1-1. Two days later, John Hendrie's Barnsley side came to Easter Road and beat the Hibees 1-0, Macedonian striker Georgi Hristov scoring when Hibs were down to ten men, as Jimmy Boco was off receiving treatment for an injury – an injury which he never recovered from and which forced his retirement. In Barnsley's squad that day, but not playing, was teenager

Marc Heckingbottom, brother of future dud Hibs boss, Paul. The Barnsley match was a memorable occasion, though not for the actual game of football between Hibs and the Tykes. Before the match, Willie Ormond's widow, Margaret, had renamed the new north stand at a ceremony attended by the other four members of Hibernian's Famous Five. From that date onwards, the stand behind the goals at the Hibs end of the stadium would be known as The Famous Five Stand. The match's build-up was actually interrupted because the PA announcer had to summon Barry Lavety from the pre-match warm-up to move his illegally parked car, as the police were going to tow it away and impound it! Nevertheless, the stand renaming was a fitting gesture to the Hibernian heroes of the olden days and also a timely morale booster for the fans.

Tuesday, 4 August saw the league campaign begin in earnest. A huge travelling Hibs support descended on Cappielow, where Hibs narrowly beat Billy Stark's Morton 1-0, thanks to a Barry Lavety strike. An away League Cup victory over Hamilton followed, which set up a tie with SPL leaders Aberdeen at Easter Road in the next round. Hibernian were then beaten 2-1 at home by Stranraer in the first home league match of the campaign. That result sent shockwaves around Scotland. Many in the media predicted that Hibernian weren't good enough to be promoted. Some even looked into their crystal balls and saw Hibs being relegated again. Almost all of the press used the Stranraer defeat as an indicator that Hibernian's time in the doldrums was only just beginning – such was their fantasy.

And so, dear reader, we come to the Hibs v Aberdeen tie at Easter Road in the League Cup, where this humble tale began. That 1-0 win over the Dons kick-started our season, even though we were thrashed in the next round by eventual beaten finalists, St Johnstone. Falkirk, our main rivals in the league, started the season very well, while we were slow but steady out of the traps. After the Aberdeen game, Hibs drew away to Falkirk, hammered Ayr United at Easter Road then drew away to Clydebank. Our next league match was at Love Street. We lost that match 0-2 to St Mirren but Mixu Paatelainen made his debut that day, finally arriving at Hibs from Wolves. Hibs then beat Raith and drew with Hamilton at home, then thumped Airdrie 3-1 at their new Excelsior Stadium. One week later, a solitary Stuart Lovell goal gave the Cabbage a 1-0 win over Stranraer at Stair Park and the result put Hibernian on top of the league, where the team remained until the end of the season. Morton were beaten 2-1 at Easter Road a week later. Seven days after that, the Hibees fought back from 3-1 down against Ayr at Somerset Park to earn a 3-3 draw. A player named Russell Latapy made his Hibs debut that day; he would go on to become a club legend.

After the 0-2 defeat away to St Mirren on 12 September, Hibs didn't lose another league match until 13 March, when Clydebank pulled off a surprise 2-0 victory. Between those two matches, Alex McLeish's Hibees went on a 22-match unbeaten run in the league, drawing just three of those matches. Contrast that run with the dreadful winless run of the previous season which caused the team's relegation. Though Falkirk kept up a valiant pursuit, Hibernian strolled their way to the title. After Mixu and Russell Latapy arrived, there was no stopping the green jerseys. Crowds went up, fans who had stayed away for years came back to watch a winning team and the club was reborn as it charged towards the title and promotion. Alex McLeish continued to strengthen the team as the season went on. A move for Bulgarian World Cup star striker, Emil Kostadinov, almost came off, but was hampered and ultimately scuppered by red tape. He had been freed by Mexican side FC Tigres after they had been unable to pay him.

Speedy winger Paul Hartley was signed from Raith, defenders Tom Smith and Paul Lovering were signed from Clydebank and right-back Derek Collins came in from Morton. Yes, Hibernian did cherry-pick some of their rivals' better players in Division One, but that's football and it's no different to what Rangers or Celtic do when signing better players from us and from their other top-flight rivals. In February, two further players joined Hibs. Alex Marinkov was a big defender who joined from Scarborough. He made his debut in a 2-1 Hibs win over Falkirk at Brockville. Also wearing the green for the first time that day was a 33-year-old midfielder who had joined from Montpellier. He had 39 caps for France and had won the European Champions Cup with Marseille in 1993 and the UEFA Intertoto Cup with Strasbourg in 1995, as well as having played in Serie A for Atalanta. His name was Franck Sauzee and his performances for the club would earn him the nickname 'le God'. With Sauzee, Latapy, Paatelainen, the other new additions and the guys who had remained since the previous season, the Hibees romped to the title, regaining their place in Scotland's top flight at the first time of asking, racking up a whopping 89 points – a record at the time. Just three league matches were lost, five were drawn, the other 28 matches were won. Hibs scored 84 goals and just 33 were conceded. The only real blot on the copybook was a shock Scottish Cup exit to Stirling Albion after a replay, but by season's end no one cared about that.

Ole Gottskalksson was ever-present that season and made amends for his errors in the previous campaign with numerous excellent saves as the team pushed towards the title. Stevie Crawford was the top scorer with 15, Lovell, McGinlay and Paatelainen each bagged 12, Latapy managed seven while Paul Hartley notched five. Hughes and Dennis were immense at the back, Sauzee gave a taste of what was to come from him in the next two seasons, while Justin Skinner was also a hero, strolling through matches as coolness personified.

The title was clinched on Saturday, 3 April with a 2-0 win over Hamilton at Firhill, with a moving rendition of 'You'll Never Walk Alone' sung at full time by a joyous Hibs support with their scarves held high. The actual title party was held on the last day of the season at Easter Road, when Hibs defeated Falkirk 2-1 in front of almost 15,000 fans. That match had a carnival atmosphere to it. Ole saved a penalty from Falkirk's ex-Hearts striker Scott Crabbe, Franck Sauzee scored a trademark thunderbolt goal and Paul Hartley got the other one. Hibernian was thus restored to its rightful place among Scotland's elite, having won the title playing wonderful football and scoring a barrowload of goals – that's a real Hibs team for you!

I'm on my way,
Soon be moving on my way,
Leave a little light on,
Leave a little light on

NOTHING BUT LOVE – HIBERNIAN FOREVER

'While I'm worth my room on this earth
I will be with you
While the Chief, puts Sunshine on Leith
I'll thank him for his work
And your birth and my birth.'

NOW, IT'S easy for fans and commentators to say that a club like Hibs should never have been in Division One in the first place. It's easier still to blame Jim Duffy for the relegation in 1998, or to say that Alex Miller's departure led to the relegation. One could even say that we as Hibs fans expected too much after what were some very good years for the team in the early to mid 90s, and that we should have listened to that old proverb 'be careful what you wish for' when some of us were calling for the boss's head in 1996. There's a degree of truth to all of that, but it's not the full story.

The story of Hibs in the late 1990s, at the turn of the century, ends like this.

Alex McLeish led Hibs in their first season in that new-fangled SPL. The gaffer gave almost all of the players who had won promotion the previous season a good chance to prove themselves in the top flight. He also strengthened the squad. To the delight of Hibs fans, young Grant Brebner did return to Easter Road once the club had returned to the top flight. Brebs would become an important part of the Hibernian team for much of the next five years. Also added to the squad were Ireland goalkeeper Nick Colgan and German striker Dirk Lehmann, the latter joining from Fulham. French midfielder Fabrice Henry came in from FC Basel while left-sided centre-back Martin McIntosh came north from Stockport County to wear the green, in a £250,000 deal midway through the season.

That SPL campaign began with a home fixture against Motherwell on the last day of July 1999. The opening track of the Oasis album *(What's the Story), Morning Glory?* was called 'Hello'. Its chorus was sung by the Hibs faithful at Easter Road before and during that league opener against Motherwell, though with different, somewhat fitting alterations to the lyrics.

'Hello, hello, the Hibees are back! The Hibees are back!'

Easter Road shook to the sound of the fans belting out their new song. It was supplemented by one of the loudest renditions of 'Hail Hail' ever heard at modern Easter Road as the green jerseys took to the field. German hitman Dirk Lehmann bagged two goals in what was a 2-2 draw on a glorious Edinburgh summer day. Dirk liked to wear tape to cover his earrings and many Hibs fans emulated that style and could be seen with taped ears of their own in the crowd at the next few matches. Running amok in the First Division, winning the title with such panache and being back in the top flight had revived the Hibs support. The fans were smiling, swaggering and optimistic again. A week later, the German striker scored again; his strike along with a marvellous double by Franck Sauzee and a late winner by youngster Kenny Miller gave the Cabbage a superb 4-3 win over Dundee up at Dens Park, in a live televised Sky 6.05pm Sunday kick-off game. A week later, Hearts came to Easter Road for the first Edinburgh derby in 16 months. Russell Latapy gave Hibs the lead with a penalty kick, and when that sweetly struck kick bulged the net behind Giles Rousset, Easter Road erupted. That penalty would of course be used in a British Telecom advert later on, with the movie alien ET wearing green and celebrating the goal, which reportedly compelled a number of furious Hearts fans to complain to the telecommunications giant and even to cancel their telephone services in disgust. It didn't matter to Hibs fans at that derby that Hearts bagged an equaliser in the second half. We were so delighted just to be back playing local derbies, to be a top-flight side again, to be the true Hibs again.

The remainder of the season went fairly well. Alex McLeish's newly promoted side had their ups and downs and finished sixth in the SPL and reached the semi-finals of the Scottish Cup – Hibernian's first big cup match at Hampden since the 1991 SKOL Cup Final and our first big semi-final since 1995.

Our chronicle of Hibernian 1992–1999 ends on Sunday, 19 December 1999 at a packed Tynecastle. Nick Colgan in goal, a back four of Derek Collins, Tom Smith, Shaun Dennis and John Hughes, a midfield of Sauzee, Latapy, Brebner and Lovell and big Mixu Paatelainen and Dirk Lehmann up front. The most ferocious, confident, dominating Hibs performance at Tynecastle since the 1970s ensued, live on Sky, in that time-slot that the green jerseys were almost invincible in. Dirk Lehmann gave Hibs an early lead, Franck Sauzee – playing in midfield in season 99/00 –

smashed a long-range effort into the same net at the Gorgie Road end in front of the Hearts fans to double the lead, and then ran the length of the pitch to celebrate his goal with the Hibs fans in the Roseburn Stand. Anything Hearts threw at Hibs was easily dealt with by Dennis and Hughes at the back, prowling the back line like two ferocious heavyweight boxers, and by Nicky Colgan, who had recently ousted Ole from the first XI. Hearts had just received an £8m investment from SMG. They'd spent a large portion of that on Rangers goalie Antti Niemi, ex-Rangers and Dundee Utd man Gordan Petric and Jamaica midfielder Fitzroy Simpson, who all played that night. They made no difference. A late goal by substitute Kenny Miller capped a 3-0 win for Hibs, the three points and the club's first victory at Tynecastle in five years. It was also Hibernian's biggest margin of victory in a derby since the 3-0 win over Hearts at Easter Road in January 1976. To the victor go the spoils and this fine win gave Hibs fans the festive bragging rights and has gone down in history simply as 'The millennium derby'.

It was a fitting way for Hibernian FC to end the 20th century. The last few years of that century had been, I'm sure you'll agree, very interesting and full of myriad emotions for fans of Edinburgh's green and white. One thing you can always say about the fine old club from Leith is that supporting them is never, ever boring. The new century would begin fairly well, too. Sauzee and Latapy would become Hibernian icons. The team would compete at the highest level in Europe once more, following a superb campaign in 2000/2001 which brought a third-placed finish, a 6-2 victory over Hearts and a noble attempt to win the Scottish Cup. We would eventually win that cup, 15 years later, on that glorious day when Anthony Stokes and David Gray ended the infamous hoodoo, and the road from 2000 to 2016 was one that would see us finally finish our magnificent stadium, invest in a new training centre, bring through a golden generation of youth players and also see us recapture the League Cup in 2007, under the masterful leadership of former Hibs player John Collins. Sure, we also suffered a relegation, dealt with the collapse of two TV deals and weathered the global financial crisis along the way, but that's just Hibs, that's the rollercoaster which Hibs fans choose to ride – and we wouldn't have it any other way.

We began the 1990s in great peril and under existential threat from Hearts and from financial bungling; we ended the 90s stronger, better and with an even greater sense of togetherness among the supporters. As you've just read, our journey through the 90s was a topsy-turvy one. There were disappointments but there was far more to be proud of. Alex Miller was a huge part of that story, the largely excellent teams he built in the 90s with such talented players entertained us, made us proud to wear the green and ultimately played a huge part in so many of our lives. What came after Alex was just as important, though. Mr Duffy did his best, Mr McLeish did better. All three of these managers were at the helm throughout Hibernian's transition to being a truly modern football club. You as a fan were part of that transition, too. You bought the tickets, cheered the goals and sang the songs along the way. We might not have won a major trophy between 1992 and 1999 but that doesn't mean that we didn't have a good time. Alex Miller, Sir Tom Farmer and, most importantly, we the fans, made modern Hibernian. So, raise a glass to the Hibs Heroes of the 90s, honour them and their achievements. They made you laugh, they made you cry, they made you smile, and they made you sing. The Hibernian players of that time are among the most iconic in the club's modern history and are still spoken about by fans with great reverence. For as long as there is sunshine on Leith and green jerseys on the pitch at Easter Road, we will remember them. That was the 1990s and we are, together, forever and ever, Hibernian FC. The Hibs Are Here …

Nothing but love gives the world some meaning
Nothing but love is the drug of Healing
Lover be soft, lover be bold
Earthquake, avalanche, volcano

INTERVIEWS

DARREN JACKSON

I'd enjoyed my time at Dundee United but I was delighted to sign for Hibernian in 1992. Alex Miller had kept an eye on my progress and had actually tried to sign me when I was at Newcastle United. I always knew that Hibs was a great club; a massive club. I already knew young Chris Jackson and a few of the other players who were at Easter Road – Chris because we are kind of cousins, the others through playing against them. I settled in quickly at Easter Road – I wasn't a shy guy and we all got on well at the club.

The double header against Anderlecht in the UEFA Cup in my first season was massive and a great experience. After the 1-1 draw in Brussels, Anderlecht's boss Luka Peruzovic came into our dressing room and complimented us; he said that it was very rare for teams to come to Anderlecht and play in such a confident, fearless, energetic style against them – usually visiting teams feared Anderlecht. We were unlucky over the two legs; they had such top players, guys like Van Vossen, Degryse and Albert. The Hibs fans were unbelievable that night in Brussels, we heard them all night – I think there were about 3,000 of them. They did us proud that night with their backing and we did ourselves proud, too.

My strike partnership with Keith Wright was a good one; we complemented each other's styles well. We had other great strikers when I was at Hibs, like Gareth, Mark McGraw and Kevin Harper, but I think if you ask most people who Hibernian's strikers were for most of the 90s, they'll say me and Keith. Keith liked to be the no.9; he liked to play along the line, getting into the box and getting on the end of chances. That really suited me playing as the no.10 slightly deeper. We combined well and scored a lot of goals – around 140 between us in the five seasons that we played together. Keith was brilliant to play with and his attitude as well as his ability were spot on – and he was a good mad Hibby, too.

My second season at Hibs, 1993/94, wasn't my best. I only scored about eight goals and was booked about 12 times! For some reason I was poor that season, I feel. I played with an injury during our 1993 League Cup Final against Rangers at Parkhead. Andy Watson, our coach, had accidentally injured my ankle while training with us, so I wasn't 100% for that game. We did okay in that final but could have done better. We gave a good account of ourselves but didn't do enough to win the cup. It was almost fate that McCoist would score the winning goal, having recently returned from his broken leg injury lay-off.

About a year or so after that cup run I was given a framed picture from our '93 semi-final win in that cup against my old club Dundee United, at Tynecastle. The picture was a framed shot of my goal celebration in front of the Tynecastle shed, which had been full of Hibbies that night. I was given that picture as a player of the year award for 1994/95 so I'd clearly improved on 93/94. That semi-final against United was a tough game – especially the midfield battle between Davie Farrell and my old pal Dave Bowman. The atmosphere was great that night, a lot of Hibbies, a lot of noise.

I was at Hibs for the last nine matches of that annoying winless run against Hearts. When we eventually ended it, we didn't have a special plan or anything, we didn't do anything differently. It was a monkey on our back, in the same way that Hibs' long gap between Scottish Cup wins was. I've played in derbies in Dundee, Glasgow and elsewhere. We knew that we *could* beat them and so when we actually did, it gave us the confidence to win three out of four derbies in season 1994/95.

In 94/95 we did well to finish third and split the Old Firm, but we could have done better. We won just three away league games and drew far too many matches, too. With a bit more luck that season we'd have really challenged for the title or at least finished second and got into Europe again. In the Scottish Cup double header against Celtic at Ibrox my friend Peter Grant actually hit me on the chin early on when the ref wasn't looking! Nowadays with VAR he'd have been off! We did very well in the drawn first match but weren't as good in the replay. It's hard to play in such big matches against the Old Firm and usually if it goes to a replay you've missed your chance to knock them out.

My dad was a mad Jambo who lived in Easter Road and a lot of his friends were Hibs fans. He always had a bit of attitude towards referees and that rubbed off on me a bit, which may explain some of my bookings! I was wrong in my attitude to referees, Alex Miller helped me with that – he even used to fine me for talking back to them! I calmed that down a bit by the time I got the call to play for Scotland. I didn't get my first full cap until I was 28 and had only been an unused squad member at under-21 level in the 1980s once or twice. When I did get involved with the Scotland set-up John Collins got me into weight training and this improved my game, my attitude and my fitness greatly.

Then later when Yogi Hughes joined Hibs, we had a thing about who was 'king of the gym' – I think he was, to be fair. I wasn't the tallest so the weight training really helped me physically. Back then doing weights was a fairly new thing for footballers to be doing.

I remember well making my Scotland B debut against Northern Ireland early in 1995. It was great to make that debut at Easter Road. Pat McGinlay and Tweedy played, too. I scored what I think was the best goal of my career in this match – possibly even one of *the* best goals, ever – but there were no TV cameras there to record it, sadly. It was a good night; there were even some Hibs fans on the east terrace! Guys like Keith Wright, Pat and Tweedy should have gotten more caps but had other good players in front of them in the queue. Kevin McAllister is one of Scotland's greatest uncapped players, too.

My Scotland journey began while I was a Hibs player. I was in that squad on merit – Craig Brown was his own man – though Alex Miller being his number two and my club gaffer maybe helped to get me noticed at first. I started for Scotland in the World Cup opening fixture against Brazil at the France 98 World Cup. To be honest, I always thought that most of the guys in the Scotland team were a higher level of player than me; I probably only started in that Brazil game because Gary McAllister was injured. We did well. It's one of the few games that I wasn't nervous before. My nerves didn't quite kick in until I looked to my left just before kick-off and saw Ronaldo! Billions of people saw that match, yet I was standing there before it thinking, 'I used to play for Meadowbank Thistle, now I'm up against Ronaldo!' My time at Hibs was a big part of my experiencing that World Cup, even though I'd left Hibs by then. That's what dreams are made of.

The contrast between our performances at Christmas and New Year of 1995/96 was stark. The 0-7 defeat at Ibrox hurt – that was the game where Gazza was booked for showing a card to the referee! Rangers had a superb team then, we were good but had an off day that day while Rangers were rampant and on form – that's how they beat us 7-0. After the fourth goal went in, heads went down and we seemed to be chasing shadows. That can happen to any team, even to good teams – but the result was still unacceptable to us. Forty-eight hours later we faced Hearts at Easter Road. We owed it to ourselves and to the fans to bounce back. I remember when Neil Pointon scored for Hearts early on, I was so determined that we should handle the pressure, so it was me who grabbed the ball out of the net right away to get the match restarted. With hindsight it was probably good that Hearts scored early that day, as it motivated us more. We'd just had a pasting at Ibrox and we didn't want the same thing happening against Hearts, so we didn't let it happen and we won the match 2-1. That was a brilliant win!

I wouldn't entirely disagree that Alex Miller was a defensively minded manager at times, but when you look at our squad in the 90s, sometimes you'd have a midfield with O'Neill, McAllister and McGinlay in it, plus Keith and I up front. Sometimes it seemed that some of the fans didn't fully appreciate the gaffer – he was a wonderful coach and I absolutely loved my five years playing under him. Alex was a superb coach and a big loss to Hibernian when he left. That's no disrespect to Jim Duffy.

The two games in the 1997 play-off against Airdrie were very different matches. Our goal in the first leg came from an own goal off my free kick. Alex MacDonald, the Airdrie gaffer, had been 'bantering' with me from the bench during the game, trying to wind me up, so that was extra motivation for the second leg. Had they not missed their penalty when 1-0 up at Broadwood we would probably have lost and gone down. However, Jim Duffy said the right things at half-time and we romped home in the second half. Some say that match was my best performance for Hibs; maybe the second half was. We won 5-2 on aggregate, 4-2 on the night and we were relieved. I'd have hated to have been part of a Hibs team that was relegated. No team is ever 'too good to go down', but in that match we certainly proved that we deserved to stay up and that we were far better than Airdrie.

There were so many good players at Hibs when I was there. Gordon Hunter was a magnificent defender. He had everything, and is another player who really should have been capped. Michael O'Neill was the best player that I played alongside at Easter Road. Richard Gough of Rangers was the toughest opponent to play against while I was at Hibs.

My favourite Hibs memory is the 2-2 home draw with Anderlecht in the 1992 UEFA Cup. Both teams just went at each other and the atmosphere was incredible with a big crowd. They were a great side but so were we. I also enjoyed our 1-0 win at Ibrox in 1995 and our 3-2 win at Parkhead in 1992. So many good memories, though.

After I left Hibs in 1997 I ended up facing Hibs a few times for Celtic, Hearts and Livingston. I got stick from some Hibs fans. At the time I did feel a wee bit hurt as I'd done my best for Hibernian for five years of my life but now I understand why fans do that and it no longer bothers me. I never took any of it personally. I left to join one half of the Old Firm then later played for their city rivals. That's football. When I was a Hibs player, the fans were amazing, always behind us and they even gave me a bit of stick during 1993/94 when I wasn't playing as well, which helped me improve. The fans were great, the people at the club were great, from the chairman Dougie Cromb to Pat Frost the groundsman. I loved my time at Hibs.

CHRIS JACKSON

I was part of the Hibs youth squad who won the BP Scottish Youth Cup in 1992. Myself and a few other members of that squad joined Hibs from Salvesen. At the time Hibernian was very proactive in youth development, with help from Club 86. Dougie Cromb and Alex Miller were both very much in favour of bringing youth players through.

The Hibs youth team had narrowly lost the 1990 and 1991 finals of the BP Cup to very strong Dundee United teams which included many stars of the future. In 92, as part of the 91/92 youth squad, I scored in our semi-final win over Dundee Utd but I missed the final because of an injury. Our squad in 92 included talented guys like Graeme Donald, Nicky Ingram, Graeme Soutar, Kenny Balmain, Graeme Love, Colin MacDonald, Paul Currie, Jamie O'Rourke (son of Jimmy), Jason Gardiner and Stevie Dallas. Jason Gardiner was a great goalkeeper. We beat Ayr Utd 2-0 at Easter Road in the final in front of a big crowd. That cup win was great for the fans as they hadn't had the easiest of times in recent years; the SKOL Cup win and the Youth Cup triumph gave everyone something to smile about.

My favourite game from my Hibs career was in September 1995 when we beat Rangers 1-0 at Ibrox. My parents and my future wife were there that day. I had been doing well in the first team but was still delighted to see my name on the team sheet for that huge match – in Scottish football it doesn't get much bigger for a player than playing in front of over 50,000 at Ibrox. Myself, Graeme Love and Kevin Harper started that day so that reflected well on the club's youth policy. That was a good Hibs team. I think we played well that day; it was very hard against a Rangers team with guys like Gascoigne and Laudrup in their ranks. I idolised that type of world-class guy when I was younger, now I was playing against them! I remember when Darren scored our penalty – the Hibbies in the bottom left of the Broomloan stand went mental! We did well to get the 1-0 win that day – we could maybe have scored more but Rangers had their chances too. We defended well. I think that was Hibs' first win at Ibrox in five years. We were delighted for the Hibs fans after that win – they pay good money to watch the team and Rangers had such a strong team back then – to win in front of over 50,000 in Glasgow must have been great for the fans, too. My mum and dad loved that day; I'll never forget them greeting me after the match outside Ibrox, those big smiles on their faces!

I remember my first goal for Hibs; I scored it at Tynecastle in a narrow 1-2 defeat back in November 1995. I'm a Hibs fan and Tynecastle was my favourite away ground to go to. Back then Hearts had their new Wheatfield and Roseburn stands, the old main stand and the Gorgie Road terrace, which had seats on it at the time. It was always a boyhood dream for me to play in an Edinburgh derby, having watched so many as a fan growing up. We were 1-0 down at half-time but in the second half we were attacking the Gorgie Road end, where our own fans were. The boss told us just to keep passing and to keep playing our game and moving. Kevin McAllister rolled the ball to me as I gave Gary Mackay the slip, so I kept going forward. I could have played in one of the strikers but I noticed that the

Hearts defence were backing off me tactically. I kept going forward then I hit a low, hard shot into the bottom corner from distance, big Gilles Rousset went for it but couldn't stop it. When I saw the ball bulge the net, I couldn't believe it – I'd scored in an Edinburgh derby. I instinctively ran towards the Hibs fans behind the goal. When you see your own supporters going absolutely crazy it's an amazing feeling. There were some Hibs fans at the front of the Gorgie End [including this book's author] who had climbed up the perimeter fence to celebrate. I then looked up to the wing stand where my parents were and saw them. As an Edinburgh lad and a Hibby, to play in a derby was brilliant, to score in one was even better. I became a Hibs fan as a teen – as a child I was actually taken to see games at both Easter Road and Tynecastle. It would have been better had we won the match but the overall experience was euphoric and truly memorable.

When Alex Miller left in 1996, I was sorry to see him go. He wasn't the only top coach at Hibs; another big influence on my career was Hibs' superb youth coach Jimmy McLaughlin.

Our first match without Alex as manager was against Rangers at home in front of a big crowd. Ray Wilkins and I teamed up in midfield. Ray Wilkins was a football icon and it was a joy to play with him. When he first signed, he was about 40 and I remember worrying about my starting place because Ray and I played the same position. Thankfully there was room for both of us. He was a great guy and was very generous with his time towards younger players like me. As for that Rangers match, we dug in and deservedly won the match 2-1. We were actually 1-0 down at one point and later on Laudrup missed the same penalty twice. The atmosphere that day was incredible. In that match I went for a 50/50 with Laudrup and dislocated my shoulder, Laudrup was injured, too, and I had to be subbed, so I had to leave the pitch via the trackside which of course meant that I had to walk past all of the away fans, who weren't best pleased about that challenge or how the match was going at all. They let me know how they felt. I had to go to the Royal Infirmary with my shoulder and my ambulance was actually given a police escort! I remember lying recovering in hospital after my shoulder had been popped back in, all I wanted to know was whether or not we had won the match. Jocky Scott was also a good coach, he gave me a new contract late in 1996.

Alex Miller was a good manager. When I was an S Form he would come and watch our youth matches. He watched reserve games, youth games, bounce games, even youth training. Often he'd take the youth training himself, other times he would just watch and observe us. Alex loves football. If Hibs were playing a match, no matter at what level, the gaffer would be there. He really wanted to build something at Hibs and youth development was a big part of his plan. He had such a sharp football brain, was very thorough and when displeased he didn't mince his words, yet was very fair, too. If you ever had a disagreement with him, he didn't hold a grudge and the next day at training was a clean slate. Some critics over the years have claimed that Hibs were defensive under Alex, but we were always encouraged to go out and win every match and to play well. He was a proper old-school football manager, he did everything, even down to things like making sure the youth players had cleaned the stadium properly. Hibs would have won more cups under Alex throughout the 90s but for some bad luck in semis and finals.

I played with some very good players while at Hibs. Michael O'Neill and Kevin McAllister were amazing,

Darren Jackson could always get us a goal and lift the team. Mickey Weir was superb on his day. Billy Findlay was an excellent young player, too, a real talent. He had so much natural ability. I'd like to have seen Michael O'Neill manage Hibs.

As to opponents, Celtic and Rangers both had excellent teams when I played for Hibs. Celtic had Thom, Di Canio, Van Hooijdonk and Cadete. That Celtic team gave us a few chasings. Then at Rangers there were superb players like Albertz, Gascoigne and Laudrup. Laudrup was just sensational; with his turn of pace, skill and movement he was very difficult to play against. Laudrup, Gascoigne and Di Canio were probably the hardest to play against. Di Canio's technical ability was off the scale.

The Hibs fans were great to me. They were so supportive. I think they like to see one of their own come through the ranks. Hibs fans love their team. I now take my son to Easter Road and we sit in the East Stand. Easter Road is a fantastic stadium and it's changed so much since my days there. I was fortunate to have the career I had. I'm a Hibs fan who played for the team he supports. So few Hibs fans get to do that – I'm proud and privileged – I lived the dream.

KEVIN McALLISTER

After I left Chelsea in 1991, I went to Falkirk for two seasons. Falkirk were relegated at the end of season 92/93; that caused financial hardship for the club and was part of the reason for my move to Hibs. I'm a Falkirk fan but Hibs will always be special to me. I signed for Hibs at the same time as Michael O'Neill and Jim Leighton. The manager just told me to play my usual wing game like I had been doing for Falkirk, and I was happy to. Michael wasn't really a winger, he was a midfielder, but the gaffer played him on the other flank from me. Michael was a fantastic player and having two wide men really worked for us as a team, as long as we got the service. We had excellent strikers, too, in Keith, Darren and Gareth.

In my first season we started on a really good run, topped the league for a while and reached a cup final. Apart from narrowly losing the final, everything was going according to plan. We were a good team. We were unlucky in that cup final against Rangers; I remember one of my crosses was cleared from the line when it was 1-1, just before Ally McCoist came on and scored the winner for them. In a way, we just knew what was going to happen when we saw Ally coming on; he'd been out with injury for so long. On another day we might've won that final as we matched a very strong Rangers team well.

In one of my last games for Falkirk before joining Hibs we beat Hearts 6-0 at Brockville; we beat them so badly that their manager Joe Jordan ended up sacked. We won quite easily that day as Hearts weren't very good at the time, and at the time Falkirk were getting relegated. A few months later I was playing for Hibs against that same Hearts team and it was different, even though their line-up was much the same. At the time Hearts had avoided defeat against Hibs for about 17 matches. It seemed that part of the reason why Hibs weren't beating Hearts was psychological; maybe one or two Hibs players had actually started to believe that they couldn't win derbies. The press and media made a big deal of that run, too. We didn't win any of the first five Edinburgh derbies that I played in, but we played well in some of those games and were particularly unlucky against them in the cup tie, the one where Wayne Foster scored a late winner. To me, our poor derby record had less to do with football and more to do with psychology. When

Gordon Hunter scored and ended that run in 1994 it felt great and I know that many of our longer-serving players felt relieved. It was actually ironic as, when we won that derby 1-0 at Tynecastle, we didn't play very well and Hearts were maybe a bit unlucky. That's how it goes though; in some games we dominated Hearts and got nothing. The derbies were always tight when I was at Hibs.

My favourite derby match was the New Year derby in January 1996. We beat Hearts 2-1 just 48 hours after we had been thrashed 7-0 at Ibrox. Neil Pointon gave Hearts an early lead and then their Swedish striker missed a good chance, but after that we bossed that match and could have won by more. As Hibs players we felt under unbelievable pressure after that 0-7 loss at Ibrox so a derby immediately after it was huge for us. I remember the referee had booked Gazza in that match at Ibrox, for 'cautioning' him after he had dropped his cards, we couldn't believe it. That derby was important to us after the Rangers loss because we felt we owed the fans a performance.

When as a team we finished third and split the old firm in 94/95 I think we managed that because we were a good team and were well organised; it's simple but true. We had a good squad so if anyone was injured or suspended that season we had able guys who could step in.

Alex Miller was an excellent coach, his training was excellent. We didn't just 'do' football; we did aerobics and swimming, all kinds of things. I know that the boss got some stick from some of the fans for supposedly being a bit negative, but when I joined Hibs, we were playing with two wingers and were more often than not battering teams when we went on the attack. The gaffer was light years ahead when it came to training. When I came to Hibs in 1993, players at most clubs would finish the season and go away for six weeks of holiday, then return to get in shape for pre-season. It was different at Hibs. Before we ended a season, we were blood-tested and fitness-tested as well as having other tests done. We were expected to keep fit during the close season, to eat properly and to be fit and ready to play by the time we returned to the club for pre-season. Each player's close-season training programme was specific to them, personalised. When we did return, we were tested all over again to see if we had stuck to our close-season regime and to see if we had remained fit. At the time it really was groundbreaking sports science. I remember when I was coaching in the mid 2000s and some clubs were only just starting to think about using such techniques. Fitness-wise, we were years ahead at Hibernian. The manager taught us a lot about fitness and coaching, and he was on his own learning curve as a boss, too, and look where that curve took him; he was at Liverpool when they won European trophies.

I played with some brilliant players at Hibs. Michael O'Neill was a truly outstanding footballer. He had a good footballing brain and could just glide past defenders and score goals. Big Keith had it all up front. He was strong, fast, a good team player and an excellent finisher. Darren Jackson was a class player and a real character on the park. He strutted about the pitch as if he owned it and you need guys like that in a good team. He could play just as well up front or in midfield. Gordon Hunter was an immense defender. Big Jim Leighton in goal was brilliant for us, so was Willie Miller. For me as a winger, playing in front of Willie was great. He could play a bit but he also took no prisoners, he was always there to win the ball back and pass it to me or to Michael. Graham Mitchell was a superb left-back, too. We had so many good players when I was at Hibs.

Hibernian is and was a fantastic football club. I really enjoyed my time there. The fans were a great bunch, always right behind us with their backing and, when needed, letting us know when things weren't working. I had an excellent rapport with the Hibbies. I was sad to move on in 1997 but the new manager had looked at the squad's average age and wanted to try something new. That's football. There was no ill feeling or anything, I left on good terms.

Asides that 1996 New Year derby win, the highlight of my time at Hibs was the 1993 League Cup run. Firhill for thrills in the quarter-finals and that dramatic penalty shoot-out, followed by that amazing atmosphere inside Tynecastle when we beat Dundee United 1-0 in the semis, with Hibs fans in all the Hearts areas of the stadium, then that brave and unlucky performance against Rangers at Parkhead in the final, I really enjoyed all of that.

DAVID 'FAZ' FARRELL

I remember my first Edinburgh derby as a player; it was at Tynecastle on New Year's Day 1992 and it was amazing. At the time it was still the old Tynecastle so you still had the old shed and the big Gorgie Road terracing behind the goal. It was a very cold, wet evening and the game was live on Sky TV. I didn't know that I was going to play in it until the morning of the match, when the manager phoned me. I'd been out injured for a while but I think the boss knew that he could count on me. It was a very fast and very physical match with tackles flying in; we were determined to take something from the match and we did when Tommy scored our equaliser with the late penalty. That was some atmosphere!

In 1993, when the boss rebuilt the midfield, I ended up playing for most of the season in the holding midfield role.

The manager never actually said to me, 'You're the new holding midfielder this season', it just kind of happened. In reserve matches I sometimes played in central midfield but also at centre-back and at full-back, so I was flexible. The new role was one that I knew I could play. In a way the boss pulled off a masterstroke by playing me there as I was 5ft 10in, strong and could jump, so I could compete physically against big fellas like Mark Hateley and Ian Ferguson when we played against them. Also, the position suited me well because I could play a bit and 'sort out' opposing players as well. I was happy to win the ball then pass it out wide to guys like Kevin McAllister and Michael O'Neill, or forward to Ted or Darren as they were great players who could do damage. The 1993 Hibs team had a lot of flair players, so I guess I gave the side a bit of balance in my ball-winning role.

As a boy in Scotland, you grow up dreaming of playing in big cup finals and at places like Celtic Park, Ibrox and Easter Road, so when I started for Hibs in the 1993 cup final against Rangers it made me very proud. I enjoyed the final itself, I enjoyed the run to the final, too, especially when we beat Dundee Utd in the semi-final at Tynecastle – what an atmosphere! The final, though an amazing occasion, ended with a little bit of disappointment. For long spells of that game we more than matched Rangers but just couldn't get ourselves over the line. There was nothing that we could've done about McCoist's stunning winner, though, that's a goal everyone remembers. It was a shame because we could have won that day.

The 1995 semi-final against Celtic at Ibrox was another massive match. I played in the first match which we drew but was dropped for the replay, which we lost. I think the manager thought I had a wee injury. That was disappointing to me, but that's football. In the first match we went toe-to-toe with a good Celtic side and matched them well, even though they missed a penalty, we proved that we could match them. Celtic were like a different side in the replay, though, they hardly gave us a kick. It was like we had used all our energy in the first match and were puffed out a bit in the replay.

In 1995 we became the last Hibernian side to split the old firm, finishing third, narrowly missing out on Europe. That's one achievement of the good Hibs teams of 1991–1995 which is often overlooked. For those four years we were a good side, we were in two cup finals and four semi-finals as well, plus we competed in the UEFA Cup, all in those four years. We had good goalkeepers, good defenders like Tweedy, Gordon Hunter and Willie Miller. Pat McGinlay was a rock, while guys like Kevin McAllister and Michael O'Neill could have walked into any team in Scotland. Nowadays, most teams see playing with just the one winger as being a bit cavalier, we often played with two! Up front we had a great blend, three very different strikers in Gareth, Darren and Keith. I don't think that period's achievements get enough recognition. For most of my time as a first-team player we were in the top six in the league, often in the top four, we even topped the league a few times!

Alex Miller was and is a brilliant football coach. His knowledge of the game is exceptional. In the 90s he was years and years ahead of his time. Back then we were using advanced sports science and blood oxygen testing, things that most other clubs didn't know about or didn't use at the time but which are now part and parcel of a football team's training regime. That probably gave us an extra edge. The boss treated everyone equally and was very thorough and methodical. I actually loved the training at Hibs. In terms of man-management, the gaffer was perhaps a bit too honest at times. Some players need a pat on the back, others need a rocket up the arse – the boss didn't differentiate, he treated all of us the same way. Overall, though, as a coach, he is second to none, and look at all we achieved in the early to mid 90s with him in charge. Would we have achieved more without him? No chance.

I was lucky to play with some great players in my time at Hibs. Steve Archibald was the best I encountered. Though I had seen him on TV and at matches when I was a lad, it wasn't until he was at Hibs that I realised what an amazing footballer he was. He had everything: ability, skill, vision, fitness and he was a great guy as well – a true pro. Later on, Darren Jackson and Michael O'Neill were superb players, but the best of the mid 90s was wee Kevin McAllister; his skill could have you up on your feet, he didn't just 'skin' defenders, his end-product, his crossing and shooting, were a joy to watch. As for opponents, the hardest guys to play against in my time at Hibs were Brian Laudrup and Paul McStay. Laudrup had everything; he was tall, fast, strong and skilful, while McStay was unbelievably talented. Paul was much better than the team he played in, totally on another level; he could have played in any league.

I loved my time at Hibernian and I felt privileged to have played for such a huge club. It's a real family club and there was always a great sense of togetherness. Hibs fans are very passionate and they are also very fair, they give everybody a chance. When I was there, there was a bond between the fans and the players that you just don't get now at modern football clubs, since training centres and big salaries have set 'superstar' players and fans that bit further apart. I loved playing for Hibs, it's a great club and I always feel so welcome whenever I go back there. The fans and I still enjoy a great wee affinity. They were always a special bunch, home and away.

GRAHAM 'MITCH' MITCHELL

For winning the League Cup in 1991 our reward was a spot in the UEFA Cup the next season. I played in the first leg against Anderlecht at Easter Road but I picked up a wee calf injury just before the second leg and missed that one. I felt that we played brilliantly in both legs, especially at Easter Road. That leg ended 2-2 but we deserved to win the match. Anderlecht had some world-class players. Degryse was a class act and the boy Van Vossen played in the same Holland team as Van Basten and Gullit, he took Holland's penalties. We were unlucky over the two legs to go out against Anderlecht; we didn't lose a match to them. The atmosphere at both matches was tremendous, home and away. The home leg actually had one of the best atmospheres I ever played in at Easter Road; it was the last European tie played at Easter Road with terracing. Back then the Belgian sides were always a tough draw in Europe; teams like Antwerp, Mechelen, Brugge and Anderlecht were formidable sides.

In season 93/94 when Kevin McAllister and Michael O'Neill arrived, we became a more attacking team. A lot of teams struggled to cope with us playing with two wingers. It wasn't just one on the right and one on the left, they swapped over sometimes, defenders don't like that. When both of them played well we usually won, we even won a lot of matches when only one of them was 'on fire'. They made a real difference. For me as a left-back, it was great to have one or both of them always willing to receive the ball and do something with it. With Keith and Darren up front, quality strikers, and those two great wingers, we were always capable of getting goals.

I actually think that we played better as a team in the 1993 League Cup Final which we lost to Rangers than we did in the 1991 League Cup Final that we won against Dunfermline! We gave Rangers a great run for their money in the 93 final and we were unfortunate not to at least take the tie to penalties. We had great team spirit and we held our own, we didn't fear that Rangers team. McCoist's winner was a great goal to win any final, especially as he was not long back from serious injury, but it would have been better if one of us in green had scored it at the other end.

A lot of the derbies in our winless run against Hearts were very close games; most of them were, in fact. I feel as if we had a bit of a mental block when it came to that fixture, it wasn't to do with our footballing ability. The papers were the ones who went on about the winless run a bit and made it into 'a thing'. It could be a bit embarrassing to have that monkey on our back. When we ended that run we didn't prepare differently for the match, we just got a long overdue rub of the green.

The 94/95 team was a great Hibernian side. Winning breeds confidence. That season we played well and we even won sometimes when we didn't play as well, too. Our top scorer was Michael O'Neill that season. When the wingers are banging in as many as the strikers you know that you have a good team. Look at Celtic in recent times: so many goals they score come from Forrest and Sinclair as well as from the forwards. Having wingers and midfielders like Michael and Pat scoring goals is worth ten to 15 points a season to a team.

Alex Miller was one of the best coaches in the country back then. You only have to look at the success he helped bring to Hibs and then Liverpool as a coach to see that. Coaching-wise, I don't think there's anyone better.

John Collins was by far the best footballer that I played with in my time at Easter Road. We were also fortunate to have had three great Scotland goalkeepers to rely on at Hibs in Rough, Goram and Leighton. Andy Goram was a class act in goal, but the best player overall was John Collins, he was on another level. As for opponents, in my time at Hibs the hardest guy to play against was Brian Laudrup. He was tall and strong but also so skilful.

I loved the Hibs fans and had a good relationship with them. Obviously, there are times when every player might get a wee bit of stick from the fans, but that's all part of being a professional player. The fans were always very fair. It's great bumping into Hibs fans – they always talk away. Joe Tortolano and I went down with some of the other ex-players like Mickey and Kano to a London Hibs function and it was fantastic; the fans still treat you as if you're still playing for the club, even now.

I was actually signed by Hibs in 1986 to play as a centre-back. I'd been playing there or in central midfield for Hamilton. I signed on the same day as Tommy McIntyre and Dougie Bell; we were Alex's first signings. Big Tam was a great player, he could play in many positions, he could pass well and he wasn't afraid to put the boot in when necessary. Gordon Hunter was another great defender; he certainly didn't hold back when tackling, even in training.

The highlight of my Hibs career was the 1991 SKOL League Cup win. There were just green scarves everywhere, en route to the stadium and inside Hampden, I don't even recall seeing or hearing any Dunfermline fans. When we got back to Edinburgh and its streets were flooded with green and white, that was just amazing. Hibernian is a massive football club. I've spoken to guys who played for Hibs after I was there and many didn't realise what a big club it is until they joined. They were a big club back then and they still are now. Look at all of the fans who were out celebrating after the 2016 Scottish Cup win. That was incredible! My wife and I were at Orlando airport when that final was being played; we had been on holiday and were waiting to fly home. I was keeping tabs on the Hibs score throughout the match but in the terminal my wife's phone lost its signal near the end of the match. I started asking people in the queue if they knew the score. Eventually I asked a guy and he had the score up on his tablet. The guy actually said that Hibs had won 3-1 and that Stokes had scored the last goal, but he was right about the outcome. The whole queue in the airport started to cheer! We were on the other side of the Atlantic but it didn't matter. I don't think all of those cheering were Hibs fans, but it was just so amazing. I wouldn't be at all surprised if Hibs were to win that cup again within the next five years.

JIM DUFFY

When I got the Hibs job late in 1996, I was a bit surprised. Back then, managers didn't have agents so Hibs had to approach my club Dundee to ask for permission to speak to me. I felt very privileged that such a huge club was interested in me.

It was and is such a big job. I came in right after Alex Miller's decade in charge of the club had ended. I actually played for Morton back in the early 80s when Alex began his managerial career there. When a manager has been at a club for ten years then leaves, the players, supporters and staff sometimes tend to have an embedded way of doing things. That's perfectly natural. You can get issues when the new manager tries to change things, though, even small things. For example, say I suggested that training begin at 9.30 or 10.30, people might've said 'but we train at 10am at Hibs', because that's when training had started under Alex. It could've been any issue, though. Alex had been there for ten years so people at the club were used to doing things a specific way. That can take time to change, though it is perfectly natural after one man has been in charge for so long. Look at the difficulties Manchester United and Arsenal encountered immediately after losing Sir Alex Ferguson and Arsene Wenger. When you take over from a long-serving manager you really have to hit the ground running or fans and critics will quickly develop doubts.

I went to a lot of supporter meetings when I first went to Hibernian and I spoke to a lot of fans. They loved their club. The fans' paramount desire was to watch an attacking team and they asked me to make sure that football was played the Hibs way – attacking, cavalier even. That's what the fans wanted and I did my very best to give the fans that. In hindsight, I probably got sucked into that whole 'the Hibs way' thing a bit too much and I maybe tried to change things more quickly than I otherwise would have.

When we were good at the start of season 97/98, we were really good. We started the season with a fully fit squad, and we were excellent when we beat Celtic on the opening day. A lot of people had written us off before the campaign even began, so a victory over a very strong Celtic team, who would win the title and who had Larsson among their ranks, was a great achievement. In the weeks after that we continued to do well, both Chic and Pat scored wonder-goals from long range. We started that season well, confidence was high. I remember a few years later when I was back at Dundee and we were playing Hibs, the great Eddie Turnbull came into the dressing room and told me that the Hibs team at the start of season 97/98 had played some of the best, most exciting football that he had ever seen. For me, that's as good a tribute to that team as you can get.

Injuries played a big part when our good form slackened. We lost big Shaun Dennis after just four or five games with a cruciate injury; he had been a revelation for us so he was a big miss. Brian Welsh, another central defender, also got injured, so did Barry Lavety. That was us minus a central defence and a top striker. I wouldn't put everything that happened down to the injuries, but the injuries certainly didn't help. We made some defensive mistakes in games and that dents players' confidence, so we had the injuries and the mistakes contributing to the heads maybe going down. Confidence is very important to a team.

When I first went to Hibs midway through season 96/97 we lost big John Hughes for two spells because of injury; he didn't return until right at the end of the season. Darren Jackson missed a few games through injury, too. Darren was probably our key player, the best we had when I first went to Hibs. He added a totally different dimension to the team when he played and he was a great influence; with Darren in the side the players believed that they could win and do well. He was on another level. He was a big loss to us when he left in the summer to sign for Celtic. There was a World Cup coming up and he was about 31 by then so it's easy to see why he wanted the move. We also lost Jim Leighton that summer, another top player. Jim had a pre-existing agreement with Hibs that he would return to Aberdeen, an agreement made before I arrived at Hibs. When you lose a top striker like Darren and a great goalie like Jim it makes things difficult, they're hard to replace.

At big clubs like Hibs, you don't always get adequate time to nurture talent, people expect results quickly. I probably rushed the rebuilding job as I was keen to do well and to make the supporters happy. When I took over at Hibs we had around 11 first-team players over the age of 30. With hindsight, I should have maybe kept guys like Kevin McAllister and big Joe McLaughlin for a bit longer, to retain a bit of experience in the squad. Gordon Hunter left as well and was a big loss both because he was experienced and because he'd been at the club for such a long time. Experienced guys are always hard to replace. I was trying to build something new with younger guys who had potential, like Paul Tosh and Davie Elliot, but the need to get results and to rebuild at the same time wasn't an easy balance to maintain. Managing Hibs is a huge responsibility; I put my hands up and admit that I got some things wrong.

Chic Charnley proved a lot of people wrong during his time at Hibs, he had tremendous ability. Pat McGinlay was a superb player. Stevie Crawford was a great talent. It was me who first tried to recruit Grant Brebner from Man Utd in season 97/98 but we couldn't pull it off at the time. Alex McLeish did eventually get him for Hibs. He had a long-standing relationship with Alex Ferguson, which helped.

The change in the transfer market with Bosman in 1995 made player recruitment a bit more difficult for a year or two. In 96 and 97 Bosman was mostly a one-way thing for most British clubs and players; a lot of players left to play in Europe and it maybe took an extra year or two before the new system became a more two-way thing and clubs in Scotland started to sign more European guys. Hibs getting Franck Sauzee in 1999 is a good example of that. In the summer of 1997 scouts and agents in Scotland were still mostly focused on homegrown players and we weren't really being approached by foreign agents at the time.

My happiest time at Hibs was during the first few months of season 97/98 when we were doing well. The fans were happy and we were happy. For a time, we played some fantastic football and scored some great goals. We really did light up Easter Road from August to October. When everyone was on top form and fit, we were a really good side.

Alex Miller did a fantastic job in his ten years at Hibs by keeping the team in the top flight and even winning cups and playing in Europe. He had time to build something slowly. I took more risks, and when you take risks, things have a bigger chance of going wrong – that's football. I wanted to give the Hibs fans what they craved, an attacking team that they enjoyed watching, and for a wee while that's what they got. I just wish that the early success had been sustainable.

When I was coaching at Chelsea a few years after my time at Hibs, I used to bump into Ole Gottskalksson a lot as he was by then at Brentford. At Griffin Park Ole was voted player of the year three or four times in a row. He wasn't a bad goalie at all, though I did used to joke with him that he'd gotten me the sack. At Hibs Ole made a few mistakes and lost his confidence, which is particularly tough for goalkeepers. The fans get on your back after a few mistakes as a footballer, and that can hurt. Jim Leighton was almost irreplaceable, so when replacing Jim I went for potential rather than for experience. As a manager I take full responsibility for how it panned out that season, I should have gone for experience. Sometimes I meet people who say that I got Hibs relegated – I sometimes say that no one gets relegated in February. There were still 13 league games to play when I left, almost 40 points to be won. I don't think I'll ever change some people's minds about that, though – that's football.

I am proud that I signed Tam McManus for Hibs. I saw his energy, his ability, his enthusiasm and his cockiness and knew that he had potential to become a great player, and he ended up as one of Hibs' top strikers for three or four years. He was gallus, as they say in Glasgow. He was effervescent, fearless and had that swagger about him. I gave Kenny Miller his Hibs debut because I knew that he was ready and that he, too, had great potential. He had the right attitude and was a great athlete. Even as a teenager his work ethic for the team was incredible, and for a young lad he was so unselfish. Defenders hated playing against Kenny, even in training, because he was so relentless and never gave them a moment's peace. We did work on his play in the box, as at first most of his good work was done outside the box, but he worked hard and developed the calmness in front of goal that was needed. I knew that he would play at the very highest level; not many players manage to play for Celtic, Rangers and Scotland and at the highest level down south. I was glad to help give him that opportunity.

Hibernian FC is a fantastic club. The renditions of 'Sunshine on Leith' after Hibs beat Hearts in the Scottish Cup replays a couple of years ago were the greatest examples of football fans singing that I've ever heard. It really gave me goosebumps. Hibs have had some fantastic sides and played some brilliant football over the years. I know Jack Ross and I hope that he does really well at Easter Road.

KEITH 'KEEF' WRIGHT

Being a Hibs fan, playing for Hibs was a dream come true for me. I remember in 1992 when we played Anderlecht in the UEFA Cup, that was a massive game for us and for the fans because it was our reward for winning the SKOL League Cup a year earlier. Both of the matches were brilliant, I loved the build-up; it was my first time playing in that tournament. Anderlecht were one of the best teams in Europe at the time and had some great players like Philippe Albert, Marc Degryse, Danny Boffin and Peter van Vossen. They were hard games for sure but we did well and didn't let ourselves down, they only beat us on away goals. The atmosphere at both matches was terrific, the home leg especially. It was the first time I'd played at Easter Road when there were our own fans on the Dunbar End. There were a few noisy away fans in the seated enclosure. We could've won that leg,; I thought Mickey was unfortunate to be sent off. The away trip was something special as well; the travel, the city and the match itself, everything, it was a great experience. We played very well over the two legs against a top continental side and that was something to be proud of for us all. The Scottish Cup semi-final we played that season against Aberdeen at Tynecastle was a close game; our matches against them usually were. It was always going to be decided by a single goal and sadly for us it was Scott Booth who scored it. Gareth was unlucky not to score near the end. There was a good atmosphere that day as it was almost a home tie for us with it being in Edinburgh.

When we were drawn with Dundee United in the 1993 League Cup semis I was delighted because I always relished playing against them and because we knew that the tie would be played at neutral Tynecastle. There was some atmosphere inside the ground during that match. Darren's goal was a beauty; he wrong-footed their whole defence and finished superbly. It was by no means a classic, it was as much a battle as it was a football match, the fans really turned up the noise that night, it was great to win a cup semi-final there. The final was a great occasion; I'm still claiming our goal! After we equalised against Rangers we had a really good spell of pressure and had a few chances, we at least deserved extra time. But I suppose the writing was on the wall when McCoist came on as a sub; he wasn't long back from a serious injury and was due a change of luck.

We topped the league for a few months in season 93/94. The only slight nuisance was our derby record; that record was largely down to one man, John Robertson. We were as up for the derbies as the Hearts players were in most of those matches, but they did just seem to out-battle us on the day; they usually had a very strong defence and midfield and were very well organised. A lot of the derbies I played in when we weren't beating Hearts were matches that we dominated but were unable to score in. I sometimes wish that I had scored more goals against Hearts, but that's football.

Looking back, it was great in the season 94/95 that we not only ended that winless run but won three of the four derbies. I scored in the 3-1 win at Easter Road in the last derby that season. Hearts were actually involved in a relegation battle at that time. I remember when I scored. The Dunbar End had been demolished so the small Hearts support was housed in part of the main stand. When I did my celebration I ran towards them and pointed downwards with my fingers, as a joke. Mickey scored a great goal that day, too. We did so well and split the old firm that season simply because we were a team full of great players and we had a great manager. We had Darren Jackson, McAllister, O'Neill, McGinlay, we had Kevin Harper coming through and Tweedy and Geebsy were great at the back. We also had Gareth and Mickey who were good attacking players. We had a great goalie in Jim Leighton. There were no 'superstars' that season, we were simply a hard-working team who liked to go forward. The two cup semi-final matches against Celtic that season were massive games; the first one was on a Friday night. I remember Ibrox was absolutely covered in green and white and the atmosphere was great. Our best chance of beating them was in the 0-0 first match; they really upped their game in the replay when they beat us 3-1 and I scored. That was a bit sad because we'd have faced Airdrie in the final and might have ended Hibs' Scottish Cup hoodoo. Looking back, it was a great achievement to finish third that season; we didn't think much about it at the time maybe because we didn't win a cup that season, but it was certainly a great campaign, worthy of recognition. We all really gelled as a squad and as a team in 94/95.

Our 7-0 defeat at Ibrox just before Hogmanay in 1995 was a real doing. Then, when we were playing Hearts at Easter Road two days later and they scored early on, we felt like we had to pull something special out of the bag, we didn't want to be haunted by a derby defeat as well. We showed a lot of character to bounce back from the Rangers game to overcome Hearts in that derby. We knew that we owed it to ourselves and to the fans to win that one.

The relegation play-off win over Airdrie was so tense. Cup finals and other big matches are tense but they're also enjoyable, you look forward to them, but the play-off certainly isn't enjoyable. So much is at stake and you really don't want to lose. As a team we didn't like the fact that we had ended up in the play-off and we were desperate to win it. Jim had signed some other strikers so I had missed a few games that season, but I was recalled for the play-off for some reason. I think the team needed its experienced players for that tie. I'm a big believer that Hibs shouldn't ever be in such positions at that end of the league and threatened with the drop. The play-off was a must-win – it was about survival. As a Hibs fan and player I didn't want to be remembered in club history as part of a side that had been relegated; it was the same with the other established players like Darren and Jim, we were determined that Hibs would still be a top-flight club by the end of the play-off. It was important that Hibs stayed up. When we won, though we looked pleased; there was no joy or elation, simply relief that we had stayed up.

Jim Duffy was my team captain when I was at Dundee, he really helped my career and was good to me. At Hibs he was still a young manager who had been given one of the biggest football management jobs in Scotland. He genuinely tried to do something new at Hibs but it didn't work. That's football. I think, longer term, his experiences at Hibs made Jim into a better manager.

Alex Miller was a great manager. He made me a better footballer and he got me my dream move to Hibs. Don't get me wrong, he could be a hard taskmaster in training and was a stickler for time-keeping, but his training was brilliant. We had all sorts of sports scientists and sports psychologists working with us, years before other teams started to train with those methods. I really enjoyed my time at Hibs under him. Look at all he achieved as a coach at Liverpool: Alex has had a great career. I think if Hibs had done better against Hearts during his time at Easter Road he'd be seen as an outright legend by all Hibs fans, though many do see him as one anyway. He built and maintained a good Hibs team on a tight budget even when clubs were having to spend millions on stadia in the mid 90s. He deserves more recognition for the joy that he helped bring to the club at times.

There were so many good players at Hibs when I was there, it's almost impossible to say who I think was the best.

I'm going to say Mickey Weir, though. He was a huge talent and he and I had a special understanding, he always knew where to find me with crosses and through balls. So many were good, though. Michael O'Neill was a fantastic player, Brian Hamilton sometimes got stick from the fans but we loved having such a good ball-winner in the side. Darren Jackson was a different class, too.

Richard Gough was a very difficult opponent. He was tough, strong, good in the air, fast and clever. He was always up for the battle. Craig Levein could be almost as formidable, as could Brian Martin of Motherwell. I always knew I was in for a good battle against any of those three!

Hibs fans were always brilliant when I played for the club. I think they appreciated that I always gave 100 per cent for the team. I still remember the reception they gave me during my first competitive start against St Mirren at Easter Road, it was brilliant. I have wonderful memories of my time as a Hibs player. Alex Miller always said that I really seemed to love playing football, he could see it on my face, and he was right, I did, and especially while I wore the green jersey of Hibs.

MARK MCGRAW

Season 91/92 was very special at Hibs. The opening day of the season when we beat St Mirren 4-1 at Easter Road was when things really started to click for us. The fans could sense it, too, I think. They were on our side and the atmosphere was fantastic. Things just kind of steamrollered from there. At the time, myself and Gareth Evans were rotating up front with Keith Wright and that was working well for us. In the 1991 SKOL Cup, though we were away from home in every round, we could feel our momentum building. Kilmarnock gave us the stiffest test in the early rounds before we encountered Rangers at Hampden in the semis. I think most people expected Rangers to beat us but we managed to defeat them on that amazing night at Hampden. I got injured a few weeks before the final and missed it, which was a bit of a disappointment, but I was still a part of it all, we won as a team. We were unbeaten for quite a few matches at the start of that season. In fact, the first match we lost was the one after I got injured; we lost 4-2 to Rangers at Ibrox. We did have a fantastic start to that season.

When we split the old firm in season 94/95 by finishing third I think our secret was that we had a large and good squad, whereas in 1991 we did well because we had a smaller, more tight-knit group of players. I had some injuries while at Hibs but I remember coming back from one and being on the bench when we played Celtic at Hampden in a league match in 95. I came off the bench and scored our equaliser; I was delighted to score that goal and see our wee group of fans celebrating. That was the last Hibs goal at the old-style Hampden. I hadn't scored for a while so I remember that one! We did well against Celtic in the cup semi-final that season but if we were going to beat them it was going to have been in the first match, rather than the replay. You don't tend to get a second chance to beat Rangers or Celtic. It was a pity as we would have played Airdrie in the final and could have won the cup that year.

I was lucky to play for Hibs when there were so many great players there. Goram, Leighton and Budgie Burridge were great keepers. Darren Jackson was a great player at Hibs; he got picked for Scotland regularly at Hibs at a time when most Scotland players tended to come from Rangers, Celtic or big clubs down south. Keith Wright was a superb player, Brian Hamilton was a bit of an unsung hero at times, we appreciated having him in the team. Gordon

Hunter was a superb defender; Pat McGinlay and Kevin McAllister were great players. Graham Mitchell was a top left-back who was unfortunate not to get a testimonial. Michael O'Neill was a great talent.

As for opponents, Richard Gough was difficult to play against but I found Miodrag Krivokapić of Motherwell to be the hardest defender to play against. He was a classy defender and was very strong and clever.

Alex Miller was a huge influence on me. He is a superb coach. I liked the training at Hibs, it was always so interesting. He definitely made you a better player. His managerial style didn't suit every player but that's football.

I absolutely loved my five and a half years at Hibs. I sometimes feel that I underachieved or could have played a bit more but I still had a good career. I loved the Hibs fans; they were so good to me, even when I wasn't in the team. In fact, I'm from the west coast but I ended up settling in Edinburgh, that's how much I loved life at Hibs.

STEVEN 'TWEEDY' TWEED

I'm a Hibs fan so I was pleased to score in that important Scottish Cup quarter-final win against St Johnstone at Easter Road. It was my first goal, but what was more important to me was that the team got into the semi-finals. Since a young age I have always thought that a club like Hibs should be playing in semi-finals and finals regularly. In season 94/95 when we split the old firm and reached another Scottish Cup semi-final, we had a great team spirit among the lads and in that campaign we weren't hampered by lots of injuries and suspensions as we would be in 95/96. In 94/95 we had a degree of consistency in the first XI and none of our best players missed much of the campaign, except Keith Wright who missed the first half of the season with an injury but did well when he returned. Our defence was excellent in that season; we kept clean sheets in 19 of our 44 matches.

We were almost late arriving at Celtic Park for the League Cup Final in 1993, because of the traffic, we were stuck on the hard shoulder for a long time. We were unlucky in that final, but the script that day was written for McCoist's comeback. I actually watched that goal the other day and noticed that there were about five of us Hibees around him and Hateley and he *still* managed to score.

When we lost 0-7 to Rangers at Ibrox on 30 December 1995, we lost so heavily for the simple reason that they had a superior team and also played very well that day, while we didn't play very well as a team. It was a massacre. We turned it around 48 hours later in the New Year derby against Hearts at Easter Road when we won 2-1, though, for two reasons. Firstly, Hearts were nowhere near as good as Rangers, they weren't even better than us. Secondly, as we had to play again a mere 48 hours after the Ibrox defeat, we didn't really have time to dwell on the defeat or think about it too much. Sometimes in football that's a good thing. We hadn't suddenly become a bad team overnight just because of one bad defeat, and perhaps it was best that our next match was against our city rivals, as we needed no extra motivation to play against Hearts.

I was very lucky in my time at Hibs to have played with such fantastic players, in all positions. I played in front of Andy Goram and Jim Leighton, two of Scotland's greatest-ever goalies. Outfield wise, Michael O'Neill and Kevin McAllister were amazing talents and Darren Jackson just seemed to get better with every passing month. Pat McGinlay was also a great player. I learned a lot from Tommy McIntyre and Gordon Hunter.

I wouldn't single out any opponent in Scotland as being the toughest to play against. Every opposition attack was different and presented different challenges, Motherwell had Arnott and Tommy Coyne, Rangers had Hateley and McCoist, Hearts had Robertson and Colquhoun. Most teams still played with two strikers back then so every match was a different challenge that I relished.

My favourite match during my time with Hibernian was in August 1994 when we beat Hearts 1-0 at Tynecastle to end our long winless run in the derby. I saw that run as something I had inherited upon my establishment as a first-team regular in early 1993 and I was determined to help bring that run to an end. My own record against Hearts for Hibs is actually quite good, right through from my youth days to my time in the first team! The media played a role in creating the hype that surrounded our run in that fixture and I didn't want that run to be part of my career or to bother the fans any more.

I always wanted to win the Scottish Cup as a Hibs fan and as a Hibs player. We could've done it in the mid 90s if conditions had been different, but I'm glad we won it eventually. After 1996 a lot of good players moved on. We had played for three seasons with two out-and-out wingers, not many teams do that now or even did that then. I remember the night at Easter Road when myself, Darren and Pat all made our Scotland B debuts, in a 3-0 win over Northern Ireland. The crowd wasn't huge but there were some Hibs fans in it. It felt surreal to be wearing the blue at our home stadium on that cold, dark evening.

The manager was ahead of the curve when it came to coaching. We had nutritionists, heart-rate monitors and all sorts of other sports science techniques at our disposal which most other teams didn't. That was all down to

Alex Miller. He was a big influence on my career and is a fantastic football coach. He even helped encourage me to study business studies while I was a player, so that I could have a skill to fall back on, and that's the field that I work in today.

The club had a really good youth system from the mid 80s onwards and our youth teams did really well, but only a few of us really went on to be regular first-team players. By the mid 90s only really myself and Kevin Harper had broken through and stayed in the team, though some of the other lads did well.

As I'm a Hibs fan myself I always got on with the fans when I was a player. I remember the 1990 Hands Off Hibs crisis well. When I was in the first team we tended to sit above Hearts in the league, I suppose at the time it was the 'natural order' of things. I love Hibs, I often go to home games and events; in fact, Easter Road still feels like home even though I don't play now. I am proud to have worn that green jersey, I wish that I'd been able to wear it for even longer.

MARTIN FERGUSON

I really enjoyed my time as a coach at Hibernian. I stayed on for a little while after Alex left in 1996 to help keep things ticking over until the new boss came in. I loved my time at Easter Road, Hibs are a great club. There was a great atmosphere at the club when I was there, the relationship between the players, coaches, staff and fans was just right. My time at Hibs is up there with the great times I had with Kirkintilloch Rob Roy as a player. At the Rabs we were coached by Andy Stevenson, who has sadly recently passed away. Andy, like Alex Miller, was years ahead of his time in coaching. We were being taught techniques such as the correct way to turn around and how to minimise wasted energy when sprinting, long before many other coaches were teaching that. At Hibs we were using these techniques and many other new training methods. We were ahead of our time at Hibs, too. Had I been full-time at Hibs we might have used even more revolutionary training techniques. During my time at Hibs I had a good full-time job and a family, and as a part-time coach you're always wary that if you go full-time it's sometimes not a secure job. Alex stuck by me and I by him for ten years, though; we worked well together. I think that I made a positive contribution to Hibernian, and was glad to.

When we finished third and split the old firm in 1995 we did so for a simple reason: we had really good players. They were talented but also hard-working and they listened in training. I always give the players full credit for all that's achieved; they're the guys who really put the effort in. We had some terrific players while I was at Hibs.

Pat McGinlay was a superb player; Graham Mitchell was perhaps underrated – there weren't many better players than him at the club. Keith Wright and Darren were great strikers, Paul Kane had immense ability, was a hard- worker and a fighter and could play anywhere. Mickey Weir was some player; when he played, he really played. I did a lot of coaching work on Mickey; sometimes he came back too deep but when he was on his game he really was up there with the best. Mickey listened to what the coaches told him and became a better player; he was a real handful for defences.

Big Tommy McIntyre was a super player for us. He was big and strong but he could also play as well: he had the skill. He could read play and control the ball. Tommy didn't just thump the ball up the park like some defenders.

Michael O'Neill was a super player, even though at times he could frustrate you. Sometimes he could be over elaborate, taking on a defender when it was perhaps easier to pass around them, but he had the skill. With his technical ability Michael could have played for any club in Britain. He had a fiery temperament but was a good lad, they all were. As a team, you can only do well if everybody is pushing in the same direction, that's important. They don't necessarily have to like each other, as long as they play as a team.

The good Hibs teams of the 1988–96 period don't get the recognition that they deserve, that's simply because most media coverage goes to the old firm. We got into Europe twice while I was at Hibs. In Scotland that's a great achievement for a club as, remember, two of Scotland's European places are almost block-booked in advance by Rangers and Celtic. We won the League Cup, lost a League Cup Final to Rangers and were in three Scottish Cup semi-finals while I was at Hibs; it was a good time, we did well, as Aberdeen and Hearts were also good back then. Rangers and Celtic get blanket press coverage no matter how good or bad they're doing, whereas non-old firm clubs have to be doing really well to get into the spotlight.

The best time at Hibs was when we won the SKOL Cup in 1991. It was the first time that an Edinburgh team had won anything in nearly 20 years. From the Gogar Roundabout right into the heart of Leith the fans lined the streets, it was wonderful – and the team and fans deserved it. I still go back to Easter Road sometimes and am always made to feel welcome.

Some of the Hibs fans in the early days didn't like the fact that Alex Miller had played for Rangers. I don't think that went down well with some of them. He worked hard to overcome that. I suppose that's football. It was sometimes the same with Hearts – if they signed an ex-Celtic player some of their fans didn't like it and the player would have to win the fans over. Alex Miller put his whole heart and soul into Hibs; there were a few times when things didn't go as well for us but Alex fought on. He was a hard worker and expected the same from the players. He didn't smoke or drink and kept himself incredibly fit. As a professional he was great to work with and Hibs were lucky to have him.

Had we beaten Celtic in the 95 Scottish Cup semis I think we'd have beaten Airdrie in the final. At the time we had struggled against Airdrie in the League Cup as they were a very physical team, but I think we'd have overcome them at Hampden because we had the best players. Of course, I'm the chairman of Airdrie now! But back in the day, they were always tough opponents, as a player and as a coach.

There was a simple reason why we struggled against Hearts in many matches from 1989–94: they were simply too strong for us physically. They had ability but they also had brute strength, we didn't have the brute strength, we were a team of ball players – even our physically big guys like Mitchell and McIntyre were ball players: tough guys, but they had more to their game than just brute strength and you wouldn't call them bruisers. Hearts had an edge over us because of that sheer brute strength. It did feel fantastic when we eventually did beat them, and ended up winning three out of four derbies that season.

Hibs have a huge support; we used to wonder where they all came from whenever there was a big match; they were a fantastic bunch. I'll always support Hibs and I love to see them doing well.

Also available at all good book stores

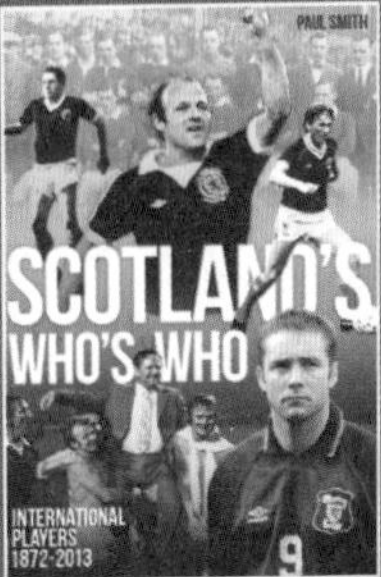

9781909178847

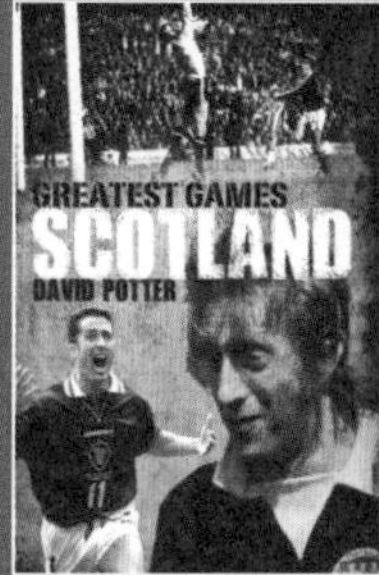

9781848182004

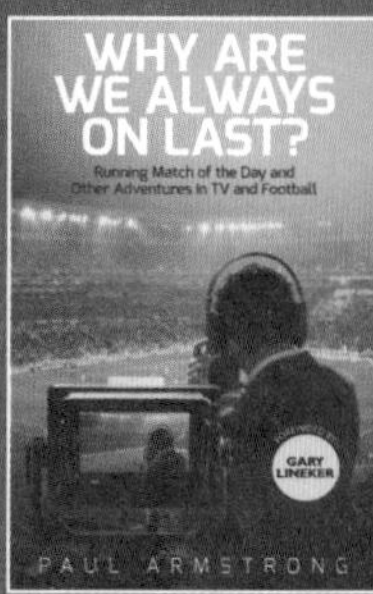

9781785314384

9781785316449

9781785316708

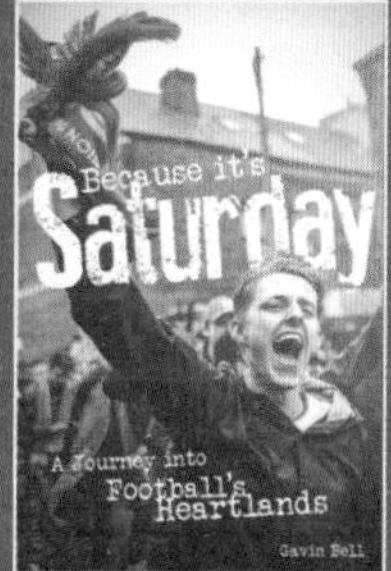

9781785316463

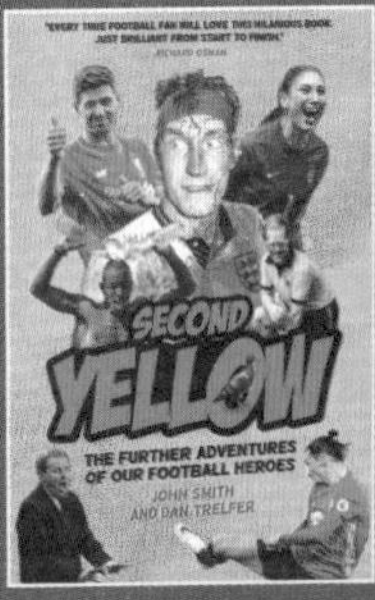

9781785316791

9781785317286

9781785316814